Laying Down My Net

Laying Down My Net

A Walk of Faith

Sue Cass

VANTAGE PRESS
New York

Published by Vantage Press, Inc.
419 Park Ave. South, New York, NY 10016

Manufactured in the United States of America
ISBN: 978-0-533-15995-6

Library of Congress Catalog Card No.: 2008901299

0 9 8 7 6 5 4 3 2 1

In memory of
my late husband.
The love of my life.

Dedicated to
all those who have
helped me on this journey.

"Come, follow Me, Jesus said . . .
At once they left their nets
And followed Him."

—Matthew 4:19–20

Foreword

The longing for real insight and honesty is a common challenge in life. Those who survive hard times often want to forget the struggle and just go on. Sue Cass has paid the price for spiritual wisdom that has transformed her life. The story of her journey is a powerful inspiration for our own breakthrough to deeper fulfillment. As a follower of the 'still small voice' she invites us to join her with the Spirit of Christ. More good things are just ahead.

—Cliff Garrison, Ed.D.
Counselor—Haven of Hope Counseling Center,
Sugar Hill, GA

Preface

The honeymoon's over and now it's time to get down to the business of growing in the relationship. I'm about to be stretched to the limits. The Lord Jesus is taking me out of my comfort zone and it isn't easy. He's not telling me anything except on an as needed basis. This is scary for me. Having less than an ideal childhood has taught me self-reliance. Independence and a strong sense of survival is a major part of my make-up.

Having to trust Him totally is foreign to me because many of the people I've trusted have betrayed me. Now I'm being told to sell my acreage and home. To leave my church family and friends.

I've been in Georgia forty years, my career has been fulfilled here, I met, married, and buried my husband here. I know how to survive, who to turn to, the weather, everything familiar to me is here in Georgia.

Being told I am moving to a distant land and destinations beyond that, yet unknown, is very much testing my faith and trust in Him. It has also created doubt in others as to whether I'm really connected with the Lord.

"You really don't believe the Lord would send you somewhere far away not knowing anyone there, do you?" "You can't go somewhere by yourself! What will you do when you get there?"

"Are you sure it's the Lord saying this?" And one brave soul, "I don't think that's the Lord telling you that at all!" I have one reply to these assaults on my faith. "He hasn't told me what I'll be doing, where I'll be living, or why He's sending me. I'm stepped out in faith. I'm being obedient to His call, and yes, I'm positive this is of the Lord!"

The Lord has said, "I am in you and you are in Me" (John 14:20) so how can I not be connected?" I see the Lord as my husband. He says that we, the body of Christ, are the bride of Christ.

I am His bride and He my Husband. As with any relationship there's a honeymoon. Our honeymoon has been great but it doesn't last forever. All marriages level off.

We learn about each other, in my case I'm learning about Him. He already knows me. There's also times of testing, highs and lows yet the relationship, if allowed, will evolve to a trusting comfortable place.

The lows are less, the highs mingle and intertwine with a sense of stability. Sharing, laughing, crying, and silent times of just sitting together being comfortable are all part of the relationship. ("I'll call you when I need you" is not a relationship.)

This is how my marriage to the Lord is. I have progressed to where I'm comfortable with my Partner. He's challenging me to greater faith. He doesn't want me to stagnate at the level I am.

To remain content with the way things are and the level of maturity I'm at does not fulfill a relational bond. He wants to give me greater understanding, to know Him better, and to draw closer to Him.

My marriage to the Lord reminds me of an old couple, married fifty years. They look at each other, say nothing, and yet one senses a rock solid something there. A rock solid tie.

They don't have to do anything or say anything and yet one knows these two are forever. That's where the Lord has brought me in our relationship. We're forever. At some point in our lives we realize life is fruitless without the Lord Jesus. What we're doing just isn't working. We aren't satisfied, we're indecisive. Feelings of hopelessness, and no direction. Then we stand before Christ asking for His forgiveness and proclaiming Him as Savior. When we do that we are placing our life into His hands.

At that moment of asking Him into our lives we are making a covenant with Him to surrender everything we have to Him. "Not My will, but as You will." (Matthew 26:39).

We are committing, promising to give Him our love, faithfulness, and obedience. The Lord asks that we throw down our nets and follow Him (see Matthew 4:19–22). I've thrown down my net. The journey is just beginning.

Acknowledgments

About fourteen years ago the Holy Spirit told me I would write a book. He keeps His promises. This is my first book. I want to give all praise, honor, and glory to my Lord and Savior, Jesus Christ. Without Him this wouldn't be possible. The Lord has brought many special people into my life. They have walked this journey with me. A special thanks to Cliff and Diane Garrison. God really knew what He was doing when He brought you into my life. You've been with me every step of the way. Laughed with me in the highs and cried with me in the lows. Without you I would never have made it this far.

Steve Wood, thank you for being so patient with me when I asked dumb questions and believing in me. You have given your blessings in all the endeavors in this ministry. I will always be grateful for that. May God give you Spiritual wisdom as you fulfill your destiny.

Kay Filosi, what a godly woman, supportive and special friend you have been. May God continue to bless you.

Michelle Barrow, I have watched you grow from a scared, fragile woman to a strong, loving adult. Your courage and determination is an inspiration to many. Your love has meant so much to me. I love you dearly.

Wanda Stemp, I was right, "She's a keeper." We've shared many miles and good times. We have many wonderful memories. May God continue to guide you and bless you. I love you.

Martha McKinnon what a special friend you are. Your faith and encouragement has been such a blessing to me. May God continue to shine His light on you and through you.

For all the men and women the Lord has ministered to through this ministry, I am so proud of you. Your courage to face the pain, to take the steps to freedom through our Lord Jesus has been awesome to watch as He heals you, touches your heart, and transforms you. Never give up for He is our hope.

To the many others, thank you for your prayers and encouragement. You have helped me grow in the Lord. The Lord asks us to love Him, trust Him, and obey Him. You have helped me do that. God bless you all.

Laying Down My Net

1

Listening to the sounds of the nurses and doctors talking at the nurses station, I'm feeling a deep sadness mixed with the overwhelming feeling of fear and sorrow. Turning from the window, I have no idea how my world is about to change. I walk over to the hospital bed.

I look down at my husband sleeping in the narrow bed with the silver rails raised high on each side as a safety precaution. I silently place my hands on the cold smooth rail. His face is drawn from the long illness he's been fighting for five years. His eyes are closed as I'm looking at him.

"How can God, if there is a God, let this wonderful man be dying of leukemia?"

Anger begins rising up in my chest. I look away, swallowing to keep from lashing out at God in my mind. Hearing Brian stir in the bed brings my attention back to the bed.

"What? What did you say, Brian?"

"I'm going to be alright, Sue-Sue." His voice is barely a whisper as he looks up at me through half closed eyes.

Tears are trickling down my cheeks. I take a deep breath, slowly letting it out. Love for him fills my heart. But then the anger rises up again. I try to subdue it and look at him.

"Brian, if there's a God, He's going to have to prove it to me!" Leaving the room tears are streaming down my face. *"Why? Why is this happening?"*

As I enter the house the phone is ringing. "Hello." "Sue, this is Mary. I'm leaving Florida and want to stay with you for a few days. Will that be alright?" "Of course."

Mary is an elegant older woman. Her husband Rick and Brian are as close as brothers and have been for years. I've

1

only met Mary once and liked her immediately. She and Rick came to visit when Brian was home, in between his many hospital stays.

Rick recently passed away from the cancer that ravaged his body; she understands my grief. When I answer the doorbell, Mary is standing on the porch. Her gray slacks and soft blue cashmere sweater complement her slender build.

As I open the door and hug her, my tears dampen her sweater.

"It's only been ten days, Mary, since he died and I miss him so much."

"Of course you do. I miss Rick, too."

The next couple of days laughter, tears, and remembrances are shared. It's a bittersweet visit. On the third morning, I crawl out of bed, yawning while walking into the kitchen to the coffee pot.

"Good morning, Mary." Mary is sitting at the table with a steaming cup of coffee. "Good morning. Did you sleep well?"

I took my cup of hot coffee over to the table. "I'm really feeling weird this morning."

"That's to be expected with all you've been through the last five years."

"I guess so. Remember me telling you a while back that a church was being built just down the road?"

"Yes."

"I have the strongest feeling that I'm supposed to go there this morning. It's really weird but I can't shake it. Would you like to go?"

"I'd love to but I really need to get on the road. I have a long drive ahead. You go ahead and I'll lock up."

"You don't mind? I just feel so strongly that I have to go to that church this morning."

2

Feeling like I'm moving in slow motion, I get dressed, and hug Mary good-bye, "Bye Mary, have a safe trip."

"I walk out the door, down the wooden wheelchair ramp, and out to the car. My mind is suddenly clouded like a heavy fog has moved in and taken over. Sitting behind the wheel and turning the ignition key there's a feeling of someone else turning the key, sitting with their hands on the steering wheel.

The car seems to drive itself. *"This must be how those out of body things are that I've heard about."* Slowly the car pulls out of the driveway and heads toward the church as though it's remote driven. Like it's on auto pilot with radar directing it to its destination.

Turning right off the main road I'm finding myself sitting in an empty parking lot in front of a church I had watched being built as I passed by on several occasions. The sign next to a grassy area reads, "Sunday School—9:00 A.M."

Anyway that's the way I'm seeing it. (I later learned the sign read 9:30 A.M.) As I look at the sign, then the empty parking lot, I am even more confused and still in the foggy condition. The car door slowly opens.

Dream-like, everything seems in slow motion. Approaching large double wooden doors it's as though my hands are detached from my body as they're pulling the door open.

Having never been inside this church before the confusion increases even more. My legs carry me down a long staircase going down to another floor. There's no one in sight. *"It's five minutes to nine. Where is everyone?"* One foot reaches the step and then another, as I slowly descend the stairs. I reach the bottom and stand still as though in a stupor.

Looking down a long hallway, one step after another, my feet carry me toward a light shining in the hall. Entering

3

a door I'm suddenly standing in front of a large mahogany desk.

While I am still feeling dazed, just standing here, a man sitting in a chair facing a computer turns toward me with a puzzled look. "Can I help you?" Standing quietly, looking at him, I'm not sure what to say.

My mouth opens and the words seem to come from somewhere else, as though someone is speaking through me. "I don't know why I'm here, but maybe you can help me."

The man is dressed in dress pants, a soft blue long sleeve shirt with the top button open. He reaches out his hand as he walks around his desk. "I'm Kirk Browning. I'm the pastor here."

"I'm Sue Cass." Again the words seem foreign.

I look around the office as he's speaking to me and I hear his words, but they aren't really registering. We're talking but my mind seems to be off in some distant land. He touches my arm gently, as though to get my attention. "Would you like to ask Jesus to be your Savior?"

Not knowing what to say and hesitating, again the words spring from my mouth. "Yes."

"Do you confess your sins and want Jesus to forgive them? Do you believe in your heart that Jesus died and arose? That He is the Son of God?"

I answer "yes" to all the questions.

I look at him and suddenly sob. "I don't know why I'm crying."

Looking at me compassionately he says, "It's been a long time coming. You have every right to cry."

I'm forty-nine years old and in this unfamiliar place I've just committed my now lonely, empty life to Jesus.

He hands me a tissue. "Would you like to be baptized this morning?"

"Yes."

He leads me toward another room. "If you'd like, you can join this class while you wait for the worship service."

"Okay."

Poking his head in the door, he says "Good morning ladies."

I stand shyly beside him. "This is Sue Cass, she'll be joining you this morning."

A lady stands. "I'm Thelma, welcome to our class." Then she introduces me to people I've never met before.

The group is sitting around a long table with Bibles open in front of them. Thelma sits down while gesturing for me to take a seat. "We're studying Philippians three." It's a Sunday school class and I don't even have a Bible.

I sit amongst them, looking down at my lap and feeling very uncomfortable. *"What am I doing here? I don't know anything about the Bible!"* Prayers are spoken and we all stand up to leave as the class ends.

Thelma walks up to me. "Do you know where the sanctuary is?"

"No." She leads me up the stairs, and we enter a large room. This whole morning feels like I'm sleepwalking, yet I'm awake.

Cushion covered chairs are lined up in neatly formed rows creating one section off to the right. An aisle separates that section from the center section of chairs and then a third section sits off to the left with another aisle separating them.

Large windows line the side walls. A large polished wooden cross is on the wall in the front of the room. It's beautiful mahogany and hangs from high up on the wall to almost touching the floor.

The sunlight comes through the windows and rests on it. As I stand here gazing up at it I'm getting a strange feeling that its arms are reaching out welcoming me. Pulling my gaze away, *"This is weird."*

I walk toward the front row of seats, select a chair, and sit down. I'm feeling very strange in this new environment, and I gaze around. People begin entering and taking their seats.

A piano, podium, and a high back chair are on the stage in front of the cross. I fold my hands in my lap, like I think I'm supposed to. I lean back against the chair and look around; I'm feeling very much out of place. *"Now what do I do?"*

A lady approaches the piano, takes her seat, and the piano music starts. A choir dressed in their long blue gowns with white collars, file in taking their positions. The choir leader motions for us to stand; everyone begins singing.

Glancing over at the hymnal of the person next to me, I see what page our song is on. The people sing without looking at the words. *"I'm so stupid. I don't even know these songs!"* Yet I am singing.

The singing stops. As I sit down resuming my "church posture," Pastor Kirk approaches the front of the podium. "We have someone who would like to join our church and be baptized this morning. Sue, would you please come forward."

I rise from my seat, and walk forward to where he is. *"Why couldn't he have done this in his office?"* Standing next to a small round table with a bowl of water on top, Pastor Kirk touches my arm softly.

Looking directly into my eyes, with about four hundred people watching he says, "Do you profess Christ as your Savior?"

I whisper, "Yes."

"Do you wish to join this body of Christ giving of your time, talents, prayers, and tithes?"

"Yes."

Pastor Kirk reaches into the bowl of water with the tips of his fingers, and moves my bangs back. He's drawing a wet

6

cross on my forehead. "Sue Cass, in the name of the Father, Son, and the Holy Spirit I baptize you. You are now a daughter of the King, God bless you." Everyone claps. Pastor Kirk smiles. "Please welcome Sue into our family." Everyone stands, clapping and smiling. Embarrassed at having all this attention directed at me, I lower my eyes, and carefully step down to resume my seat.

Driving home, "*Oh Brian, I wish you were here. I just got saved. The most important decision I'll ever make in my life and you can't even share it with me.*"

I pull into the garage that's separated from the house and walk toward the house, looking around at our home. "*We helped build this.*" I am feeling an emptiness and remember how we cleared one acre and left the other five acres natural with their tall pine and oak trees.

The path we'd cleared through the dense trees leading to the creek is narrow. The creek winds its way through our property disappearing around a corner to grace the adjoining land. "*I remember when we cleared that path.*"

I stand, gazing out at the woods. Wild dogwood trees are scattered throughout and come alive with pink and white blossoms. Their branches reaching out over the path make an umbrella of beauty.

Wild ferns spotting the moist ground mingle with a variety of wild plants and saplings that fill nature with wonders and color. Deer, birds, rabbits, squirrels, and occasionally a possum wander out into the open spaces of the yard.

I turn my gaze to the front yard with a twitch of a smile. "*I remember when I first saw that wild persimmon tree with the dogwood keeping it company.*" The long rock-lined driveway leading to the newly paved road has finally been graveled.

I look over at my wishing well in the center of the front yard. "*I worked my butt off making that.*" I remember how

I'd taken an old metal barrel and cemented rocks that I'd dug up in the woods all around it, and getting my Dad to build the roof with its little bucket hanging in the center, and planting ivy around its base.

I take a step closer to the front of the house. My railroad tie borders are lined along the front of the house. *"Brian and I almost killed ourselves placing those there."* The flower gardens nestled behind them are filled with plants that bloom leaving a fragrance lingering in the air.

"I love those Azaleas, Rose of Sharon's, and Rhododendrons. They're my pride and joy." The tree-lined property line, separating our property from the neighbor, shades the ivy at their base. The grass is manicured, I did that last week. *"We put a lot of work in this place."*

I slowly walk toward the back door and pass through the chain link fence we had installed. A large rose bush covers a length of it and in the summer months it produces large beautiful roses. *"I've blessed many women with fresh bouquets of these fragrant roses."*

We've put a lot of work into making this our little haven. Brian loved it as much as I do. But now it seems vacant of joy, laughter, and love. With a sigh, I walk up the ramp, feeling sad and empty. I enter the now silent home.

I walk into the living room and sit down on the couch with a heavy sigh. *"Brian, there's no one to share this with anymore. I feel like an old dead hollowed out tree. I died with you, now what do I do?"*

I'm not aware that a transformation has already begun in my heart, mind, and soul. *"I thought I would be jumping around. Excited, have happy feelings. I don't feel anything. It's weird. I just got saved so why don't I feel any different?"*

I lay in bed several nights later, tears streaming down my cheeks, soaking my pillow. *"I can't do this, Brian, I don't know how I'm going to live without you. I want you back!"*

My sobs tear through the night. I lay here feeling very empty. "*I just want to die! God kill me so I can be with Brian.*" Suddenly thoughts of suicide start taking form, my mind reels with thoughts of how I can kill myself.

I open my eyes, wiping away the tears. Suddenly startled, I'm staring at a man standing in my bedroom doorway. He's huge! His head reaches the ceiling. He's dressed like the knights of old time with silver armor covering his body. A helmet hides his face. One arm is hanging straight down his side. The other arm is bent at the elbow with his hand resting on a long sword in a sheath hanging at his side, his stiff armored body erect. I can't see his face but a fierce power radiates from him.

All thoughts of suicide vanish! Sitting straight up in bed my heart stops in mid-beat. Staring at this person standing in my doorway, my tears suddenly freeze in their place.

A tidal wave of fear courses through me.

"Do not be afraid."

"*What the hell?*"

Sitting as still as a dead man I can't believe what I'm seeing. His body almost engulfs the entire doorway.

Looking past him on one side of his armor, fear wells up even more. Leaning against the corner of the hall wall behind him is a figure. A very mean looking man-like figure. His eyes are glowing red. His body is red, two small red horns are stationed on top of his head.

He looks like the characters drawn of the devil, but this is no cartoon! He's glaring at me with hatred that would melt an iron kettle into a puddle of smelt. "*I'm dreaming! This can't be real! Wake up!*"

"You are safe. No harm will come to you." The warrior in his full armor moves into a full on guard stance blocking the doorway so the devil can't enter. "Go to sleep, you're safe."

9

"This is one hell of a dream!" Feeling wonderful peace suddenly flow through me, I scoot back down under the covers. I fall soundly asleep.

2

This isn't the first time I've experienced the supernatural. Looking back I remember listening to the respirator that whooshed and clanked as it rushed air into Brian's lungs. Standing beside his bed weary and tired, the tubes going in and out of his body were beyond anything I've ever experienced. I was holding onto the railing of his bed and once again watched my beloved husband's chest rise and fall to the rhythm of the breathing machine.

I've never experienced what is known as a vision. I'm totally unaware of such a thing really happening to people. I've heard of people that say they have visions, but they're those "religious kooks."

Suddenly, without warning, I'm standing on the sidelines of a marathon being run. I'm cheering as I'm seeing Brian come down the middle of the paved road. There are no other runners around him.

He's wearing the same running shorts he's worn when he ran the Boston marathon and many other marathons throughout the years. The tennis shoes are his favorite, and his striped tank top hangs loosely.

After running many miles there's no sweat. His head is held high. His shoes, shorts, and tank top are brand new. His shoulders are not slumped, but appear quite relaxed. He's approaching the finish line of what is a long race.

Standing at the finish line I can see the chalk line drawn across the road. As he approaches the finish line his head turns. Looking straight at me, arms raised high in a sign of victory, "Sue-Sue, I made it. I've crossed the finish line." His foot suspended above the finish line begins to fall on the other side of the line and as suddenly as the vision appeared, it disappeared.

I was back standing beside his bed listening to the hospital sounds. While I was standing on the sideline watching my husband run the race in the vision, I didn't realize the doctor and nurse had slipped into the room.

Doing what doctors do, checking blood pressure, handling I.V. lines, quietly turning off the respirator as I had requested. No more beep, beep, beep of the heart monitor. No sounds of whooshing air being pushed into now still lungs. Brian has died.

I'm totally bewildered. I'm so engrossed in what just happened in the vision, I'm not aware of the doctor's hand gently on my shoulder. *"I've really lost it. This has just been to much, for too long. I've really gone crazy."*

With thoughts of the vision I've just had and the numbness engulfing me at knowing my husband is gone, I can't even cry. Arriving home, I almost run into the bedroom where a picture hangs of Brian crossing the finish line in the Boston marathon. I stop in front of it.

Standing here looking at it, I see his head is down, sweat pasting his hair to his head. His arms, legs, and torso look as though he's just run in a downpour of rain. His whole body slumped and exhaustion is so evident I can almost feel it through the picture.

His old torn running shorts are soaked, his tank top plastered to his body, his old running shoes look like they're on their last race. Body slumped forward, arms hanging loosely, he's crossing the finish line.

Standing frozen before the picture I can't believe my eyes. I was sure, at the hospital, that I was somehow seeing this picture. *"This isn't what I saw!"* My mind is whirling.

Goose bumps the size of ostrich eggs rise up all over my body. Talking out loud to the silent room with pill bottles lined up on the chest of drawers. Bed made neatly with a potty chair sitting alongside it. Bandages and tapes scattered across the dresser. His wheelchair folded and resting against a wall. "What the heck is going on?"

"This isn't what I saw at the hospital! Brian's arms were up, not dangling at his sides. His clothes are brand new, not sweaty, old, and worn. There's the number he wore pinned to the front of his tank top. That wasn't on him at the race I experienced at the hospital!"

I'm now convinced I've gone over the edge. Sitting down, the tears of loss and confusion come. Sobs of grief and despair flood through me like a dam that's been held back, finally breaking and all the pent up roller coaster emotions come flooding out.

Seeing Brian cross the finish line into eternity was my first vision but it wouldn't be the last. The Lord has already started proving to me that He is very real. The first vision I had as a new Christian was on the Walk to Emmaus.

A spiritual retreat through my church. On my knees praying I'm suddenly in the Spirit. (Taken into a spiritual realm.) In the vision I'm standing at one end of a large grassy field and see Jesus across the expanse.

He has His arms reaching out toward me waiting for me to come into them. Running toward Him, crossing the field, I reach Him and throw myself into His waiting arms. My head is cuddled in His neck as His arms embrace me.

I'm sobbing hysterically and pouring out my heart to Him. All the hurt, the pain, the atrocities that have been done to me throughout my life. I can feel His beard against my cheek. Holding me close He lets me pour it all out while never saying a word.

13

The vision ends and I find myself on my knees with my forehead pressed to the floor bawling my eyes out. I'm at the foot of the cross that's standing across the room. How I got there, I have no idea.

That wasn't where I was when I began praying. Jesus must have supernaturally picked me up and placed me at His feet. This vision was very significant to me. It's what I have needed all my life. To embrace my real Father.

I was raised in a most unpleasant environment. Abused physically, emotionally, sexually, and psychologically for the first eighteen years of my life. Fear, bruises, and a teeny tiny bit of hope was my world.

The only tiny bit of hope I felt was filled with hatred and wanting revenge. "When I'm old enough, I'll make them pay!" I held onto that for many years. I didn't know what love was or how a father should act. "Train your child in the way he should go . . ." as the Bible says (Proverbs 22:6) was totally foreign in our home.

Embracing my real Father for the first time is an experience I'll never forget. The Lord allowed me to embrace Him within my spirit. I can still feel His beard on my cheek at times.

In the months to come I've learned the Lord gifts us in many ways. I see angels, I pick up a pen to write and it flies across the page. Sometimes it writes so fast I can barely hold onto it.

Words and scriptures fly across the paper telling prophetic warnings, spelling out past events, giving loving encouragement to me as He takes me through the healing process from my abuse, and specific messages to various people in leadership, including my pastor.

I show the writings to my pastor. "Sue, this has to be from the Holy Spirit. I know your background and you just don't know these things. It fits scripture perfectly."

"I keep telling you, I hold the pen, He does the writing." Not being familiar with Bible scripture, I don't know if it lines up with scripture or not, that's why I'm taking them to him. I want to make sure I haven't gone crazy because I don't have a clue what it's talking about.

At first Pastor Kirk thinks it's "automatic writing" as is done in the occult world. He quickly deems it's coming from the Lord because the many messages that are given are Biblically accurate. We realize it is a genuine gift from God.

I've just bought a motor home and named it "The angel Buggy." It's parked beside the garage. I'm sure glad it's there because another experience leads me running to it. Standing at the foot of my bed preparing to go to bed, *"Something feels strange in here. It's giving me the willies. What is it?"*

Arms over my head with my nightgown suspended in mid-air, *"I don't like this, this is scary!"* A very strong sensing of horrible evil is filling the room. Looking around I see only the dresser with the jewelry box, Bible, and a figurine sitting on top.

The bed, chest of drawers with its small T.V. and a couple pair of shoes and my slippers thrown on the floor. No human around except me. My three dogs stretched out on the bed sound asleep.

I can't see anything out of the ordinary but feel goose bumps rising, covering my arms. *"What is this? I'm getting scared. Head for the motor home! Get out of here!"* I quickly tug my nightgown down over my body, slipping my feet into slippers, grabbing a robe. "Come on Jacob, Dusty, Rocky, let's go! We're sleeping in the motor home tonight!"

I grab the motor home keys off the key holder on the wall, slamming the back door, running for the motor home. I unlock the door. "Come on guys. We'll stay in here."

I lock the door behind me so nothing can get us. *"Boy, it's cold! I better get my heavy afghan for the bed if we're*

15

going to sleep in here." I reach into the storage area and pull out the large heavy afghan, spreading it over the other blankets on the queen size bed. "Okay guys, let's hit the sack. I think we're safe."

Waking to sun shining through the window, stretching, I'm tired but at least I finally went to sleep. Opening the motor home door and feeling a little scared to go back in the house, I step out.

With the dogs at my heels, I hesitantly walk toward the house. "Guys, be on guard. If there's anything in there, attack!" *That's a joke. They'll lick whatever it is to death.*

Entering the house through the back door, walking cautiously room to room, I don't sense anything. No evil lurking. *"I don't understand this. What the heck was that last night? I don't feel it now so I guess we're alright."*

Experiencing these supernatural occurrences is driving me nuts! I'm not acquainted with the supernatural having not been raised in church. Even if I had been many churches don't recognize or teach about such things.

The Twilight Zone theme song comes to mind, "Do-do-do-do, do-do-do-do," with its eerie music. When I tell others about these experiences I get a look that speaks volumes. "Sure you heard that! Oh, we understand completely," as they give each other the look of "she's really nuts."

God also says in scripture, "My sheep listen to My voice . . ." (John 10:27) When first hearing a voice in my head, I'm thoroughly convinced I've really gone nuts. All this Christian stuff is driving me crazy!

Seeing angels, a warrior in full armor in my bedroom. The devil glaring at me, a pen that writes on its own with me only holding it. Evil lurking in my house, I'm sitting at a table in a restaurant with one of the ladies from my Sunday school class.

I am hesitantly looking at her sitting across from me at the table and taking a bite of my sandwich. I get up the courage to ask as I'm wiggling in my seat a little: "How do you know if God is speaking to you?" *She's going to think I'm nuts.*

Cocking her head to the side, she answers "God speaks to people in different ways."

"What do you mean? How?"

"Well, in some people they get a sensing inside. Like down in their gut. Others hear Him through reading the Bible. It's like the words jump off the page."

As she takes a bite of her sandwich she's looking at me quizzically. "Music speaks to others in their heart. Some, I've been told, actually hear His voice."

"*Oh my gosh!* You mean they hear in their head, a voice speaking?"

"From what people who hear His voice have told me, yes. I don't hear His voice. I feel a sensing in my spirit."

My mind is whirling. *That might be what I'm hearing. I'm not telling her I hear a voice. I already feel like some lunatic, I sure don't want her thinking I am, too.*

I am watching T.V. "*I love you.*" *Now I know that didn't come from the T.V.!* I pick up the remote control and click it off, listening. "*I love you, Sue.*"

I snap my head around to see if anyone's in the room. "*Is that You, God?*" "*Yes, it's Me. You aren't crazy.*" The Lord begins speaking to me and I begin to believe it's really Him and start listening.

The more I'm convinced it's Him I start talking to Him. He gives me advice, helps me to understand scripture, guides me, and sometimes orders me. Because of my upbringing—being told to do this, that, or the other—I'm not used to being asked to do something.

I was always ordered around. No choice. Do it and ask no questions. The Lord speaks our language. He knows what we're used to and uses that familiarity to communicate. Many times He tells me what to do, whatever it is He wants done. Usually He doesn't tell me the reason He has for my doing it. *"I want you to go to the Christian bookstore. I'll show you what I want you to buy when you get there."* "Yes, Lord, I'm on my way."

It's amazing to me that He always comes through. Walking into the bookstore an unseen Man directs me to a porcelain statue of Him holding a cross. *"Buy it."* "Okay." I walk to the counter with the statue in hand, reach into my purse, and pull out a twenty dollar bill. "I think this statue is so pretty."

The cashier smiles and hands me my change. Carrying my wrapped statue to the car. I say *"Thank you, Lord, I really like this."* I'm not aware the Lord is teaching me obedience and trust. In my mind He's just blessing me because He likes me.

During the past year I've begun to trust the Lord more and more. That's huge for me! I don't trust anyone. My husband taught me about unconditional love and I trusted him.

Anyone else? I expect to be hurt so I keep my distance, physically and emotionally. "Don't let anyone close and never tell too much. They'll use it against you." Sitting in my Sunday school class, listening and discussing scripture, a point is made.

"God knows everything. He even knows what we're thinking." *"If that's true then I might as well tell Him since He already knows."* From then on I tell Him exactly what I think.

"I'm angry at You right now and I don't want to discuss it." "Lord, I'm feeling down. Will You give me Your comfort?" "Can You lay down beside me? I just need someone to hold me."

I've actually felt Him lay beside me with His arms around me. "Lord, can I go to the beach? I need to get away for a while." "What should I do about this?" "Am I really supposed to forgive her? Did you hear what she said?" "You make me so mad!"

I've learned the hard way I can't cross an invisible line with the Lord. I can get angry, express my anger. But there's a point where I've gone too far. "That's enough!" The Lord's stern reprimand shuts me up in a split second.

I'm so shocked at the sternness in His voice that I don't even ask for forgiveness. In the first place I'm too angry. In the second place, I'm so shocked because I've never had Him speak to me like that before.

Having been taken to the woodshed, as we call it here in the south, I feel the sting of His reprimand. Finally calming down, "Lord, I confess. I was really mad and I shouldn't have said what I did. Please forgive me. I won't do that again."

My walk with the Lord, having a relationship with Him, is just plain hard at times. From childhood I've learned to be independent, stubborn, and stand my ground. I didn't survive by being a "wimp."

Now that I'm an adult, I make the rules that I want to live by. I go where I want, I buy what I want, I say what I want. Tact is not one of my better qualities. What someone else thinks doesn't matter.

I say what's on my mind and if they don't like it, too bad. If I don't want to do something, I don't do it and to heck what others think. This attitude gets me in so much trouble!

The Lord's ways are very different from mine. A whole lot different! He cares what I think and how I act towards others. He wants His gentleness to be my gentleness. He's teaching me that and I'm going kicking and screaming all the way.

I am walking down the hall at church and talking to a friend. "If I had known being a Christian is this hard, I never would have become one!" Janice, walking from the other direction, has heard my comment.

She stops directly in front of me. "Yes you would, Sue. You can't turn back now. He's got 'cha!" As a "baby Christian" I'm learning scripture as I study at home.

Listening in the Sunday school class, talking with other Christians, and getting other points of views has also helped me. Now that I'm studying scriptures I'm more aware when others say something about a scripture and it doesn't line up with what I've read in the Bible.

I listen intently to the pastor's sermons. It seems like every one of his sermons are directed straight at me. It's really unnerving. I stop him after a worship service. "Pastor Kirk. Why do you do that?"

"Do what, Sue?"

"Direct your sermons straight at me?"

This self-centered, bull-headed baby Christian is learning, the hard way, this Christianity stuff isn't as easy as I thought. It's about me but not in the way I want it to be. Jesus wants me to be like Him.

That's very hard for me to swallow, but He's not giving up on me. No way!

3

This year has been a real learning experience for me. The people in church have truly embraced me and continually nurture and love me. I'm not used to this kindness or attention but I'm learning slowly to accept it.

I didn't get hugs growing up. That wasn't a part of my upbringing. Quickly learning the Christian people are huggers, it seems like handshakes or a simple hello doesn't suffice. They grab hold of me and like it or not I'm being hugged. I'm very uncomfortable with all this hugging business.

A tall, heavyset man named Bruce reminds me of a great big teddy bear. He usually greets me in passing but I try to steer clear of him. His smile is friendly enough, I don't feel a real threat but after all he is a man!

Walking past the Sunday school classrooms Bruce is approaching me. He walks straight up to me. Thinking nothing of it as he comes face to face with me, I just expect the usual "hello" and start to say, "hi."

His arms open wide and before I can protest he has me in a bear hug. I absolutely freeze! I'm as stiff as a board and scared out of my wits. Trying to remove my face from his belly, struggling to break away without just socking him in the gut, he suddenly releases me, smiles, says hello, and walks away.

"After that little incident, I'm steering clear of him! Waaaay away from him! I have no intention of putting myself in his path again for a repeat performance." It doesn't always work. Turning around from speaking to someone I bump into him.

"Here we go again, the bear hug!"

He releases me, smiling. "Hi Sue. It's good to see you."

"What's with this guy?" Bruce continues to find me when I'm not expecting him.

Each time is the same but his hugs are more gentle. I don't feel trapped, manhandled, or in any way offended by his attention now. I meet up with him in the hall once again.

"Hi Bruce."

"Sue, I need to talk to you for a minute. Do you have a minute?"

"Sure. What's on your mind?"

He looks a little uncomfortable. "You know when I first started hugging you?"

"Yes."

"Well, the Lord told me to do that. He said He wanted to teach you that there are safe hugs and was using me to do it. I know you were scared to death. I'm sorry."

I am laughing. "Oh really! I guess you aren't a pervert after all."

He laughs, giving me a hug. He's now continuing down the hall. I'm not threatened by him at all now. Because of the Lord using him in teaching me all men aren't going to hurt me, I'm not so uncomfortable when men indicate they want to give me a quick hug.

I still assess the situation and who's about to hug me. Total trust isn't always healthy trust. Over all though, I don't fear like I did for so many years. When I see Bruce now I just expect a friendly hug.

The Lord is showing me He will use others to help me. Sometimes it just scares the hell out of me, too.

Having gone through the stage of shock at losing my husband, feeling loss, aloneness, and missing him terribly is almost more than I can bear. *"Brian, I miss you so much. "Do they celebrate birthdays in heaven?"*

"*What do you do in heaven? Did Jesus meet you at the gates of heaven? Are you playing tennis? Chess? Do they have marathons there?*" Anger begins to wiggle in. Blaming God, not only for the abuse I suffered as a child, but now for my husband's death.

I shake my fist toward heaven and screaming, "You took Brian to punish me for all the years I wasn't a Christian!" Breaking into sobs, laying on my bed, I'm convinced that's what God did just to get back at me.

Anger slowly subsiding, I'm worn out from the hysterical outburst. I finally go to sleep only to have fitful dreams. "*I'm alone, Lord. Nobody would understand and I won't share these feelings with them. You know when I showed any emotions as a kid what happened. God, I really need you!*"

There are days I'm okay. Then more outbursts. "*I wish I was dead! I want to be with Brian!*" "*Look at that couple! We're supposed to be like that!*" The hurt at seeing others lovingly laughing and holding hands brings sadness and anger mixed together. "*It isn't fair!*"

Then guilt begins to plague me. If I want to die shouldn't it be so I can be with Jesus? I'm confused. At this time in my grief I'd rather be with my husband. Yes, Jesus is there and I'll get to be with Him but my focus is more on being with Brian. "*Lord, I'm sorry. I want to be with Brian. I know You'll be there, too.*" "*I understand.*"

Gradually the months of sadness, misery, and grief become farther and farther apart. "*I miss him so much, Lord.*" "*I know. You'll be okay.*" Accepting he's gone, I've begun turning to the Lord more and more.

My relationship with Him is getting stronger as I look to Him and lean on Him. Twirling around in a circle in my living room I say, "Lord, see my new dress. Do You think it's pretty?" "What should I have for dinner tonight? You can come if you want to."

A big part of my relationship with the Lord is communication, in thoughts and speech. "Thank you Lord for this parking space, that flower is so pretty. You did good! I don't understand what You're showing me. What are You doing?! This doesn't make any sense at all!"

We talk about many things. It isn't a one-sided conversation. *"Don't be scared, I'm here." "I have given man free will. "You are My daughter, I love you more than you'll ever imagine." "Trust Me."*

"Then where were You when I was being abused?" *"I was there."* A mental picture plays out in my mind. Jesus is on His knees praying. His face uplifted toward heaven. Tears are streaming down His face as my father abuses me. Red hot anger flares up. "That's all You did? You just prayed!"

I haven't fully grasped that Jesus intercedes to the Father on our behalf. He gives us free will and if we choose sin He honors our free will to do that. It doesn't mean He likes it.

Other times I'm crying out to the Lord. "God, please help me!" Yet many times I'm laughing at what He's said. He has a wonderful sense of humor and in my mind's eye I can see Him with His head thrown back, laughing with me.

The visions, things He says to me, His love and comfort leave me in awe and "Wow!" is commonplace. I feel His hand on my shoulder at times, reassuring. *"It'll be okay."* It's as though a real hand is touching me and at times I even reach up and put my hand on His.

I am sitting on the couch in thought. *"Lay down."* Laying down, closing my eyes I'm once again transported into a vision. This vision isn't like watching a movie as in some of the visions I have.

In this one I'm actually participating in the vision. It's me in the sky feeling the air around me as I'm flying over the tree tops. Clearing the tree tops looking down at sand dunes,

I'm marveling at the rolling of the sand and various patterns the sand makes as I glide above them.

Off in the distance is a large gray cement building. *"Is that a warehouse? A school? I wonder what it is."* Then in a blink of an eye I'm standing in front of a worn, tattered, green door at the building front.

It has no windows and I'm still not sure what it's used for. Jesus is suddenly beside me holding a key. The door is closed. *"Will you walk through that door without knowing what's on the other side?"* Looking up at Him and a little hesitant I say, "Okay."

I am waiting, expecting Him to open the door. *"You have to open the door, Sue."*

"Will you come with me? I won't do it unless You're beside me."

"Yes." He hands me the key.

Placing it into the lock, cautiously pushing the door open, I don't know what to expect on the other side. I'm surprised when I see nothing. The Lord is looking down at me. *"Are you willing to step over this threshold?"*

Looking at Him, feeling the trust of being with Him, He and I step over the threshold. The vision ends. Still laying on the couch I can't move. I'm off somewhere in a Spiritual realm that the Lord has not brought me out of.

Suddenly the phone is ringing. Jerking up to answer it I'm hardly able to speak. I feel like I'm just coming out from under anesthesia.

"Hello."

"Hi Sue. It's Nancy. Were you sleeping?"

It takes a few minutes for the fog in my mind to lift.

Not everyone experiences visions, hears the Lord's voice, sees angels or senses evil presences. Several Christians I know personally do. How many actually hear angels? I don't know. Some of us do.

I am laying in bed after a Christmas Eve service. *"I hear music! Where's that music coming from?"* I listen more intently to see if I can locate where it's coming from. *"That's absolutely beautiful!"*

The music gets a little louder. *"It's an angel choir!"* For some reason fifteen hundred comes to mind. *"It's an angel choir of fifteen hundred angels! Woooow!"* They're not singing Christmas songs like we're used to but praising the Lord Jesus using songs I've never heard before. Possibly no one else has ever heard either.

I've never heard anything so beautiful. The music is so clear I can actually hear the words they're singing. *"I should write the words down."* But being so mesmerized by the beauty of the song, I just lay there listening.

I drift off to sleep as the choir fades away. *"Oh Wow! Thank you Lord,"* is my last thought. When I wake up, *"Was that a dream?"* I don't think so, I really did hear those angels! People sure won't believe I heard an angel choir."

4

My hairdresser and I have become very close friends. We're chatting when she looks at me rather seriously. "Sue, I just found out I have breast cancer. I'll be having surgery Monday."

Eyes watering, I can hardly speak. Hugging her, tears start sliding down my cheeks. She knows Brian died just eleven months ago. "I know you'll be with me in your heart. Don't come to the hospital. Randy and I will be fine."

It's been six weeks since she's had surgery and started her chemotherapy and radiation treatments. I walk into the beauty shop to get my hair cut. "Hi Sue, I'll be with you in just a second."

I can tell she's worried about something. Beckoning me over to the chair, sitting down, she wraps the plastic cape around my shoulders. Looking at her in the mirror, "Rebecca? What's wrong?"

"Randy and I are having to leave our apartment. You know he's been out of work. I don't know what we're going to do or where we'll go."

"You'll go to my house and live with me until Randy goes back to work!"

Tears trickle down her cheeks as she hugs me from behind.

"You and Randy start moving your stuff in my house tonight."

Upon returning home I'm clearing out dresser drawers so they'll have more room in the guest room.

Arriving with two suitcases and a couple of boxes Rebecca sits down on the couch as Randy sets them in the bedroom. "Sue, sit down, I need to talk with you."

I see concern etched across her face. "Rebecca, what's going on?"

"I have to have a bone marrow transplant, Sue. It will be done at Emory and my doctors are the same that Brian had. Randy and I will understand if you can't handle coming to the hospital. In fact we don't want you to."

Shocked. I can't even speak. No comforting words, no hugs. I can't even cry as I'm looking at her. I know all too well what it means to have to have a bone marrow transplant. I witnessed too many of them on the cancer floor when Brian was sick.

Rebecca has been at Emory a week now. *I need to go to the hospital and see Rebecca at least once.* Driving to Emory, walking through the hospital corridors, I don't need directions to the fourth floor.

As I'm passing the nurses station I hear, "Sue? What are you doing here?"

"Hi Dr. Flemming. I'm here to see Rebecca."

He looks at me sympathetically. "Haven't you had enough of this place?

I smile weakly and walk into Rebecca's room. "Hi, how are you doing?"

The hospital smells, calls over the P.A. system, hearing patients retching, and the soft conversation between patients and families are all too familiar sounds and I'm wanting to run as fast as I can.

Standing at her bedside, the beep, beep, beep of the heart monitor is almost more than I can stand. The I.V. lines hanging from the pole with bags of saline solution, liquid food, all are reminders of another time. *"I never should have come."*

Pushing herself up slightly in the bed she says, "Randy isn't here right now. He'll be here later."

Shifting from one foot to the other, I can't stand still. It's almost like my feet have a mind of their own and they're screaming, "Run!"

"How am I going to leave without hurting her feelings? I've only been here fifteen minutes. I can't stay here! This is one of the same rooms Brian had." A nurse walks in. Touching Rebecca's hand I say, "I guess I better go and get out of the way."

"I'm glad you came by. I'll be home soon."

I hear the car pull up to the house. *"Rebecca's home!"* I run out to the car, helping Randy walk Rebecca into the house and to bed. "Can I get you anything? Do you need a pitcher of water?"

Weakly smiling she says, "Thanks, I'm fine."

Rebecca and Randy have been with me three weeks now. Coming home from church and walking into the house, there's a feeling of heaviness in the atmosphere. Entering the living room, Rebecca and Randy are sitting on the couch talking softly.

"We have to tell her."

"Tell me what?"

With concern on her face Rebecca pats the couch. "Sue, sit down. We have something we need to tell you." Feeling as though the floor is about to cave in, I can tell something is very wrong from the looks on their faces.

Rebecca looks at me, the lines of weariness creasing her face. "Sue, the bone marrow transplant didn't take." Shock courses through my body. I can't breathe. The words seem to knock the breath right out of me.

I'm dumbfounded. I can't cry, speak, or get up to hug her. A feeling of panic is rising up in me. *"I gotta' get out of here! I can't take this! This can't be happening.*" Without saying a word, I'm running to the safety of my motor home.

Throwing myself on my bed, I'm able to let out the fear, the knowing, crying so hard I have to run to the bathroom to vomit. I know all too well what happens when a bone marrow transplant doesn't work.

"*NO! NO!*" My face stuffed in the pillow. "*Fix her! You're all powerful, You can do anything! Damn it, do something!*" Tears flow like a waterfall. "*I can't go through this again! I'm out of here!*"

I run into the house, throwing clothes in a pile. "*How much food can I get in the refrigerator?*" I better stop and fill up with gas. Don't forget dog food. *Oh God you can't be letting this happen again! Why? Everything I love you take!*"

Rebecca is sitting quietly on the couch with her face in her hands. Randy is pacing. "Randy, I can't do this! I'm leaving. I'm sorry, Rebecca. I'm going to Destin, Florida. I'll call when I get there."

Randy turns to look at me. "Do you know how long you'll be gone?"

"No! When you see me, you'll know I'm back."

Rebecca lifts her head, looking at me with understanding in her eyes. She knows I'm running away.

I've already put the groceries in the motor home refrigerator. Carrying my clothes, several tapes so I can listen to music, Rocky, Jacob, and Dusty are already sitting in their favorite places.

Rocky likes to lay on the couch with his head resting on his small pillow. Jacob sits on the bench on one side of the table where he can watch out the window. Dusty lays stretched out on the bench on the other side of the table.

Occasionally, he'll ride in the passenger seat across from me. All three are expectantly waiting for the engine to be fired up. They know when Mama is going in the motor home they'll be going with me. It's our home away from home. Relaxing under the awning of the motor home with the waves gently caressing the beach, the dogs are sleeping at my feet. A gentle breeze makes the scalloped edge of the awning dance.

People begin pointing at a dark ominous cloud off in the distance. The man with a fifth wheel trailer parked next to me is standing at the end of the motor home. He turns toward me. "A big storm is blowing in! You can see it's headed straight for here. Lady, we're all packing up! You better do the same."

Everyone starts packing up to leave. *"I don't want to go home yet!"* I look out across the water and see the black cloud rolling toward us. *"Doggone it! I've only been here a week."* I look back toward the black cloud that now looks like a tidal wave rolling toward us. *"Yea, maybe I better go. That sucker looks mean!"*

I reluctantly store pots and pans, the radio, items off the table and various things that have been sitting out. I unplug the power lines, septic hose, and water line. "Come on guys. We have to go home now."

Arriving home the house is silent. *"Where's Rebecca and Randy?"* Seeing a note on the table I pick it up. "Sue, I just can't do this to you. It's too soon after Brian's death. We've moved into a house. Randy got a job." Laying the note down, I know she's dying and she knows it, too.

I've waited three days before going to visit her. I'm not sure I can face this yet again but deciding to go I follow the directions to their house that Randy gave me on the phone.

I sit beside her hospital bed that's been moved into her new home, and point to the head of her bed. "Do you see the angels, Rebecca?"

"Yes. They're beautiful. I'm so anxious to be with Jesus." Her voice is barely a whisper.

Continuing to look at the head of her bed I'm seeing three angels hovering just above the bed. Oh they are so beautiful in their flowing white gowns. Their wings are large. Each wing is stretched to full bloom making a beautiful cascading shelter of white flowing feathers as each wing touches the tip of the next wing encircling the head of the bed where her head rests.

Rebecca's eyes close. Kissing her forehead I quietly leave her room. Arriving home, sitting down at the table, I'm suddenly seeing into the spiritual world. A beautiful purple light is spiraling toward heaven.

It races heaven bound, followed by a pure white light that's beside, mingling with, and swirling with the purple light. Immediately I know it's Rebecca's spirit. I jump up and shout to the heavens, "You go girl! The angels can't even keep up with you!"

I throw the front door open and step outside, waving as though Rebecca is waving back at me. "Hurry up angels or she'll beat you to heaven. I love you, Rebecca. Tell Brian I love him and still miss him."

I pick up the phone as it rings. "Sue, Rebecca just died."

"I know, Randy. I watched her go to heaven."

Through his tears he said, "You what?"

"I saw Rebecca go to heaven. I know what time she died. I'll explain later, Randy."

That's another gift the Lord has blessed me with. It's called "Seeing the Spirit." The Lord opens my spiritual eyes which allows me to see into the Spiritual realm.

We have our human eyes but we also have spiritual eyes. In my case, I see only what He wants me to see and some things I'd rather not see.

It isn't imagination. With visions, if it were imagination, I could just sit down and think, "Okay, what trip shall I take today? I've been over trees and a desert. How about an island someplace?" or "I think seeing someone go to heaven would be cool."

A man at church had severe back pain. His pain was so great and for so long he tried to commit suicide. I was sitting in my office when Pastor Kirk stuck his head in. "Sue, start praying! Jack just tried to commit suicide. I'm on my way to the hospital."

As he rushes out the door, I look down at the open pages of my Bible where I was reading Psalm 31. Verse four and five jump out at me. "Free me from the trap that is set for me, for You are my refuge. Into Your hands I commit my spirit; redeem me O' Lord, the God of truth."

Just as I'm reading it the Lord lets me see into the spiritual realm. Jack's spirit is jettisoning to heaven. Then he and Jesus are standing facing each other talking. As I'm watching them talking I can't make out what is being said, except for one statement, "It isn't your time."

"Sue, go to the hospital. Jack just died. His wife will need you." "Yes Lord, I'm on my way." Running to the car, it's a fifteen minute drive from the church. *"I better hurry. I don't know if anyone else is there."*

I ask where Jack is at the information desk. "He's in the Intensive Care Unit. Second floor." Walking quickly down the second floor hall I can see Jack's wife is leaning up against the wall.

Just as I'm approaching her Pastor Kirk walks out from the Intensive Care room. Surprised to see me he says, "What are you doing here?"

"The Lord told me to come. Jack died and He wanted me to be here for his wife."

A look of absolute astonishment comes over Pastor Kirk's face.

"He just died about fifteen minutes ago. They've brought him back. He's alive." His facial expression absolutely screams of bewilderment and astonishment. "Praise God. I guess I can leave then."

That isn't something I just imagined. At the exact time Jack died the Lord told me he died. The Lord's voice can be pretty powerful or a soft whisper. When He said to go to the hospital it wasn't a soft whisper. He meant, "go to the hospital and go now."

No one can conjure up a vision. It comes from God. Otherwise it's a daydream, imagination, or wishful thinking. It's the Lord's decision when and if we'll have a vision, a mental picture, a night vision, or even certain dreams.

Visions and sudden mental pictures are pretty frequent occurrences for me. One of God's gifts that He blesses me with. The mental pictures are like snapshots. Suddenly I'm seeing Jesus at a potter's wheel molding clay.

Almost as quickly as it appears, it disappears. Even though it's a sudden snapshot it has a message. In this one the message is loud and clear, "We are the clay and You are the potter." (see Isaiah 64:8).

It seems the Lord likes to catch me at the least likely times. Walking across my living rom with a book in my hand, sitting down on the couch to read, the next thing I know, I'm waking up from having been in hell.

The Lord once again has taken me into another experience through a vision. In this vision faces are floating around in darkness. Some I recognize and others are strangers. Mouths are open as though they're screaming, yet there's no sound coming from them.

They all have a look of agony and desolation. Lost, terrified expressions on their faces as they float around listlessly with seemingly no purpose or direction. The appearance of desperate begging in their eyes as they look at me is almost more than I can bear. Even in the vision.

As the faces disappear into the black abyss more float out of the darkness. I've never seen anything as black as what I'm seeing. Pitch black doesn't even begin to describe it and the horror on the faces is terrifying.

The faces disappear and a small white church comes into view in the midst of the blackest black anyone can imagine. It has the box-style shape as do so many small country churches.

It has a little porch on the front to protect its worshippers from the elements. Three small steps lead up to the front door. A small steeple with a cross on top stands proudly at the forefront of the roof.

Slowly the church starts turning in a circle. The counter-clockwise spinning picks up speed. It seems like in just a matter of seconds the church is spinning very fast. It's become a whirling blur and suddenly flies off its axis and spins off into the unending blackness.

The vision continues and suddenly I'm standing in flames. Flames reaching up higher than my head. Flames licking at everything but me. Looking above me, around me, the flames are blazing on all sides and above me.

An angel standing beside me in the flames says, "I'm with you. It's going to be okay. You won't be harmed."

Amazingly I don't feel the heat, I'm not burned. The hairs on my arms aren't even singed, yet I'm totally surrounded in red hot fire. The vision ends.

5

I am talking with Pastor Kirk in his office. "Sue, why don't you start your own support group for women that have been abused as children?"

Not having told anyone about my abuse, other than my therapist and Pastor Kirk, I'm very hesitant to do that.

"Call around and see if there are any. Georgia Council on Child Abuse may have one. But I doubt if there are any Christian-based ones. We could have one here."

"Maybe it would help me to join one and see what exactly goes on in them."

I walk out of his office. *"I'm not sure if that's really what I want to do."* Revealing such a thing is quite scary. Trust, guilt, and shame are strong issues survivors have.

"Sue, call and see if they have a support group." "Lord, I'm not sure I want to do that." "Trust Me, it will be okay." Getting up the nerve, picking up the phone, dialing, a soft voice answers the phone. "Hello, Georgia Counsel on Child Abuse. Can I help you?"

Scared to death, the words don't want to come out of my mouth?

"It's okay. Take your time."

Tears begin running down my face, my hands are shaking, almost whispering, "I was sexually abused as a child. I'm wondering if you have a support group I might join."

"Yes, but it has a year waiting list. Would you like to add your name to the list?"

"No, thank you." Relieved, I hang up, letting out a big sigh. *"Good! I don't have to do that!" "Oh yes you do."*

For almost a year the Lord has me going to a variety of conferences and seminars pertaining to abuse. Suddenly it seems like everywhere I turn there's a conference being pointed out to me. *"I want you to attend that conference."* *"But Lord." "Go!"*

Each one piques my interest more. The best part is I don't have to reveal my abuse unless I want to. Which I don't. I'm learning a lot about the healing process victims go through. Which helps me better understand my own issues.

Large groups, as well as small groups of people, attend these various conferences. One seminar I attend is a small gathering of professionals. Psychiatrists, social workers, pastors are seated. Like me they're here to learn more about abuse victims and how to help them.

Going from one person to the next in introductions, "Good morning, I'm Dr. so and so." "I'm a social worker with such and such county." "I'm Pastor so and so at such and such church." Then it's my turn. *"Dear Lord, why in the world did you send me to this one!"*

I feel totally out of place. I inhale deeply and wish I could suddenly disappear. "I'm Sue Cass. I'm just a little ole Christian that wants to start a support group in my church."

All eyes are on me as they clap, give encouragement and smile friendly. *"Phew! I guess they don't think I'm an idiot after all."* The conference lasts all day and I've learned a lot.

"I want you to give a testimony at church." "No way!" "You'll be fine. Trust me." By now I'm calling Pastor Kirk by his first name. He isn't hung up on having to be called pastor and most of us address him as Kirk.

Our congregation is like family in many ways. Of course if we introduce him to someone we call him pastor.

Stopping him after church I say to him, "Kirk, the Lord wants me to give my testimony at church. Would I be able to do that?" Hoping against all hope. I'm hoping he will say no.

"I think that would be wonderful! How long do you need and when would you like to give it?"

"*Oh God, why are You doing this to me?*" "*Trust me.*" I pick up the pen to begin writing my testimony. "*Lord, You better write this. I sure can't.*" The pen begins to fly across the paper and the next thing I know I'm standing in front of the congregation.

Twenty minutes later as I leave the podium, there's polite clapping. Some give me nice comments, some are encouraged, yet some have felt uncomfortable about the testimony.

I'm not surprised because many don't understand that abuse was done to us. We're unwilling participants. I am sitting in Kirk's office talking about my testimony. "Sue, I wasn't going to tell you, but I think you need to know. Some of the women came to me complaining after your testimony."

"Why? What'd they say?"

"They feel this is no place for that kind of thing. They said, we don't need *that* stuff here in the church!"

"What did you tell them?" I am flabbergasted.

Leaning back in his chair he said, "I said, well, ladies, if hurting people can't come to the church for healing, where else can they go?"

"Way to go! Thank you for backing me up." I am now grinning.

From the moment I walked away from behind the podium that morning, the shame I've felt for so many years is gone. Having stood before four hundred or more people telling my story of abuse and how Christ has been healing me, the Lord just lifted the shame.

"*It's time to start a support group, Sue.*" "*Lord are You sure about this?*" "*I want to use your pain to help others.*"

"Oh God, now what do I do?" *"You'll call it the Angel Ministry. The support group can be called the Angel Group."* Giving me step by step instructions the Lord tells me what materials to buy and how many Bibles, pencils, and journals I'll need. Buying poster board and cutting it in half, He tells me what to put on posters to hang in the church inviting women to come to the group.

"I've never even been to a support group, Lord. How in the world am I going to pull this off?" *"I'll get you someone to lead the group and you co-lead it. That way you'll get acquainted with how it's done."*

The Lord, as usual, does exactly that. He supplies me with a Christian woman to lead the group. The support group is going well. Sitting at my desk preparing the material for tonight's group I can hear Kirk on the phone.

I wait a few minutes until he was finished talking and walk across the hall to Kirk's office. "Do you have a minute, Kirk?"

"Sure."

I sit down in the leather chair in front of his desk. "We need a counselor in here. These women need more than just a support group. You yourself call this church 'the church of the walking wounded.' Everyone would benefit."

"You're right. I'll pray about it."

In less than a month the Lord brings us a married couple who are licensed counselors with plenty of experience. Kirk pops his head into my office. "We have two counselors that are joining us. This is Benjamin and Carol Banning. Because of limited space they'll be sharing your office with you. Is that okay with you?"

"Sure."

"Oh great!"

Arriving early in the office I'm rearranging the furniture. Moving the desk, adding a love seat, dragging a book case in to help with whatever books and items they might have.

"Hi, are we disturbing you?" Looking up, Benjamin and Carol are standing in the doorway. They're a nice-looking couple. Both appear to be in their late fifties. Carol is tall with slightly graying hair.

Her tan slacks and soft green sweater is quite attractive on her and complements her complexion. Benjamin is a tad shorter than his wife. Wearing dark gray pants that fit his slim body and a patterned short sleeve shirt, he's holding a small stack of books.

An aura of calm confidence comes from both of them. "No. I was just trying to rearrange things. What do you think? Will the bookshelves be enough?"

Ben steps closer, looking past Carol." "Yes, that will work out just fine."

Carol is standing just inside the door slightly in front of Benjamin. Stepping farther into the office she's looking around at the various things hanging on the walls. On one wall hangs a large poster of an angel.

On the wall next to the desk, a small sign, "Angels at work—Prepare for random miracles" is held up by thumbtacks. Just below that is another sign, "Hangeth in there."

Framed certificates showing the completed training I've had decorate the wall near the window. "It's so nice of you to let us share your office. We appreciate that." "No problem, Carol."

"*Okay Lord. You answered my prayers, now help us figure out how all of this is going to work.*" Ben sits down in the chair after placing the books he's carried in on the bookshelf. "Let's see how we can all meet the needs we have for the use of the office."

Carol and I sit on the love seat. "What are your needs, Sue?"

I tell them about the ministry, the support groups. "I'm in and out. I'm not in here all the time but I think we can work something out."

"How would you feel about our putting a sign on the door, counseling in session?"

I look at him and then Carol. *I know they need privacy but how's that going to affect me?*

"That will work, then I'll know not to enter. *Oh Lord. What happens when I need the office?* After discussing everything I'm realizing this is going to be a big adjustment for me. I'm not too pleased about how this is going to interfere with my work but there isn't much I can do about it.

Within a couple of days they settle and begin counseling with people who have a variety of needs they want help with. Ben and Carol do individual counseling as well as couples and premarital counseling.

I rush down the stairs to get some things out of the office and find the "Counseling in Session" sign hanging on the door. *"I knew this wouldn't work!"* It's been "my space" for some time and I'm finding it more challenging than I thought.

My self-centeredness peeks its head up from time to time. Under my breath I'm grumbling and moaning. *"You'll get used to it, child."* *"Yea, right!"* I've finally gotten used to having to share my office and we're able to cohabitate quite well.

I'm still frustrated at times when I see that sign on the door when I really need something out of the office. Especially if it is pertinent to the group I'll be leading tonight.

I've come to like Benjamin and Carol a lot and I'm feeling more comfortable around them. I've begun calling Benjamin, Ben. Having been told about the ministry I do, they're very supportive.

This is a real blessing to me because on occasion I need their advice about something that arises in the support group. If someone needs a counselor outside the group I can suggest them along with others I have listed as counselors.

The support group is going pretty smoothly. We have ten women in the group and we're about three months into the material and discussions. Bonnie, the counselor that has been leading the group, announces she'll be moving soon.

"Now what, Lord?" "I want you to take over and lead the group." "Are You kidding me? I can't do that! I'm not ready." "Yes you are!" "Well, You better do it through me because I sure don't know how." "Trust Me."

Obviously the Lord already knows Bonnie is leaving because He provides me with another lady to help lead the group almost immediately. Susan is a small woman. I'll guess she's five foot one or two. She appears to be very delicate and soft-spoken. A godly woman.

She's like a soft warm breeze that gives reassurance and comfort to all around her without saying a word. We've now been leading the group about a year together. Her little flared skirt softly swishes as she walks up to me. Eyes twinkling she says, "Let's do it."

Susan and I seem to be made for each other. Laughingly I call her the "good cop," and me the "bad cop." Her soft-spoken words are quite different from my blunt, no nonsense manner.

The ladies feel at ease with her but some are intimidated by me. We absolutely complement each other yet are so different in ministering to the women. She's as serious as I am about dealing with the issues at hand but I come across more forceful, even though I don't mean to.

Our personalities are very different but the Lord has brought us together and He certainly knew what He was doing. We almost read each other's mind. I fill in thoughts where she leaves off and she does the same with me. It's uncanny.

She and I are anxious to begin the new group coming in. On the first night, sitting at a table situated in the center of the room, we've prayed for guidance, wisdom, and healing for each lady.

The chairs are pulled out from the table to invite those who enter. Closed folders are on the table in front of each chair containing information about what we'll be doing during the course of the next five months.

A small leather bound Bible, journal, book marker, and small inspirational card are on the table at each seat. In the center of the table a small vase with a silk rose flower sits between a box of tissue and a basket filled with pencils.

A lady walks in that we haven't met. "Hi, I'm Candice. Is this where the Angel Group support group meets?" She isn't a bit shy as most of the women are when they walk through the door.

She sits down across from Susan. *"She's going to live with you." "Dear Lord, what are You doing? What do You mean she's going to live with me? I've never seen this woman before." "You'll see."*

As we're waiting for the others to arrive we make small talk. "My two daughters and I are living in my truck. I have a job but I don't have enough to support us. They live with their father but I have them on the weekends."

Again, the words come out of my mouth that are not mine. "How old are your girls?"

"The oldest is eleven and the youngest is seven."

"I live very close to here. Why don't you follow me home. You can stay with me, if you want. If it doesn't work out you can leave." *What am I saying?* Once the other ladies arrive we begin.

"Ladies, I'm Sue Cass and this is Susan Frost. We'd like to welcome you to the Angel Group. We're a Christian-based support group. We support each other as we go through the healing process. We aren't going to preach to you, but we do seek the Lord's healing."

We pause to give them a moment to think about that. "We're not a therapy group although some of you may need extra help on the side. We ask for a five dollar donation each night. It helps with the supplies we need. If you can't afford that, you're still welcome in the group."

One lady looks bored, the others are attentive. "Everything that is said in this room is strictly confidential. What's said in here, stays in here! Is everyone clear on that? Absolute confidentiality is a must!" My voice is now quite stern. When it comes to confidentiality I make no bones about it.

Heads nod. "Let's go over the boundaries we have for the group now. We do not tell what I call horror stories." Looking around the room I can see each is paying close attention.

"We don't need to know the specifics of your abuse." Looking around the table the ladies seem a bit more relaxed at hearing the boundaries so far. "We all have anger. You will be allowed to express that anger, but you will not be allowed to direct it at any individual in here."

Everyone is silent. I sense a little tension in the air so "Good cop" steps in. "Ladies, we're providing a safe place for you to be able to laugh, cry, and bare your heart. We're all here to support each other."

Susan glances at me. It's a signal for me to step back in. "Starting here, I'd like each of you to introduce yourself and tell us a little about yourself. Include in your introduction, 'I've been abused.' "

Looks of horror and disbelief are aimed at me. "The first step to healing is admitting, out loud, that you have been harmed, hurt as a child. You've been silent about it too long."

Pointing to the first lady sitting next to me, "Let's start with you." When all introductions have ended I say, "I'd like to tell you a little about myself and then Susan will tell you about herself."

"I was abused as a child." Continuing with a short testimony about myself the women are listening intently. Susan begins and tells about herself. Taking the lead once again I say. "Everyone in here has suffered as children. We're all here to seek God's healing for the issues we have from that abuse." All eyes are focused on me. "Some of you may think there's no hope. Susan and I are living proof that there is hope. The Lord has brought healing to us and is enabling us to be able to help others."

"God will do the healing if you give Him permission. That doesn't mean you can sit back and do nothing. He does His part and you have to do your part." The body language of one lady is obvious that she'd rather be somewhere else.

Susan steps in. "This is a healing process, ladies. It isn't going to be easy but with God at your side and each other to lean on, you can do it. Does anyone have any questions? Okay."

She hands each person paper and pencil. "I would like for each one of you to write down ten positive things about yourself. I'll give you a few minutes." A stunned look appears on all faces.

Glancing at Susan we both smile with a knowing look. This isn't the first time we've brought this challenge before a group of hurting women. We've found most never consider the good within themselves.

The hour and a half that is allotted quickly comes to an end. Susan closes with prayer and the ladies begin gathering their things together. A few say thank you but most quietly head for their cars.

When all have left Candice stands waiting for me to gather my things. Getting into my car and she in her small pick-up we pull out of the church parking lot. I am driving home with Candice close behind. *"Sue, There is to be no drugs, no alcohol, and no men allowed. That's the rules I'm setting up."* "Yes Lord. *That suits me just fine!"*

Candice moves in with me and I'm realizing pretty quickly this is not going to be as easy as I thought. She's as sweet as can be and I really like her but living with anyone can be challenging at times.

Walking into the kitchen I think, *What's that smell?* Glancing around, *Oh good grief! She's left the pot on the stove and all the waters boiled out!* Running to the stove, I turn the burner off. *"I'm going to strangle that woman!"*

She's laying in the bathtub during a lightning storm. "Candice, get out of the tub! Do you want to get fried?" Through the door I hear a splash.

"Oh, I'm okay. Don't worry about it."

"Candice, please! I don't want a dead body in my bathtub."

Suddenly, while I'm standing at the door, a very loud clap of thunder rattles the windows. The bathroom door flies open and almost knocking me over, Candice flies across the hall butt naked to her room. Not being used to having kids around, the weekends with the girls are nerve-racking for me at times. Their room looks like a tornado hit it, they eat like horses, and argue with Mom and each other.

Over all, I guess, they're just normal kids. They do help me in the yard at times and we get in water fights with the hose. They like to go to the creek at the back of the property so it isn't all hair-raising.

The girls want to go in the Angel Buggy camping so bad they can hardly stand it. While I'm having a quiet time in my safe retreat from them, in the motor home, I notice four little eyes peeking through the door.

They see that I've spotted them. "Can we come in?"

I'm not too happy at having my seclusion interrupted. "Yes, come on. What do you want?"

Candy steps inside. "We've never got to go in the Angel Buggy. Will you take us someplace?"

Seeing the pitiful look on their faces almost makes me bust out laughing. "I only take angels with me in the Angel Buggy. Are you angels?"

Candy, the younger one, looks at me sheepishly. "We can be."

"Okay, prove it!"

I am trying not to laugh. "If you don't get in any trouble, keep your room clean for the next two weekends you're here, I'll take you in the Angel Buggy for three days camping."

You've never seen two more behaved and sweet little darlings during these past two weeks. I walk into the girls' room. "Do you have your things ready for tomorrow?"

Candy, looking so innocent, replies "Yes, can Mary Lou go with us?"

"Is she an angel, too?"

Her eyes are wide and she has a very serious expression on her face. "Yes. She sure is. Me, too!" Giving in and not about to try to handle three kids, I insist the two mothers come along.

Three adults, three kids, three dogs, and lots of "Yippee" we're off to the lake. Wet bathing suits soak the floor, towels thrown everywhere, sneaking in to get a coke when being told they can't have one. A weekend I won't forget any time soon.

Candice walks into the living room where I'm sitting. "I found an apartment and I'm going to start college."

"That's great. When do you start?"

"I'll be moving into the apartment next week and school will start in a couple of weeks."

I was looking over at her as she sat down on the end of the couch. "Is this what the Lord wants you to do?"

"It's a Christian college so I feel like it is."

Reaching over to her, I say, "Can I give you a hug? I'm so proud of you.

"You're leaving the nest the Lord has provided for you. I'll miss you. You've been here just over a year. You're almost like wallpaper." Laughing she squirms on the seat. "Candice, you've come a long way. The Lord has done a lot of healing in you."

As Candice carries the last suitcase out the door I have mixed emotions. Relief for one thing. No more kids. But more than that I feel a sense of peace about her. The Lord has done His work while she's been here. I feel humbled to be a part of that.

6

Kirk is standing before the congregation. "I'm going to Israel in February. If there's anyone interested in going, see me after the service." I've never considered going to Israel. "Sue, how about going to Israel?"

"I don't know, Kirk. How much does it cost and when exactly are you going?"

"It will about eighteen hundred dollars and we leave February eighteenth. We'll be gone ten days."

"Okay, I'll pray and let you know." Praying and opening my Bible for my nightly reading, "Where would You like me to study tonight, Lord?" No answer, but I find myself going to Matthew chapter twenty-eight.

As I'm reading all of a sudden verse seven jumps out at me: "He has risen from the dead and is going ahead of you into Galilee. There you will see Him." "*Lord, are You telling me You want me to go to Israel?*" I already know the answer because of being given that scripture.

"Kirk, I'll be going to Israel with you."

"Wonderful!"

I'm beginning to get excited about the trip. Where there was no desire, now excitement is building. Kirk announces there's a meeting for the instructions for the trip. About forty people from various congregations show up. Kirk gives us the particulars of meeting at the airport, what to take, and approximate amount of money for tips, water, etc.

I have bought the largest suitcase I can without it being larger than what we were told and started packing. "*I'm so excited I can hardly stand it. Oh Lord, I'm really going to the Holy Land. This is unbelievable.*"

Sitting in the gate area where our flight is leaving from, gathering around to pray for traveling mercies, everyone is excited. The excitement is palpable. "We'll be boarding flight 384 to New York's Kennedy Airport in about five minutes. Please have your boarding pass ready for the agent at the door."

Boarding the plane and getting my carry-on baggage stored and seated, I'm off on the first leg of my journey. *"Thank you Lord for this trip. I am so blessed to be going to Your Holy Land."*

Arriving in New York, changing planes turns out to be more of a hassle than we expected. Finally arriving at the Royale Jordanian Airlines gate, *"I'm tired but I'm glad we're finally going to be on the plane to Amsterdam."*

Same thing as before. "This is flight 963 to Amman, Jordan with a stop in Amsterdam. We'll be boarding shortly. Have your boarding pass ready for the gate agent."

Amsterdam is a short stop for refueling and catering the food for the flight before taking off for Amman. It's an all night twelve hour flight, so most of the group sleep. Not me. I can't sleep so as soon as the service is over I'm pacing the aisle, standing in the galley chatting with the flight attendants.

I talk with the flight attendant who has just pulled the beverage cart into the galley. She picks up her cup of coffee. "You said you flew for Eastern?"

"Yes. I'm retired now."

I spend about fifteen minutes talking with her. I return to my seat, close my eyes, try to take a nap with no success. Not realizing the time change is more than I thought I finally give up on the napping. I have no idea there will be little sleep for the next ten days and my pacing continues as everyone else sleeps.

"Welcome to Amsterdam, ladies and gentlemen. We'll be on the ground for an hour if anyone would like to step off the plane and stretch your legs. Please stay in the gate area."

"*Thank God we're here! I'll just stay on board and walk around here.*" The excitement I felt leaving Atlanta is long since gone. I'm exhausted. When everyone has re-boarded the captain comes on over the P.A. system, "The flight to Amman, Jordan will be four hours and fifty minutes."

"*I can't believe we have another five hours to go!*" The pacing continues after a beverage service is completed. "Welcome to Amman, ladies and gentlemen. Have a nice day."

We board a bus to take us to customs which turns out to be a small building with armed men leaning against the outside wall. Because I have a bottle of water in my hand I'm searched and made to take a drink of the water.

We're finally back on the bus for the forty minute ride to the hotel. I enter my room. "*Thank you Lord! Now maybe I can get some sleep. Oh darn it! We're supposed to meet downstairs for dinner in an hour. If I crash now, I'll never wake up.*"

Dinner includes camel meat, and various dishes I have never heard of along with some American food. A taste of the camel meat leaves me wanting to spit it out. Arriving back to my room I think, "*I'm going to sleep for two days! I'm exhausted!*"

I wake up to car horns and trucks going by. "*It's morning already? Didn't I just go to sleep ten minutes ago?*" Turning the faucet on to take a shower the water pours out orange.

Even though I have brought adapters for the outlets I can't get my blow dryer to work. Giving up and throwing on some clothes I'm rushing downstairs for breakfast. "*Thank God I recognize this food!*"

We've all boarded the bus and in spite of little sleep everyone is excited to finally be on our way. Our guide for the next ten days picks up the microphone. "We'll be going to the Dead Sea first, folks." Clapping and excited shouts fill the bus. Blurry eyes are long forgotten.

The bus pulls to a stop. "Folks, the Dead Sea is the lowest point, above water, that you'll ever be on, on this earth. Its elevation is approximately thirteen hundred feet below sea level."

"Oh, wow!"

Kirk turns in his seat. "Hey, Sue, I want to see you floating on the mud."

"What are you talking about?"

"You can float on the water but there's also a place where you can float on the mud."

"You're kidding! I think I'll opt for the water."

He then announces to all of us, "If you're going in the water you'll need to wear shoes. The rocks are sharp. There's showers over there for when you get out and want to change into dry clothes."

I look down at my tennis shoes. *"If I do that I'm going to squish around in them all day. I don't think so!"* Big mistake. Wading out into the salty water that the guide told us is eight times greater than the ocean's salt, I'm laying back.

Floating on my back is like being suspended in air almost. My back is barely in the water. I turn over onto my stomach and pose like an airplane. "Kirk! Take my picture for me. This is incredible. I can't sink if I tried!"

I get out of the water, carefully watching where I'm stepping. *"Oh yuck! There's grease all over me. I feel like a greased pig. Where's that shower?"*

I walk into the shower room. "Lady, did you notice your foot is bleeding?" Looking down, sure enough. I've cut my foot. *"Next time listen, dummy! Kirk didn't tell us those rocks are pure salt and sharp as a razor."*

Getting back on the bus my foot is still bleeding and one of the men offers me a bandaid. Bandaging my foot I'm now able to relax and write in my journal. *"The Dead Sea takes in water from the Jordan but never releases it. Nothing lives in that water. Lord, my spirit used to be just like the Dead Sea. Thank You for bringing me to life!"*

During this trip I'm writing down everything, including all the information our guide gives us while others close their eyes and take a short nap. *"I'm sure glad I brought this notebook."*

Passing through the Jordaean Wilderness, where Jesus fasted and prayed for forty days and forty nights and then was tempted by the devil (See Matthew 4:1–11), camels graze along the side of the road. A child waves as we pass by.

We tour the ruins at Massada, watching shepherds tending their flocks of sheep, and arrive at Old Jericho. Over the guide's speaker, "This folks, is where Zaccaeus climbed a sycamore tree to see Jesus as He passed by through Jericho on His way to and from Jerusalem. Old Jericho is 9000 years old."

"The walls around Jericho are not here! They were 'tumbled down' in the Old Testament." (See Joshua 6:5.) Entering New Jericho we pull into the parking lot where we'll have lunch.

"Oh look everyone. We can ride a camel!" Sally looks at me grinning. "I don't think so, Sue. You go ahead if you want to."

"I'm going to ride that camel! I'll never have another chance like this."

The man who guides the camel has it lower onto its front knees and helps me up. *"OOOOOOOOH, what have I gotten myself into this time?* The camel begins to rise back up to a standing position.

"Oh God help me! I'm going to fly right off this camel on my head. Just like in my dream last night. Why did I ever decide to do this?" As the camel sways back and forth I'm hanging on for dear life.

"*Thank you God for letting me do this. Not many people can say they've ridden a camel. NOW GET ME OFF THIS ANIMAL!*" Emma approaches me. "How was it, Sue?"

"Fun, scary, I won't ever do that again!" I was laughing. "Let's go eat."

Arriving at the Sea of Galilee we're given time to rest in our rooms. "*I can't believe I'm standing on a balcony with the Sea of Galilee right at my feet. This is just too cool!*"

Waking up at 4:00 A.M. I feel like I've slept in. "*I want to go get some pictures of the sun coming up.*" Walking along the shore of the Sea of Galilee I'm snapping pictures right and left.

The sun peeks up, rising a little higher, then shining brightly across the water. "*Oh Lord. This is just absolutely beautiful.*" I hear a hushed "Sue!" Looking up, Kirk is leaning over his balcony waving at me. I wave back. "*I guess I'm not the only one messed up with this time change.*"

Walking into the hotel restaurant for a cup of coffee, others in the group start straggling in. From the looks on their faces they haven't gotten much more sleep than I have.

Finished eating we're climbing back on the bus. Kirk counts heads to make sure we're all on the bus. "Did anyone get more than forty-five minutes of sleep?"

Laughing, Peggy pops up, "You mean it was that long?"

"Folks, Tiberias is the only original city that's still here." We arrive in Sepphoris; Jesus' mother was born here. Then Capernaum, Jesus' home. The hub of His ministry. Continuing on, Gidera; Jesus cast the demons out of the man and sent them into the pigs over the hill into the water.

"*I can't believe I'm standing here looking over this cliff where He sent the demonized pigs! WOW!*" Next stop, "*I'm standing right here where Jesus fed the five thousand! Oh*

Lord, I am so glad you had me come here. I am just blown away!"

We're now arriving at the Mount of Beatitudes. Kirk walks up to me. "Would you like to give a short testimony about why you came here?"

"Are you serious?"

"Yes."

Kirk has everyone gather around and I stand next to him. I am standing before the whole group with the beautiful scenery behind them. "I didn't grow up in the church and I've only been saved two years. I came here for the sole purpose of being Baptized in the Jordan River."

Everyone is looking at me. "When Kirk Baptized me I didn't know what was going on. Now I do! I'm so blessed the Lord brought me here. I can't believe I'm really here and I can't stop bawling!"

Everyone is laughing. They certainly know the feeling. "Now darn it, when are we going to get to the Jordan River?" They all laugh and we return to the bus. Climbing back on the bus I'm feeling so filled with the Holy Spirit I can hardly stand it.

I notice the bus is slowing down. *"Oh my Lord! We're at the Jordan River! YES! I want to be Baptized in the very spot where John the Baptist Baptized You. You know this is the whole reason I wanted to come here. Thank you, thank you, thank you."*

I enter a small building to change into my bathing suit. *"I wonder how many will be Baptized."* Walking out to small bleachers, everyone in the group is sitting quietly. They've been given long white gowns to cover their bathing suit. Expectation and excitement fills the air.

Kirk steps up to me. "Here Sue, put this on over your swimsuit." I am waiting my turn and swiping at my tears. "Sue, it's your turn." I walk into the water toward the two pastors who are in up to their thighs, and I stand between them. "Sue Cass, do you profess Jesus Christ as your Savior?" "Yes."

Each pastor places one hand on the back of each shoulder and the other holding my upper arms. "In the Name of the Father, Son, and Holy Spirit I Baptize you." Suddenly my heart stops, I can't breathe. I'm in a watery grave.

I don't know how long I'm under the water. Raising me back up to a standing position I'm still not breathing. I'm not even sure my heart has started beating. Standing here like a rock of salt, suddenly, like a baby being smacked on the butt upon leaving its mother's womb, sucking in a deep breath, I let out a squall.

Kirk, knowing this is the main reason I came, is standing on the bank with his arms open to give me a big hug. All I can do is cry as he hugs me. *"This sure isn't anything like when Kirk Baptized me!"*

Acts 1:5 says, "For John baptized with water, but in a few days you will be baptized with the Holy Spirit." I'm convinced the Holy Spirit Baptized me and imparted His gifts on me today.

I changed back into dry clothes and we're back on the bus. Silence permeates the bus. I think everyone is trying to absorb all that just happened. Not only emotionally but spiritually.

"But if anyone causes one of these little ones who believe in Me to sin, it would be better for him to have a large millstone hung around his neck and to be drowned in the depths of the sea." (Matthew 18:6).

I am leaning against a huge millstone called the olive press. *"I absolutely have to get pictures of this to show the ladies in the Angel Group. They'll love this!"* A very large cement tub with a "core" in the center stands before me.

A huge donut-shaped stone rolls around inside the tub with a pole going through it. Donkeys are tethered to the pole and walk around and around causing the "donut" to mash the olives leaving the olive juice to flow out a small spout into buckets. *"I'd hate to be those donkeys. This is huge!"*

We arrive in Cana of Galilee where Jesus performed that first miracle at the wedding feast, changing water into wine. (see John 2:1–11). We enter the small room that looks similar to a chapel; an altar stands at the front.

In a V shape, rising above the altar, are large clay water jugs. "Folks, the largest jugs are used for purification. They're the real thing. Archaeologists uncovered them in some of their digs."

Stepping toward the door to leave, the guide gives us a mischievous smile. "Legend has it that there's a spring that whoever drinks of it will be married within a week. *"I wonder what happens if you bathe in it but don't drink any of it? I think I'll steer clear of it regardless!"*

Kirk walks to the front and stands in front of the altar. "Those of you who wish to renew your wedding vows may do so." *"Right here! Right where Jesus did His first miracle! Oh wow!"*

A sadness washes through me. *"I'm not married any more."* But it leaves as quickly as it came. Couples step forward, standing side by side they recite their wedding vows. Stepping back it's all tears, hugs, and kisses.

"For those of you that are single and wish to marry Jesus, I have a ceremony for you, also." *"Ohhhhh God, please don't let my knees buckle."* Going forward, standing before the altar, tears course down my cheeks.

"I take You, Jesus Christ, as my husband. I will love You, honor You, and obey You, forever more." I can hardly step back because I can't stop crying. When I married my husband I took those vows very seriously. How much more these mean to me. It sure gives love, honor and obey a whole new meaning!

On to Cessaria, where the book of Acts took place. *"I can't believe I'm standing on the sand of the Mediterranean sea."* I knew when I left Atlanta I would be picking up rocks and little things to bring home so I have zip lock bags with me that I carry everywhere we go.

I reach into my bag and pull one out. *"I'm going to fill it with sand. Jesus walked on this sand, I'm not leaving without some!"* Because we're scattered out along the beach, Kirk gives a whistle to get our attention.

"The sack lunches are over here. After we eat we'll be going to the Church of the Shepherds." Sitting under an original cistern eating my sack lunch I think, *"I'm actually on the Mediterranean Sea!"*

I carry my bag of sand and get back on the bus. "Look. Sue is already writing in that journal of hers." I just smile and keep on writing. *"They'll wish they did when we get back home."*

Arriving at the Church of the Shepherds we all gather around. It's a cave just like the one Jesus was born in. Standing at the entrance, we're all in awe. The next stop is the olive wood factory.

"Folks, this is where all sorts of items are made from the olive trees. We'll be here for two hours. Shop till you drop!" Walking through the doors and glancing around. I suddenly feel like a starved dog in a meat house. "Man! This is better than Walmart!"

Everyone bursts out laughing and we start our shopping. The place is huge and two hours just isn't going to do it. Carved statues of Jesus, bowls, crosses, communion sets, Bibles with carved olive wood covers.

Beautiful stuff. You name it, it's here. I wander around the store and want everything I see. "Anyone have a wheel barrel I can borrow?" Laughter echoes throughout the room. I'm in hog heaven!

I see a carved communion set. *"I think I'll get this for Kirk as a thank you. Three hundred dollars. I don't think I want to thank him that much!"* I turn away and continue to the next display.

I pick out a carved Jesus statue, a communion bowl, and hold up a small carved camel. *Just to remember my wild ride.* I'm going to shop 'til I drop. Noticing a glassed-in display, *"I have to see what's in there."*

I stand before it, gasping at its beauty. *"This is the most beautiful item in this store."* "Martha, come look at this carved Last Supper. It has every piece and is gorgeous!"

I look at the small price tag laying beside it, twelve hundred dollars. "You know, Martha, it's worth every single penny. Look at how meticulously it's carved. Every detail! I wish I had a mantle and twelve hundred dollars."

Martha takes one more glance. "It is beautiful for sure. I don't have that kind of money either." Glancing back as I walk away, "I sure wish I could buy it." I continue to fill my buggy with souvenirs I want for myself and selecting a variety of small items for friends. *"I have no idea how I'm going to get all this stuff home but I'll worry about that later."*

I get back on the bus with all my bags of goodies, standing at the front of the bus holding my bags above my head. "Hey, anyone want to buy my clothes?" Laughing, Jim shouts, "No. We thought you'd buy ours!"

Heading back to the hotel I can finally settle down and continue to write in my journal. Others are using the time to rest their eyes. Some talk softly and occasionally I hear a giggle.

At the Nativity Church, I can't begin to filter my feelings. Placing my hands on the star on the floor right where Jesus was born is beyond any words. I can't even speak. Tears stream down my face.

There's a reverent hush with only the sound of sniffles trying to be muffled from all of us. *"The King of kings and Lord of lords, my Savior was born right here on this very spot I'm touching."*

I want to continue to kneel here and just praise Him and worship Him. We have to move on so others waiting in line can experience this incredible spiritual moment. To me, this is the most spiritual encounter on this trip so far.

It even tops being Baptized in the Jordan River. I've never dreamed, even in my wildest imagination, I would be here with my hand resting on the very place where Christ was born. All I can do is choke back the sobs coming from my heart.

Sitting quietly on the bus with Martha and shaking my head in amazement, I say, "Everywhere we go makes the Bible come alive. We're walking through those pages, not reading them, but walking the same places!"

"You're right."

I lean back on the seat. "Before we would only imagine what they must be like. What they would look like if we would see them. I'm walking, Martha, stepping right where Jesus stepped! If this is a dream, I hope I never wake up."

Kirk steps to the head of the group as we're walking through a narrow passage-way in the marketplace. "Stay in the group so we don't get separated in the crowd." We walk along looking at various tables filled with souvenirs. "Oh look! Widows mites. Kirk, Can we stop for a minute? There's bags of widows mite coins."

I pick up a small bag of them. "I'd like to get a bag of them so I can give one to each widow at church." While purchasing my bag of coins I say, "Sir, do you know how much one of these coins represent?"

"It's worth one, one hundredth of a penny."

"Oh wow!"

"I tell you the truth, this poor widow put in more than any of you." (Luke 21:1–4) Jesus told the people this when He came to the Temple and saw a poor widow put her coin in the basket and I've just bought some!

Each day is filled with new sights, new experiences, and more bawling. As our tour continues we arrive at Nazareth. *"Oh wow! This is where Jesus grew up. I think He gave His first sermon here, too."*

Stopping at Mary's well is incredible, where Gabriel told Mary she'd give birth to Jesus. Standing in front of the well I'm a little shocked. It looks like it's metal and shaped like a toilet seat only with a narrower lip.

The guide tells us, "You can take a drink from it, it really is clean." Being assured it's okay, *"I'm not going to pass this up."* I push the mental image aside, fill my hand with the water and take a drink. *"Tastes just like water."*

Some of the little towns we pass through or stop at, shepherds are leading their flocks of sheep right through the middle of town. *"We sure don't see that in Georgia!"* I'm really not too surprised when we reach the Wailing Wall. *"This looks just like it did on T.V. that time."*

Jewish people are bowing before the wall in their traditional rocking back and forth. Looking around, some are sitting on their suitcase rocking in prayer. Silently approaching the wall and placing my hands against it, I'm praying a prayer of thanks giving to the Lord.

Having been told ahead of time we can write a short prayer on a small piece of paper to stick in one of the crevices in the wall, I take my small paper out of my pocket and stuff it in one the cracks. *"There's thousands of little papers in the cracks!"*

Everyone has had a chance to pray at the wall and now we return to the bus. We're leaving to head for the Via Dolorosa. In my most wild dreams I've never thought I'd actually walk this same path that Jesus carried the cross on His way to death.

I can't believe this! Walking the "Trail of Suffering" as it is also called, I can already feel the emotions stirring. The whole group starts down the path, which isn't really a path like we would think of one. It's wider than just one person walking it, but enough for a cart or a Man with a large cross.

Kirk begins by leading the group. "Don't touch the walls. They're made of shaved and splintered glass imbedded in stones. To touch them is certain cuts." The group spreads out walking at our own pace.

The path has been paved, not dirt, but the impact is still overwhelming. Wanting to have alone time with the Lord I'm walking quite a distance ahead of the group. Overwhelming emotions of every kind are coursing through me.

Tears flow freely and I can't stop them. I stop dead in my tracks about halfway down the path. *"I can't stand this any more! Lord, what is going on? I don't understand all these emotions, what am I feeling?"*

"I walked your path of suffering with you all those years, now you're walking Mine." Oh, talk about losing it! Collapsing right here on the ground, bawling and bawling and bawling.

I can't stop crying. The others catch up to me but think nothing of my tears. We're all bawling as we walk the rest of the way down through the narrow streets through old Jerusalem.

Passing by the very spot where Mary reached out to her Son as He was passing by with the cross on His bloody shoulders, the tears continue to flow. I think everyone is bawling.

As if this isn't enough to wipe me out, riding a short distance on the bus we're now entering the Garden Tomb area. There's a hushed reverent atmosphere. The birds are even hushed.

Looking around, beautiful trees and flower gardens are everywhere. As we walk toward the tomb various groups of people scattered about are praying and softly singing worship songs.

The combination of various languages spoken and sung at one time is awesome. Kirk moves to the front of our group motioning us to gather around. He whispers, "We'll gather here. Try not to spread out too much. Please be very quiet as you can see others are worshipping."

Softly we begin to sing. One of the ladies gasps as she's looking up at the sky. Looking up to see what she's gasping about, right above us is a large beautiful rainbow. We're all stunned and can't believe there's a rainbow appearing out of nowhere right here above us as we're singing.

It's only there for a few seconds and disappears as quickly as it appeared.

We are standing here continuing to look up. Everyone starts whispering at the same time, "Did you see it?" "That's just too awesome!" "I wonder if the other people saw it." "Glory be to God."

There's no explanation for it appearing other than God hearing our songs of worship and wishes to bless us. Boy, He has certainly done that! We all know the rainbow represents the covenant God made with us.

"I have set My rainbow in the clouds and it will be the sign of the covenant between Me and the earth." (Genesis 9:13–16.) In hushed reverence we softly resume our singing.

After taking communion in front of the tomb, each one of us enter the tomb one at a time. We step into the small opening, eyes adjusting to the semi-lit space. *"There's the actual ledge my Savior was lain on."*

Hardly able to breathe, not from the close space but from the spiritual explosion within me, there are no words. Leaning over and placing my hands on the ledge, the bawling starts again.

"I can almost see Him lying here and I just want to touch Him." The tears won't stop and walking back into the sunlight as others look at me, I can't speak. The Holy Spirit wells up inside me so strongly sometimes I just flat out cannot form a word.

There's nothing that can be said. I'm finding this happens at several of the places we're visiting and it's not just me. The Garden of Gethsemane has the only living witness of Jesus praying at the rock.

It's a three thousand year old olive tree. It stands majestically, with its gnarled, twisted trunk. It's encased in a fence so the tourist can't touch it. Oh if this tree could talk! It might tell us about Jesus sweating blood as He kneels at the rock in prayer.

Standing looking at the very rock leaves me speechless. I can't see the blood drops but in my mind's eye I can see the agony He must have felt. "Not My will, but Thy will be done."

Entering an open area Kirk tells us, "Break up in small groups, spread out on the grounds. I'd like for you to confess your burdens to the Lord, then to each other. Meet back here in forty-five minutes."

Boy, do I ever confess my burdens! *"Take me home Lord. Life in this world is just too hard! I just want outta' here! This is the perfect place to just beam me up."* Crying I tell the others what I just prayed and that my husband has recently passed away.

They're giving me sympathetic hugs and words of encouragement. "*All I do is cry! For crying out loud is this trip going to be nothing but bawling!*" Some of the tears I shed come from emotions. Others are welled up and poured out from my heart. Loving my Lord.

Stopping along the river where Jacob wrestled with the angel we don't get out of the bus. The river looks similar to some of the trout streams in north Georgia. (see Genesis 32:1–30)

The valley of the shadow of death is really a valley. Mount Nebo, we're standing where Moses was shown the land of milk and honey. Because of his disobedience to the Lord he would never enter it. (See Deuteronomy 34.)

Walking with Jesus, Him meeting me here, is more than I can even explain to others. It's the most awesome trip I've ever taken. I've been to other countries, toured the cities of Rome, Paris, Madrid, London. Nothing! Nothing, compares to this experience.

In front of the hotel we're gathered around to start our trip back to Amman, the first leg back to the States. Waiting for our luggage to be boarded, a bomb loudly explodes just a few blocks away.

Everyone jumps, startled. Looking around to see where the blast came from, bags are suddenly being thrown in the luggage bin. "Get on the bus quickly!" The guide turns to Kirk. "We have to get to the border before it's closed! Once it's closed there's no telling when it will be opened again."

Kirk shoos us into the bus. I'm scared to death. "*Dear Lord, please get us out of here!*" The bus speeds through the streets. We've finally reached the border and are having to wait in a very long line as each vehicle is being thoroughly searched.

The soldiers finally wave us through and we all give a large sigh of relief. We're safe as we cross over into Jordan. We're the very last vehicle to cross the line between the countries when the border is closed. *"Thank you Lord for getting us out of there. I just want to go home to Georgia."*

Picking up a newspaper in Amman, the headlines read, "Twenty-six killed, seventy-seven injured in bombing." We're all relieved to be out of Israel on our way home, but there's a sadness amongst us as we board our flight in Amman.

I've been soaring with the eagles for the last ten days, experiencing so many spiritually awesome sights and feeling the Lord's presence every step of the way. To be leaving with the horrible sound of a bomb and people being killed brings me back into the present world.

The Lord is continuing to prove to me that He is real. Very real! He hung on that cross in Golgotha (see Mark 15:22) and ascended to heaven three days later . . . For me.

"He has risen from the dead and is going ahead of you into Galilee. There you will see Him." Amen and Amen.

7

"Praise God we're home!" Getting ready for Church, *"I'm so tired and this jet lag is awful. I must have woke up a hundred times last night thinking I'm still in Israel."* My body still screaming for sleep, it's time to go to church.

"Thank God the church is close by or I don't think I'd make it. Okay car, you took me there once, now do it again." Walking into the now familiar church and taking a seat, Karen approaches me. "Oh Sue, how was Israel? We're so glad you're back. I heard about the bombing."

"Tired but I'm fine. Thank you." Cindy walks up. "Welcome home. I hope you had a good trip." Everyone's greeting Kirk and I. We're the only two from our church that went to Israel. Kirk, standing before the congregation, says "We had a wonderful trip and it's good to be home. Thank you for all your prayers."

"We just got home last night, how in the world can he look so rested?" One of the ladies from the choir steps forward and the music begins.

With a voice like an angel she's singing "Via Dolorosa." Again the tears stream down my cheeks. I'm back on the Trail of Sorrow feeling all that Christ did as He carried that cross.

In my mind I'm once again touching the star on the floor where He was born, standing with my hands on the ledge where His body was lain, being Baptized in the Holy river.

I'm still hearing Him say, "I walked your path of suffering. Now you're walking Mine." I'm right back in Israel with the emotions flooding out. *"I thought all the bawling was over with!"*

Looking at my angelic singer through my tears, she's not looking at me as she's singing. *I'm going to fall out in this floor if I don't stop this crying! Oh God help me. I don't want to make a fool of myself.*"

Without saying a word people next to me and behind me are stuffing tissue in my hands. Their compassionate acts are touching, making me bawl even more. The song ends and the choir begins singing.

Sitting here blowing my nose, wiping tears, and sniffling, it doesn't bother anyone but me. Kirk is teary-eyed, wipes his eyes, and clears his throat before resuming the service.

After the service, I hug my angelic singer and I am still choked up. "It was beautiful, thank you." The emotions, memories, and pictures in my mind have not left just because I am no longer in Israel.

The entire impact of the trip hasn't settled in yet. It's going to take me a while to process everything and sort through the emotions as well as all the pictures and notes. First I need sleep!

Arriving home after church I'm wiped out, physically and emotionally. I glance at the several rolls of film and my notebook laying on the table. "*I'm going to eat and then go to bed! I can take care of those later.*"

Waking up I realize I've slept for twelve hours. "*Good grief, what day is it? I can't believe I slept that long! I'm still tired but I better get unpacked.*" Laying out all my souvenirs on the bed, the tears begin again.

My carved camel, the beautiful statue of Jesus. All bring the memories flooding back again. I take my zip lock bag of sand, pour a little in several different bags, then set my bag of widows mites next to it and continue to lay out the gifts I brought back for a variety of friends. "*I'll take these to church Sunday.*"

I put my clothes away, stack the dirty ones on the floor that need washing. *"There's no way I'm going to do laundry today!"* I throw them in the basket. *"I don't feel like eating, I'm going back to bed."*

This continues for several days. I'm walking around like a zombie or in a trance. Kirk seems to handle the jet lag very well. Not me! It's taking me a couple of weeks to get back into a normal routine.

I go to the mall, buy a couple of albums that I can add pages to if I need to, and pick up my pictures from the photo store. I'm heading home, excited to begin the journey again. Sorting through, typing up the sequence of events, the darn tears start again.

It's as though the Lord is walking through His Holy Land with me once again. *"Oh Lord, I am so grateful You took me on this trip."* *"Would you like to go back?"* *"NO! My heart couldn't take it and my tear glands would never survive."* I hear His chuckle.

After sorting through the pictures, typing up all the information, and placing them in the sequence we traveled it, I'm reading through the completed albums. Step by step, if someone opened them they would walk the incredible journey with me.

Each time I take out my albums and begin the journey again, the tears flow. Memories flood my mind as I lay my finger gently touching the picture where Christ laid, where He walked.

Memories that will follow me to the grave for this walk with the Lord is like none other. Reading about it in the Bible is one thing. Holding His hand and walking through history is much, much more meaningful. My Bible study is yet another walk down memory lane.

8

After taking a break over Christmas and New Year's the support group has begun once again. During my time in Israel Susan has lead the group, finishing up the topic on guilt that we had been working on when I left.

Susan fills me in on some of what was discussed. She had asked the group, "When you were five years old how could you have stopped the abuse?"

Everyone gave a reason. "I told my mother but she didn't believe me."

"He threatened to kill my family and it would be all my fault." "He said it was all my fault. I asked for it." "He said it was our secret." Gently Susan asked, "So if no-one would help you, how could you stop it?" Silence.

I walk into the room. "Hi everyone. I'm back and had a great time." Getting everyone settled in, Susan reads the devotional for the evening. I take out my picture of the huge millstone. "How many of you have ever felt you wanted revenge against your abuser?"

All hands are raised. "I want to show you a picture. Remember the scripture that talks about anyone leading one of these little ones to sin? The one where the Lord says he would be better off with a millstone hung around his neck and drowned in the sea?"

All heads nod and everyone's attention is peaked. "I have a picture here that I took in Israel of exactly what the Lord was talking about. I'll pass it around and you can see what a millstone really looks like for yourselves."

Handing the picture to Peggy, it's slowly studied by each woman as it's passed to the other. "Wow! That's huge!" "I wish they had these here." A few chuckles, jokes, and wise-cracks are made as to what to do with the millstone.

"How many would like to use this millstone?" Laughing, a few raise their hands. The picture is returned to me and I lay it on the table. "Now! Shall we start the topic we'll be discussing for the next couple of weeks?"

Sally is still laughing about what she'd like to do with the millstone. "What's it about?" Susan and I look at each other and almost bust out laughing. "Ooooh I think you'll like it. Forgiveness!"

Laughter and joking is suddenly gone. There's a nervous energy that has welled up. Susan smiles sweetly. "Now ladies. Forgiveness is very important for your healing. It's paramount. After all Jesus forgives us." No one is anxious to start this topic.

I pick up my water bottle and take a sip. "Forgiveness is hard. Especially when we've been abused and betrayed so horribly. But it's a choice. You aren't saying that what was done is right. It doesn't mean you have to like your abuser or have anything to do with him or her.

"Forgiveness is for you. As long as there is unforgiveness, that ties you to the one who hurt you. You want revenge. You want to make them pay. Whether it's through hatred, hanging a millstone around their neck and drowning them, or any other way.

"Who does that hurt? As for the abuser, he may not even know you're forgiving him or even care. You walk around with all this anger, bitterness, and hurt and he's off having a beer in Tahiti. Forgiveness says, I'll leave their punishment, the judgment up to God which frees you.

"Colossians 3:24–25 says, 'It's the Lord Christ you are serving. Anyone who does wrong will be repaid for his wrong, and there is no favoritism.' That also goes for all us.

Our sins are just as harmful as other's sins. We're sinning by not forgiving."

Looking around the room Susan and I see looks of discomfort on some of the women's faces. "Forgiveness releases you. It isn't about your abuser. It's about you! You can choose to allow the person to maintain control, even if he/she is dead. Or you can choose to forgive and be set free."

An angry outburst. "He doesn't deserve to be forgiven!"

None of us deserve to be forgiven but the Lord forgives us and tells us to forgive others. He will cleanse our heart if we allow Him to by confessing our sin and asking Him to forgive us.

"I would like for you to take a pencil and we have paper, if you don't have any. Ask the Lord who He wants you to forgive tonight. Whatever name comes to your mind write it down.

"We're going to give you the opportunity to forgive that person, or persons. When you've made your list bring it to one of us and we'll help you in prayer to forgive that person.

"This is very important. Your healing will not progress significantly unless there is forgiveness. Please be silent so as not to disturb others. After you've met with us you may leave quietly. Here's your homework assignment and we'll see you next week.

"I'd like for you to write a letter to your abuser." Heads fly up from writing down names they already know they need to forgive. Looking at me like I've lost my mind, I ignore the looks.

"This letter will not be mailed! Pour your heart out. Tell that person exactly what you want to say. Don't hold back anything! Bring it with you next week and if you want to share you can. You don't have to."

Sitting quietly, heads are bowed. One lady after another stands, bringing her list of people to forgive to Susan and me. The impact of this is so strong, many are crying as we're leading them through prayers of forgiveness.

None of them are able to forgive their abuser but that will come. It takes time but this is the first step toward that goal. Having the opportunity to forgive the ones listed on their sheets is powerful! There's no doubt burdens are lain at the feet of Jesus tonight.

Low self-esteem, guilt, shame, unforgiveness, how God sees us, and several other issues are issues we're confronting in the group. Educational material is given out as well as videos being shown to help them better understand what they're feeling and why.

We discuss, laugh, cry, and support each other. Some get really mad and that's dealt with within the group. Acceptance and love are extremely important. The women that come to our group usually haven't experienced unconditional love.

We give that by not judging or condemning one another. Listening and offering support helps to do that, too. Some women are telling for the first time that they've been abused. It's very difficult for them. Some have had some counseling.

As the leader of the group it's my responsibility to not only offer support but to lead them in their journey to healing through the Lord Jesus. I take that responsibility very serious and it is awesome to watch as each woman has a "light bulb moment."

This whole topic of forgiveness is stirring up a lot of anger in me. It's doing a number on me, big time! I go home after the group, and lay in bed. *"Lord, how can I sit there and tell these women they need to forgive when I don't want to forgive my own father?"* *"You're not doing it. I am."*

"They're so angry! And so am I!" *"I know. You also must forgive."* *"I don't want to forgive him! He doesn't deserve it and I don't want You to forgive him either! I hope he burns in hell!"*

I am watching the T.V. news. "We have just received a tornado warning for Douglas County. Take cover immediately." Grabbing my Bible, my purse, and a picture of Brian I head for the closet. "Dusty, Rocky, Jacob, get in here!" Closing the closet door and hovering in the back of the walk-in closet I'm shivering from fright.

The dogs begin panting from being in the small closed space. "You can't go out yet, guys. It may not be safe." Doggie breath finally gets the best of me so I open the closet door just enough to let them out, or at least breathe outside the closet.

I hug my treasured items to my chest crying and praying. *"Lord, please don't let me die in this closet. I don't want to die hating my father."* *"Tomorrow Sue, I want you to go to your father. You are to forgive him to his face, not here in this closet."* Still crying, *"Okay."*

I feel like it's safe to come out. I go to bed; somehow I'm able to sleep.

I waken to sun shining in the windows. *"I feel like I've been run over by a train!"* Going through the motions of dressing, getting some breakfast I find myself getting in the car to drive to the small southern town where my Dad lives.

Again my mind has been invaded by a fog moving in. The car is steering itself and I'm just sitting here with my hands on the wheel and foot on the gas. About halfway to my Dad's home the car is wanting to turn around.

I am fighting the steering wheel, talking out loud. "Lord! You better do something if You want me to go the rest of the way. You better make this car go there." *"Pull into this chicken stand."*

I pull up in front of a small drive up type chicken place. *"Go get some chicken for you and your Dad to eat."* I leave the car, and go to the window. "I'd like a large box of chicken, mashed potatoes, and green beans. I'll have an apple and a cherry pie, too, please."

I get back in the car with the large dinner. "*Okay Lord. Now what?*" The car pulls back onto the road and heads in the direction we were going. I pull into the long dirt driveway and park the car in the shade of a large oak tree. "*Well, here goes, Lord.*"

I walk toward the front door. "*What am I supposed to say to him?*" "*Trust Me, I'll be speaking through you. You need this, Sue. Not for your father, but for you. You need to tell him you forgive him.*"

The fog suddenly clears in my head as I'm knocking on the door. Opening the door, Daddy stands looking at me. For just a second I see fear in his eyes. "*Has the Lord prepared him for this? He didn't know I was coming.*"

"What are you doing here?"

"We need to talk, Daddy."

Stepping inside I say, "I brought us some chicken. Have you eaten?"

"No."

Setting the chicken down on the table and getting silverware and plates, I dish out the food.

As we're eating, I look over at my aged father. "Last night I was sitting in my closet because of the tornado warning. I told God I didn't want to die hating you. Why Daddy? Why did you do those things to me?"

There's no anger whatsoever in my voice. The words are coming, but seem like they're coming from somewhere else. "You wanted it." Several more excuses are given and with each one the Lord speaks through me. Taking a bite of my chicken I can only sit here and look at this man that is my father.

For so many years my life was at his mercy and for many years I've hated him. I've wished more times than I can count he'd burn in hell and here I am, being pleasant and asking the most painful questions I've ever asked in my life.

"Daddy, I want you to know. I forgive you. I forgive you for hurting me in all those horrible ways. I forgive you for not being the father you should have been. I forgive you for everything you ever did and even the things you didn't do."

I haven't shed one tear. Which is abnormal under these circumstances. Calm is enveloping me like nothing I've ever felt before. Daddy sits with his head lowered, a piece of chicken half eaten in his hand, tears streaming down his face. "I'm sorry, Sue. I never meant to hurt you. I don't know why I did it."

Never expecting he'd admit it, I've just received confirmation, admittance, and something most survivors never hear, an apology. I look at him as the tears continue down his face. *"There's a part of me that hates him but there's also a little part of me that still loves him. He's my father."*

The realization almost knocks me off my chair. I place the remainder of the chicken in the refrigerator. "I guess I need to go." Standing up slowly, it's his turn to look like he's the one hit by the train. He follows me out the door.

We walk to the car. "Daddy, I loved you as a child and I love you now. What you did was wrong and it almost destroyed me. Because I've forgiven you doesn't mean you're off the hook. You still have to answer to God."

Driving home I can hardly see the road for crying. All the pent up emotions that have lain dormant for way too many years pour out. I walk into the house, sit down at the table, head in my hands. *"I can't believe I just forgave him."*

I feel almost numb. *"Lord, You're right, some place way down in my heart I do love him."* The tears of sorrow, relief, and pain flow for many hours leaving me emotionally and physically drained.

It's been eight months since confronting my Dad. He's now been diagnosed with prostate cancer and it's spread throughout his body. On one of his doctor visits the doctor and I are talking in the hall while Daddy is getting dressed. "Your father has about six months to live."

Daddy and I have discussed the options for his care and he's decided to live in California with my sister. Sometime later the phone rings. "Hello."

"Sue, Daddy is in the hospital. He only has a couple of days to live. Do you want to talk to him?"

"Yes." Holding the phone to his ear, I can hear him breathing.

"Daddy? I know you can't talk so I want you to just listen. I love you. Will you please forgive me? Please ask Jesus into your heart." No reply. I hang up the phone. "*Why in the world would I ask _him_ to forgive _me_? I haven't done anything to have to ask him to forgive me!*"

"*Yes you have.*" "*Like what?*" "*You hated your father. You cussed him, you berated him to others. You did not honor him as your father.*" "*Oh!*" As I enter the house with my arms full of groceries, the phone is ringing. "Hello."

"Sue, Daddy gave his life to Christ last night."

Tears begin to slide down my cheeks. "Praise God! How? What happened?"

"I asked him if he'd like to give his life to Christ. To ask Jesus to forgive him and save him? He whispered yes."

I can hardly talk as she continues. "It's the oddest thing, he said I forgive you for everything. I have no idea where that came from. Anyway, I even got a nun in here to make sure I heard right."

Tears are flowing down my cheeks. "I have prayed for him for so long. I can't believe he finally did it." "I know. I never thought he would either. I have to go. Bye."

Twenty-four hours later I'm sitting at the table having a cup of coffee. The Lord lets me see into the spiritual realm.

I see Daddy standing just outside the hospital. An angel is standing on each side of him. "It's okay, come with us." Daddy is looking around, confusion written on his face. "Where is this? Where am I?"

The angels gently coax him with loving hands on each of his elbows. "It's alright, we'll take you." Daddy takes a couple of cautious steps forward, still trying to figure out where he is.

"Where are we going?" With angelic love, compassion, and soft gentle voices, "Come with us." As I'm watching this incredible event I almost feel the confusion he's feeling.

I want to reach out to him and help him make his journey. The angels gently continue to coax him on. Looking around like a very lost child daddy takes a few steps forward.

It's obvious he's lost and confused in these surroundings. The angels continue to hold his elbows gently, coaxing him farther and farther until the three of them slowly disappear.

A cold cup of coffee in my hand, I feel like I'm coming out from under a sedative. I set the coffee cup down and lowering my head onto the table, I cry tears of joy.

9

Walking into the support group room, the ladies are gathered around the table. "Good evening ladies. I hope everyone had a good week." Everyone gets settled with their notebooks, water bottles, and cokes.

I take my seat. "Let's start with our devotional. Colossians 3:13, "Forbearing one another, and forgiving one another, if any man have a quarrel against any: even as Christ forgave you, so also do ye.""

Looking down the length of the table I feel a little nervous tonight. "We've been discussing forgiveness this past week or so and I'd like to confess something to you." After hesitating a moment, "I've never forgiven my father."

Two women exhibit shocked looks. "I've been talking to you about forgiving your abuser and I've felt like such a hypocrite." I hesitate for a moment to keep the tears in check. "When we first started on forgiveness I went home and was really praying. Then when the tornado warning came I ran into my closet for safety."

Everyone is looking at me intently. "I was scared to death! I was in the closet bawling, shaking in fear, and about to suffocate! It's not that big of a closet." Nervous laughter ripples around the table. The heavy tension in the room is eased some.

"During all that I started praying and ended up asking the Lord to not let me die. That I don't want to die hating my father." It's so silent we can hear a pin drop.

Taking a deep breath, a sip of my water, I continue to tell them what happened and how it ended. Some have tears in their eyes. Others look stunned. Some look at me with an expression of, "Boy you sure are brave!"

Looking at each one I'm also seeing hope! The Lord can lead us in forgiveness and what forgiveness can lead to. "Ladies, I never realized there was a shred of love in me for my Dad."

Susan sits quietly. "The Lord brought that out for me to see. It doesn't matter how much bitterness, hatred, or hurt we have because of what was done to us. We trusted them. They betrayed that precious trust. Since that day, my Dad and I have been having a father/daughter relationship. We've never had that."

Tears well up in my eyes again and stalling I take another sip of water. "I feel so free! I can't even describe the weight that has been lifted off my shoulders. There's such a tremendous feeling of relief. It's hard to explain."

"I've harbored hatred for all these years. In one afternoon the Lord freed me of it with three words. I forgive you." I change the subject. "Now, how many of you wrote the letter to your abuser that I asked for last week?" All raise their hands.

Each woman that wrote her letter expressed great relief. Since the letter is not going to be mailed they have felt free to express the hurt and anger. Some cry as they read their letter to the rest of us. Some express anger. But all benefit from writing them.

The Easter break is over and some of the previous women return. Susan and I have found that when the topics begin to get what we call, "deep," some of the ladies won't come back. They just aren't ready to deal with some of the "deeper" issues.

Of course we encourage them to seek counseling and continue to participate in the group. Some just run. When we start again after a break we sometimes get women that haven't attended before.

Sitting around the table are some of the women chatting about what they did over Easter. Looking up from my papers I notice two ladies standing in the doorway. One is encouraging the other to come in. "Just see what it's like. You don't have to stay if you don't want to."

Susan stands up and walks over to the ladies. "Hi, I'm Susan. We'd love to have you join us. Won't you come in and sit down. I'll sit beside you." She gently coaxes the shy young woman into the room.

Taking a seat the young woman lays her head on her arms on the table. *"She looks like a little wounded bird."* I can tell she's terrified. *"She's going to live with you. Wait until next week before approaching her. She needs your help."* *"Oh Lord, what are You doing?"*

I walk over to the young lady. "I'm Sue. Susan and I lead the group. You're welcome to participate or if you'd rather just listen, that's okay, too. Would you mind telling us your name?"

Lifting her head just a little she replies, "Brenda Michaels."

"Welcome to the group, Brenda. We're happy to have you." Brenda lays her head back down. The group begins discussing the assignment they had before the break. And the following week, Brenda returns.

"Hello Brenda. We're happy you came back to join us this week." Taking a seat, giving me a weak little smile, her head goes back on her arms as it was last week. After the devotion is read, I ask the women, "What specific problem have you noticed in the past week?"

The discussion begins as each lady expresses some concern. Brenda sits up in the chair but says nothing. Looking at Brenda I'm sensing she might want to say something but is afraid to speak up. "Brenda? Is there anything you have concerns about right now?"

Tears fill her eyes; she hesitates and doesn't say anything. Charlotte scoots the box of tissues in front of her. "Here's some tissue, it's okay. We aren't going to bite." Brenda takes some tissue.

She glances around shyly. "I don't have any place to live. I was staying with my counselor for a few days but I can't stay there forever."

"You were right Lord. I'm looking at my next roommate."

I glance at Susan and then back to Brenda. "Brenda? How can we help you right now?"

"I don't know. I have Lupus and have to have chemo once a week. I don't know what I'm going to do!"

The tears flow, head back on the table, she cries and cries. Looking at her, *"Lord, I can't do this! She has to have chemo. I can't go through that again! I can't help her."*

"Yes you can, Sue Cass! I will be doing it through you. You'll be fine." Looking at Brenda, my heart goes out to her but the memories of Brian and Rebecca being so sick flood my mind. *"Lord, are You sure about this?"* *"Yes! Talk to her after the group."*

"Brenda, I'd like to talk with you after the group, if you don't mind." She nods her head without looking at me. After the others leave, Susan and I walk over to Brenda. She's still in her seat, blowing her nose.

I sit down beside her. "I'm a widow, Brenda. I live alone and if you'd like to come home with me you're welcome to. I have a spare bedroom and you'd have your own room and bath."

She looks at Susan. "You'll be fine with Sue. I've known her for a long time."

Looking back at me Brenda says, "I guess so. Thank you."

She follows me home and sits on the couch in my living room.

"Would you like something to drink?"

"No thank you."

Trying to ease her anxiety I tell her, "This can be a trial period, Brenda. You can stay as long as you want or if it doesn't work out then you can leave. I just have three rules for living here. There are to be no drugs, no alcohol, and no men."

"I don't do drugs, I don't drink, and I don't date."

"Good! Then everything will work out. I'll show you your room, where the linens are, and your bathroom. Make yourself comfortable."

I am sitting at the table having my morning coffee. "Good morning, Brenda. Did you sleep okay?"

"Yes, thank you." She's arranged for friends to take her back and forth for her chemo treatments so I don't have to.

Coming home from her treatment she's as white as a sheet. She walks into her bedroom, crawls under the covers, and huddles there all curled up in the fetal position.

"What can I get you? Is there something you need?"

She quickly sits up, grabbing the plastic kidney-shaped container and vomits. My heart just absolutely cries for her. Remembering Rebecca and Brian, how sick they were, my heart turns to mush.

Brenda is defensive and I recognize the fear in her eyes. I know she's afraid I might make her leave. She's only nineteen years old. She's still adjusting to living with an older woman.

She asks permission for doing just about everything. "Can I go to the grocery store?"

"Brenda, I'm not your mother. You're a big girl, you can come and go as you please."

"I know you're not my mother! I was just trying to be considerate!" The sarcasm is unwarranted but I ignore it. The Lord helps me be patient and ignore a lot of things I normally wouldn't. "*Lord, is she ever going to trust me?*" "*Give her time.*"

Brenda is laying in bed after another treatment. "Do you have any pickles? I just want something salty." "You really should try to eat something." Knowing all too well that just the smell of food can set off a bout of vomiting. I leave and go for the dill pickles.

I've learned that with each of her treatments she can crave a variety of foods. Pickles and watermelon seem to be her favorites. Watching her eat a large slice of watermelon, "*Lord, I love this girl. She's so naive, so wounded, and yet like a little girl.*" "*You're doing fine and she'll be okay.*"

10

Many times I consult with Ben about some of the struggles I'm having. He has not only become an office partner but my counselor. He's joined forces with the Lord and is walking this journey with me.

Between the two, Ben and the Lord, I don't have a snowball's chance in hell of avoiding the issue at hand. Ben can immediately tell if something is wrong or heavy on my mind. "What's going on, Sue?" Sitting down, I begin spilling my guts.

When the Lord "drops a bomb on me," as I like to call it, Ben is always there to help put the pieces back together. Many times the Lord will suddenly reveal something significant when I least expect it.

It can be one of those "WOW!" moments or something that just rips me apart. Placing dirty dishes in the dishwasher, *"Take your wedding rings off."* Holding a dish in mid-air, "What? Why? No, I can't do that. Please don't tell me to do that."

"Take off your wedding rings! They're getting in the way of what I want to do. Place them at the foot of the cross." Running to Ben, "The Lord's telling me to take my wedding rings off!"

I am crying. "Ben, I can't do that! You know what these rings mean to me."

"Why do you think He wants you to take them off?"

"He said because they're getting in the way of what He wants to do. Which doesn't even make any sense. He said I'm to lay them at the foot of the cross."

"What do the rings represent to you, Sue?"

"They're my wedding rings! Brian and I were married eighteen years. Why should I take them off? I still consider him my husband. Just because he died doesn't mean I'm not married any more."

"Is there any other reason you don't want to take them off?"

"Well, if I'm wearing wedding rings then guys aren't going to hit on me. They're safety. Plus they're my wedding rings that Brian gave me!"

"Maybe that's why He wants you to take them off. He is your protector, not the rings."

"I just can't do this! It isn't fair that He even wants me to! I'm not going to do it and if He wants to hit me with lighting then oh well."

Tears are streaming down my face as I drive home. "I can't do this, Lord. You don't understand." *"Yes I do. Brian was your god and now it's time you make Me your God."*

I realize what He's said is true. *"Brian has been my god. That's true. I worshipped that man. But I still can't do this."* I've struggled, fought, argued with the Lord's request for three days. Sitting in my office. No one else around, not even Kirk. *"Lord I can't."* No answer.

I slowly walk into the sanctuary, and stand looking at the large cross on the front wall. Tears begin flowing. Reaching to my left hand and fingering my wedding rings, one slow step after another, I've reached the cross and stand before it.

I sit down on the floor at the foot of it, sobbing, slowly removing my precious rings. Hardly able to see through the tears, I reach out and lay them on the floor beneath the cross.

Sitting for a long time crying and crying, I stare at my rings laying on the carpeted floor. I'm not sure how long I've been sitting here but I am finally able to stand on wobbly legs. I reach down, and pick up the rings. *"I'm not leaving them here."*

Laying the rings on the dresser at home, the day is shot. Grieving has once again set in. *"It's like he just died again. This is worse than when I buried him."* Crawling into bed for the night I'm laying here sleepless.

"Maybe I can just wear them for tonight and take them off in the morning."

I slowly get out of bed and walk toward the dresser. I stand here looking at my rings laying next to my jewelry box.

Reaching out and taking the rings, I slowly place them back on my left hand and get back into bed. Laying my head on the pillow with a sigh, I feel so much better now that my rings are back where they belong.

I close my eyes and wait for peaceful sleep to come. *"I SAID TAKE THEM OFF!"* This is no loving, gentle voice. It's a harsh demand that jettisons me out of bed and straight to the dresser.

Before I can say, huh-o, these rings are back on the dresser. This time to stay. Crawling back in bed, stuffing my face in the pillow, I'm bawling as though I just came from my husband's funeral.

I've cried and looked at my rings a dozen times over this past week. Walking into the office, Ben is sitting at the desk. Reaching across the desk to get something, he looks up. "You're not wearing your wedding rings."

I reach over to feel my now barren finger. "No. I did what He told me to do."

"How does that make you feel?"

"Angry that He'd even make me do it!"

"He didn't make you do anything, Sue. You chose to be obedient."

"If you'd heard Him demand me to remove them after I put them back on you wouldn't think that." Knowing me as well as he does, he knows I'm in a fighting mood. Smiling, he returns to what he was doing and I get the stack of papers I came for and leave.

For weeks now I've been fingering my left finger where my rings are supposed to be, according to me. Driving through a small strip mall, "*Go in that jewelry shop.*" Pulling up to the front and sitting in the car, "*I don't think this is of the Lord. He said to leave them off so I'm not going to be fooled.*"

Leaving the parking lot, driving to the grocery store, "*Why would He want me to go in the jewelry store? If it was Him.*" Returning home with my groceries I'm still puzzled about why the Lord would have me go to a jewelry store.

Driving through the same parking lot. "*Go in the jewelry store.*" "*Okay. But if this isn't of You then I ask You put a stop to it right now. This is torture!*" I walk into the jewelry store and approach the counters with diamond rings.

"Can I help you with something?"

"I don't think so. I'm just looking right now. Thank you."

Why am I looking at these? Oh this one is pretty. I really like it. "Sir, can I just look at this ring?"

"Of course."

He opens the cabinet, brings out the ring I've pointed out, and he sits it on the counter.

Picking it up and examining it more closely, there's several diamonds. Some round, some baquettes, and one small marquee in the center. "Can a larger marquee be put in the center instead of this little one?"

"Yes, how large are you talking about?"

"One carat."

"Yes, that will fit nicely. I think it would look lovely. Do you have it with you?"

"No. I'll have to think about this. That's a pretty hefty price tag you have on it."

I am sitting on the edge of my bed. "Lord, was that You that sent me into the jewelry store?" "Yes." "Why? You said I couldn't wear a wedding ring anymore." *"Take your ring and go to the jewelry store tomorrow. I want you to have My wedding ring. Remember, we got married in Cana."*

I can't even answer I'm crying so hard as the memory of standing in the chapel speaking vows of marriage flood my mind. I take my precious diamond ring out of the jewelry box and get in the car. "Is this really You Lord? This isn't just me wanting to do this?" *"I love you."*

I enter the jewelry store once again.

"Oh, you've decided on the ring?" I place my ring on the counter. "Can I see that same ring again?"

"Sure." He reaches into the showcase, pulls it out and places it on the counter. "It is a lovely ring."

I pick the ring up once again. "It's beautiful." I hold up my wedding ring and point to the marquee. "This is the diamond I'd like in the center of that one."

"Oh that makes this ring look so much nicer. This is a beautiful diamond. Of course we'll deduct the cost of the smaller diamond since you're using your own."

"How long will it take? When can I pick it up?"

"Oh, it will be ready in three days."

I write a check for the deposit, turn and slowly walk back to the car, still not really sure if it's the Lord telling me to do this.

I am feeling guilty for taking the diamond Brian gave me out of my ring. *"Brian, please don't be mad at me. The Lord said to do this so you can blame Him."*

I pick up the ring as scheduled and place it on my right ring-finger.

On the way home, *"The marquee represents your marriage to your earthly husband. The others represent your marriage to your heavenly Husband."* Holding my hand up as I'm steering with the other, "It's beautiful, Lord."

"The various shapes of the other diamonds represent the various facets of my love. I love you very much. You don't realize how much." Stopping at the church, *"I hope Ben and Carol are in."*

I enter the church and walk down the long hallway to the office. *"Oh good. They're not in session."* Ben and Carol are sitting on the love seat discussing something. They both look up as I'm entering. Holding out my right hand I say, "Ben, Carol, Look what the Lord gave me."

Ben takes my hand. "That's something! How did this come about?"

Carol takes my hand. "Oh Sue. That's beautiful!"

"Well, it's a long story. But to make it short, He said it's my wedding ring from Him. Remember I married Him when I was in Israel?"

Ben's looking at me with a questioning expression. "Okay Ben. That's what He said. The big diamond represents my marriage to my earthly husband, Brian. The other diamonds represent my marriage to my heavenly husband. Him!"

Carol leans forward to look at it again. "It is beautiful. He must love you a whole lot." "He must. I'm sure glad He paid for it, this sucker cost a fortune!"

Sitting in my Sunday School class, I flash my right hand under everyone's noses. "Look what the Lord bought for me?" Getting many looks of, do-do-do-do-do-do-do, "Well He did!"

Then there's the "WOW" comments. I've decided Christ loves to watch my reaction at these moments. I think He says, "Hey angels, gather around and watch Sue's reaction to this!" "Oh WOOOOOOW!"

Of course I share these wow moments with Ben and Carol. I have deep respect for them and we've become friends. If Ben isn't available Carol and I will discuss whatever is on my mind.

I don't go to them about just my stuff. There's many times I consult with them about an issue that has come up in the group. "How do we handle this type of anger?" The days of my resentment and fussing about the office sharing are long gone.

Since becoming a Christian and giving the Lord full and complete permission to do whatever He knows I need in my healing process, the slow process of overcoming the issues of my abuse have escalated tremendously.

It isn't an easy process by any stretch of the imagination. There's a lot of pain to deal with, to face. So many lies having been told to me, or insinuated, that have to be revealed, also lies that I have believed.

"You aren't worthy." "You're trash." "If you hadn't done . . . then . . . wouldn't have happened." "God isn't going to help you!" "If you want something you better get it yourself. Nobody else is going to give it to you."

The one that really hurts is, "If you want me to love you, you better . . ." Distrust, self-reliance, control are instilled. Self-esteem is shattered. Because I've been told everything is my fault, shame and guilt are also ingrained.

Hatred for myself and even my body. All these things affect everything I do in relationships. Being told, "Forget it! It happened a long time ago." It's like being raped all over again. The list can go on forever.

All have to be dealt with and it takes time, a lot of effort and persistence on my part. Crying, anger, grief over a lost childhood, thoughts of suicide and even attempted suicide.

Just because I became a Christian doesn't mean that everything is forgotten and the world is all hunky-dory. The Lord said it is a renewing of our minds. Not amnesia. Greater understanding is one of the important things that has really helped me.

Understanding the significance of what I believed or didn't believe. I believed God hates me, I'm damaged goods and no one can love me. I'm dirty is a common thought. I'll never amount to anything. Hogwash! That isn't how God sees me.

In church, listening to the sermon, praying, talking about God to others has helped. For a short period of time I absolutely cannot call God, "Father." It just won't come out of my mouth. Every time I hear the word, "father," my guts do a flip flop.

I've had no idea the impact a biological father, or any father figure, has on how I see God the Father. If my father is untrustworthy, controlling, absent, manipulative, domineering, that's how I will perceive God.

I believed God is just like my father for a long time. It's so ingrained it's hard for me to sometimes believe otherwise. It has been so important for me to study the Word. To hunt for the truth about who my Heavenly Father really is.

I'm trying to dispel the lies from the truth. Not easy! *"I'm not like your earthly father, Sue."* Believing the lies can destroy a child! It's taking me years to learn the truth.

Then having a really hard time believing the truth. *"I love you more than you'll ever imagine. Trust Me."* Hearing the Lord tell me over and over that He loves me is hard for me to believe. *"How can He love me? I'm damaged goods."* *"Trust Me. I love you."*

It has taken me a while to learn that He does love me. The most life-changing event in my Christian walk is when the "God loves me" smacked me right in my heart. ME!, the "dirty one," the screwed up "nut case." The one that doesn't deserve love from anyone. "God loves ME!"

Walking into my Sunday school class after having this revelation smack me in the heart, I'm looking at all the ladies sitting in the room. "You know what? God loves ME! I don't care if anyone in this room loves me or not! God loves me!"

The women are absolutely speechless. They're so surprised by my proud disclosure they're just sitting with gaping mouths. Turning and strutting out of the room I'm feeling very much loved, by God.

Arriving home, Rocky and Jacob greet me. "Where's Dusty, guys?" Walking around the house calling for him, he doesn't show up. "Dusty? Dusty? Where are you?" Getting increasingly worried I can't look for him any more. It's gotten dark.

Getting up early Dusty still hasn't returned. Now I know something's wrong! I walk down the path toward the creek. "Dusty? Dusty?" Searching for three days now I'm not giving up!

Continuing to search the woods, Rocky runs over to something, stops, and is whining. Walking over, there's my precious little Dusty. Kneeling down beside his lifeless body the sobs come.

Sitting down next to him, with Rocky on one side of me and Jacob on the other, the sobs grow stronger and stronger. Seeing bite marks all over his little body, wanting to scream but not able to, leaning over and laying down on the ground, the silent screams are within.

Getting a shovel and old sheet, returning, the digging is difficult. Tears blind me, sobs rip through my throat. Laying my sheet wrapped "baby" in his small grave with a cross marking the spot, a feeling of emptiness engulfs me.

11

Brenda is staying with friends for the week. The house is silent and after a busy week, *"I'm going to just sleep until noon if I want to!"* Snuggling down under the warm blankets I'm sound asleep before my head even hits the pillow.

"Wake up!" Startled by the loud demand I'm wide awake. Eyes blurry, looking around the room to see who hollered at me. Finding no one here, I turn over to go back to sleep. *"Get up! We have work to do!"* *"Oooohhh, do I have to?"* Now I know I'm not dreaming. That voice is very familiar.

I drag my body to sitting position, feet dangling over the edge of the bed. All I want to do is get snuggled back under the blankets and fall back asleep. *"You're going to start a magazine."*

"I'm WHAT? You have to be kidding! I don't have a clue how to do that." *"I know. I'm going to show you how. Get up."* Turning on the coffee pot, *"I can't believe You want me to publish a magazine!"* *"Trust Me."* Pouring myself a cup of coffee, *"Now what?"* *"Go to your word processor and type what I tell you."* *"Okay."*

For most of the day we're at the dining room table. He's telling me exactly what to do and how. What to type, where to put it, each step as we talk. I haven't even bothered to get dressed.

This is a most incredible experience. I feel like Jesus is right here at my table. Pointing, directing, joking, laughing, talking. It's like we've been best buddies for years. When I look across the table I can't see a human but it's as though one is right here beside me, leaning over my shoulder. *"Move it just to the right. Now center that here." "This is incredible! I can't believe we're really doing this!"*

"Golly! It's almost four o'clock! I haven't even gotten dressed. Oh well, this is more fun." If anyone hears me they'll think I'm crazy. Here I am talking to someone that can't be seen. Do-do-do-do-do-do-do."

The layout of the little magazine is almost finished. At least the outside of it. "Hey Angels, come watch and see Sue's reaction." *"You'll call it Angels by Grace."* "OOOOOOH WOW! That is just tooooo cool. I LOVE it." I can hear His laughter and maybe even some angels laughing with Him. Another "WOOOOW" exploded from my lips.

"I want you to ask the ladies in your group if they will write a short testimony to put in the magazine." "Okay." *"The Holy Spirit will also put in a Word. You'll call it Pen Tips."*

"What am I supposed to do with this when it's finished?" *"You'll be mailing it to many people."* "And just who are these people and how do I know who to mail it to?" *"You'll see."*

I wake up early after sleeping like a log. *"Get your phone book."* "Well good morning, Lord." Again I'm talking to this invisible Man as though He's standing right next to me and everyone can see Him through the window.

"The regular book or the yellow pages?" *"Yellow pages."* Laying open the phone book I turn to the section where psychiatrists, counselors, and so on are. *"I'll show you which ones to list."*

I've spent this past hour listing each name, address, and phone number the Lord's been pointing out as I run my finger down the columns. The rest of the day I'll be going through the day as though it's a "normal" day.

Since becoming a Christian I'm not even sure there is such a thing as "normal days." I never know what the Lord is going to have me doing next or where He may take me in visions.

In group, "Ladies, I have something I'd like to talk to you about." Having looks of huh-oh on their faces, I can't help but laugh. I haven't even told Susan about the magazine yet.

"The Lord is having me do a small publication. It's going to be called 'Angels by Grace' and what I would like to ask of you, is if any of you are willing to write a short testimony to put in the publication."

"You don't have to if you don't feel comfortable doing that. I won't use your name if you prefer not to have it on your testimony. I can use initials, no name, or first names. I'll be putting testimonies, poems, drawings, and other things in the publication."

"It will go to doctors, pastors, any place that deals with sexual abuse. It will have a list of books that will be helpful and a section listing support groups around the area, if there are any. There'll be a lot of neat stuff. Please pray about it."

Going through the books I have in regards to abuse I begin the "Book List." Asking the Holy Spirit to write His Word for the publication I'm amazed at how quickly He gives me His word of encouragement for the Pen Tip page. This is definitely a "God thing."

Placing all the testimonies, poems, and a drawing together, the publication is coming together nicely. *"Oh Lord, You were right. This is going to be so good."*

"Pastor Kirk, I have something I want to show you." I hand him the rough draft of the Angels by Grace, and wait for him to read through it.

"Sue, this is wonderful. What are you going to do with it?"

"It's going to be mailed to whoever the Lord leads me to mail it to. If I supply all the paper can I use the copy machine here?"

"Sure. How many do you think you'll be making?"

"Right now I have twenty-five names to mail it to and then some copies will be left in the narthex for others to pick up. Of course you'll get one and the ladies in the Angel Group."

I go back into my office, and Ben and Carol have come in. "Look what the Lord is having me do! I think this is so cool!" I explain how everything happened and where the publication will go. Ben looks up. "I think it's great." Carol agrees.

Brenda returns home from visiting her friend and finds me hard at work at the dining room table. Paper, edited and types pages stacked in the order for the final print. She walks over to the table where I'm hunched over working. "What are you doing?"

"I'm putting together the Angels by Grace I told everyone about in the group." She starts to pick up one of the articles. "Huh uh. You can't read it until it's finished and passed out to everyone. You'll just have to wait to get one with everyone in the group."

Walking away she says, "Whatever."

Brenda has learned to trust me and isn't so fearful. She's still on guard but we have become very close. I still struggle with her sarcasm on different occasions but have more or less accepted it. The Lord continues to tell me, "Ignore it." So I do.

She has somehow wiggled into my heart and has become almost like a daughter to me. We have fun playing Yahtzee, Scrabble, and various board games. She comes to me for advice on occasion.

As I lay in bed reading scripture Brenda walks in. "Can I talk to you for a minute?"

"Sure." She lays down across the end of my bed. "What do you think about me going to work part time?" As we're talking several angels are lighting up the ceiling.

"Brenda!" I point to the ceiling. "Do you see the angels?" Rolling over onto her back and looking up at the ceiling she says, "No." "They're all over the ceiling! You can't see them?"

"No."

I am amazed that I see them and she doesn't. "How can you not see them? The whole ceiling is lit up from them?"

Giving me a grin, she sings, "do-do-do-do-do-do-do."

"Get outt'a here and go to bed."

"Lord, why can I see this stuff and others can't? I don't understand that. If You do it for one then You do it for others. Why can't she see the angels?" "That's not her gift."

Many nights Brenda and I stretch out on the bed and just talk about a whole array of topics. Sometimes we pray together, other times we're like teenage girls at a slumber party.

The nights we spend chatting until three in the morning wipe me out. Even though it's fun and I really enjoy our chats this old body is a whole lot older than hers and needs its rest.

Some of our conversations are pretty serious. Catching me lying on the couch she sits on the edge looking at me. I can see she has something important on her mind. She's had a rough week with doctor appointments.

After waiting for her to bring up whatever is bothering her I ask, "What's up kiddo?"

Hesitating, then looking at me, then the floor she answers, "Sue, I just want to be normal."

"Of course you do."

"I want a husband and kids. A normal life! I've had this stuff since I was thirteen years old!"

"I know, Brenda. What exactly is Lupus? I don't know much about it other than you having to have chemo, and that it's an auto-immune disease. But what exactly is it? Let's go sit at the table and have some tea. You can tell me about it."

We sit down at the table with our ice tea. "It's an auto-immune disease. There's two kinds. One is called Discoid Lupus. That one basically affects the skin. It isn't as bad as the other one. It doesn't involve the organs.

"The other type is Systemmic Lupus. That's what I have. It attacks the organs and joints. That's why my joints hurt so much some times. My kidney function has already dropped."

I stop the tears from forming as she continues. "My one kidney is only operating at forty percent. If it goes to twenty-five percent I'll have to have dialysis." Because Brian also had kidney failure caused by the Leukemia I know all too well kidney failure isn't good!

"So is chemo the only thing they can do for the Lupus?"

"I'm on Prednizone and you know I have a whole pharmacy of drugs I have to take. Sometimes it goes into remission and I don't have to take chemo for a while."

"So, what causes it?"

"They say it's inherited. My great, great Aunt had it. You wanna' play Yatzee?"

I realize she doesn't want to talk about it anymore. "Sure, I'll get it."

Weeks pass. Brenda walks in from one of her doctor appointments. "I don't have very good news." She's standing in the doorway of her bedroom.

"What did the doctor say?"

"My kidneys are shutting down and I may have to go on dialysis."

Tears well up in my eyes and I hug her. "I'm so sorry. You've been through enough." She's uncomfortable with my hugging her. She isn't used to displays of affection, especially from me.

"I didn't mean to make you cry."

"Brenda, it's just damn unfair!" I walk back into the kitchen. *Lord, why? She's only a kid! She's been through enough! Won't You do something?*

Knowing dialysis is only temporary until a transplant can be done, it's testing my faith. *I just don't understand You! You healed everybody under the sun, even brought people back to life when they were dead!* "Why don't You heal her?"

"Some are healed to show My glory. Others are to be a witness to others showing My strength." "I'm not sure I fully understand that but if You say so. All I know is I want You to heal her."

She doesn't know how many times I've lain in bed crying and begging the Lord to heal her. *"You're all powerful. You can do anything You want!* I'm trying to understand things I may never understand.

The kidney failure is escalating which means more pills and more frustration. Fatigue has really set in. Not only from anemia but from the kidneys worsening. Some days she isn't able to get out of bed or lays on the couch.

I understand all the fatigue because of having been through it with Rebecca and Brian. The Lord told me when Brenda first moved in, "I didn't teach you all those things for nothing. They aren't just for you."

I now understand better how He will use not only our pain, but the knowledge He gives us, to help others. I learned a lot in caring for Brian and Rebecca. I realize fully why Brenda was brought to me.

She needs love, acceptance, and someone who understands the complications of what's she's going through and given the support she needs. Many times she's come home frustrated as well as upset. "You're the only one I can talk to about this, Sue. Nobody else understands. You've been through it with Brian and that's a big help to me. Thank you."

The longer we live together, the more respect I have for her. Taking care of Brian for five years has helped me tremendously in being able to care for her when she needs help.

I'm facing a young woman that has fought for eight years and my heart continually cries for her suffering. Even though she'll get depressed at times and has her "down times" from treatments, she keeps on, keeping on.

She's had part time jobs, she's gone back to school to get a degree. She continually tries to live as normal a life as possible. In appearance she doesn't look as though she has any medical problems. That can't be farther from the truth.

The disease is rampaging through her body but looking at her one would think she's as healthy as a horse which results in people being cruel in their statements at times.

Comments such as, "You don't even look sick! It can't be that bad" or "You just need more faith!" Cruel judgments are often spit out as well, "What bad sin have you committed? You have to repent!"

Each time one of these occasions arises I try to comfort her and encourage her. Sometimes it's difficult to get her to talk about it but there are other times her anger flares up and I certainly understand that.

She tries so hard and yet there's so much out of her control. She'll be enjoying school or her part-time job and then have to quit or withdraw due to an illness that isn't even her fault.

A monster that has almost taken over her life is cruel in my book, yet her determination and the Lord's strength keeps her going. I can't help but admire her courage. Watching this young woman go through this illness is tearing at my heart.

I just can't understand why the Lord would allow anyone to have to suffer like this. *"Why Lord? Why do You allow us to suffer?"* *"Sue, suffering is to draw people closer to Me."*

"Doesn't suffering also cause people to get mad and turn away from You?" *"I have given man free will. It's their choice to come to Me or to walk away from Me."* *"If they walk away doesn't that make them their own god?"* *"Yes."*

The response to the Angels by Grace publication is great. Word of mouth, having them in various counselors' offices, doctors allowing them in their waiting rooms, has helped to spread the word.

Complimentary letters, testimonies and praise be to God, some have asked the Lord to be their Savior, all because of what they've read in this little publication the Lord got me out of bed for.

All this has made the Angels by Grace a huge success. The Lord isn't through proving He's real, not just to me but to many others, too. In Sunday morning service Kirk stands before us.

"There's a team of us going to Russia as missionaries. We are in need of funds if all of us will be able to go. I'd like for you to be in prayer and let the Lord lead you in how you can help."

"You can help through prayer or a financial donation. The people in Russia are in dire need of the gospel. Please pray about it." Walking down the hall toward my office, *"I want you to write a check."* *"Okay."* *"I'll tell you for how much."*

Stepping into Kirk's empty office, I write the check for what the Lord has indicated. Wednesday morning as I'm walking into my office I hear, "Sue?"

"Hi Kirk."

"I want to thank you for the check you wrote. You're not going to believe what happened."

"Oh yea. What?"

"I took the check to choir practice and held it up. I said someone donated this amount and what would happen if it was matched."

"So what happened?"

"As a result of your obedience to the Lord all five of us are going to be able to go to Russia!"

"That's great! Now I know why the Lord had me write it for that amount." It was the exact amount we needed.

Going about my business I've forgotten about the Russia trip. The team has been back two days. As I pass Kirk's office, "Sue, can you come in here for a minute?"

"Sure, What's up, Kirk?"

"Sit down, I want to talk to you for a minute."

Taking a seat in front of his desk, he looks at me from across his desk. "Do you know what the biggest social problem Russia has?"

"No."

He looks at me intensely. "Sexual abuse and alcohol."

"You're kidding!"

"Remember me telling you I was going to take some of the Angels by Grace with me?"

"Yes."

"Well, I did. We were handing out Bibles to a group of women and the interpreter read one of the articles to the women."

"Oh wow!"

"She's having them interpreted for them and wants me to send one each month."

Tears well up in my eyes.

"I'm not done yet. The next day we went back to that same place to hand out more Bibles.

"Several of the women that were there the day before were there this time, too."

"And?"

Leaning closer to me across his desk, "They formed a support group and named it, Ashes to Beauty."

Now the tears are flowing. He reaches in his desk and takes out a small package. "They wanted you to have this. It's handmade."

I take the package and rip the paper off. "Oh my gosh! It's a small quilted square with an embroidered church! It's beautiful."

"They said to give it to you. It's the church they worship at."

Swiping at my tears, I ask, "The interpreter is going to have the Angels by Grace translated for them?"

"She sure is. I'll be sending her one every month so I'll need two when you have them ready."

"This is just phenomenal! I had no idea what was going to happen just because I wrote that check. This is just too awesome. Kirk says, "See what obedience can do?" Hugging my little handmade quilt I say, "Thank you Lord. This is just too much."

Susan steps into my office. "Hi Sue. Have you got a minute?"

"Sure."

She sits down on the loveseat. "We need to pray about starting another group. We have several names on the waiting list."

"Okay."

Having the Lord's blessings on an additional group we begin a second group. Part of our purpose in having another group is to train one of our members to lead a group in her community. More support groups are desperately needed.

Things at home have begun to change. Brenda asks, "Sue, can I talk to you a minute?"

"Sure."

"I'm not coming back to Angel Group."

This doesn't surprise me. "Is there any particular reason you want to leave?"

Looking down at her feet Brenda says, "I just don't want to go anymore."

"*Lord, what do I do? I know she's running.*" "*She'll be fine.*" I've noticed that gradually Brenda has been staying with friends more and more and for longer periods of time.

One day I answer the phone. "Hi Sue. If it's okay with you I think I'll stay another three days with Lisa."

"That's fine, Brenda. But I need to ask you something."

"What?"

"Are you wanting to move in with Lisa?"

A long silence. "Yes."

I sat down on the chair near the phone. "Okay, when would you like to pick up the rest of your things?"

"I'll come tomorrow."

Hanging up the phone I have no idea why she's decided to move.

"*Lord, is this what You are leading her to do?*" "*No.*" "*Have I done something wrong? Have I hurt her in some way? What do I do?*" "*Do nothing. It's her decision.*" Sitting alone in the house, feeling the silence all around me I still can't figure out why she suddenly wants to move.

Brenda being gone has not ended our relationship but it has had a bruise. Why I don't know. I lean back on the sofa,

"Why'd she leave Lord? We got along great. I know she needs people her own age. I hope I haven't hurt her."

I go into the office. "Ben, can I talk to you? Do you have about three days?"

He laughs and leans back in his chair. "What's going on?"

"Brenda has moved out."

"Oh, is that something you knew she was going to do?"

"No. That's why I don't understand it. We've been getting along great and poof, she wants to move."

"Have you asked her why?"

"Yes, but she won't say why. I don't know if I said something, done something, what."

Crossing his feet at the ankles I can tell he's settling in for this conversation. By now he can read me like a book. During the next hour and a half we're talking about it. "I'm proud of her, Ben. She's grown in the Lord, she's gotten some healing, and she's finally gotten where she trusts me."

Ben listens as I rattle on. "I really admire her, she's gone through so much and yet still has a good attitude about it all. I miss her, Ben. She's like a daughter to me. She's been living with me for over a year now. I just hope this is the right decision for her."

Ben sits up straight as he uncrosses his feet. "That's something she's going to have to determine."

"Thanks Ben, I guess I better let you get back to work."

12

I am driving down Georgia 400. *"If you could have any kind of house you wanted, what would you want?"* Thinking about it, "Oh gee. I don't know. Let's see."

I'm talking out loud as though Jesus is sitting right next to me. "I'd like four bedrooms. That way if You brought someone to live with me I would still have a guest room for visitors."

"Okay, what else?" "I'd like a large bathroom with a whirlpool. I just have to have a whirlpool, Lord! Another bathroom for guests and a two car garage attached to the house so I don't have to walk outside.

"A large yard like I have now and maybe just two acres instead of six. A larger laundry room, kitchen, and a good size living room with a fireplace."

"Is that all?" "Yes, I think so."

Thinking it is just another conversation while driving, I've already put it out of my mind. Two days have passed and while going into town for groceries I recognize the all too familiar voice. *"If you could live anywhere you wanted, where would you live?"*

Assuming He's talking about somewhere in Georgia. "Wherever You want me." I arrive home, put the groceries away and walk through the living room. "Now that Brenda is gone, this would be a good time to perk up this house."

Going throughout the house and deciding my bedroom and the living room need painting more so than the other rooms, I go back into town to get supplies for both rooms.

Waking early I've spent the whole day painting the bedroom. Crawling into bed, it doesn't take long for me to fall soundly asleep. A very lifelike dream takes form. In the dream I'm standing before an altar with a man beside me.

I'm in a wedding dress, he's tall and slender. He's dressed in black jeans, cowboy boots, and a freshly pressed shirt. We're facing the altar and I'm seeing us from the back so I can't see his face.

His black, neck length, professionally trimmed hair peeks from under his black cowboy hat. A voice in the dream says, "His name is Mr. Sage." Suddenly awake and sitting up in bed, *"That was weird."*

While I stand on the ladder painting the wall, *"You know you're not painting this for yourself. You're fixing it up to sell."* I recognize His voice. "That's okay," and I finish painting.

I've begun wallpapering and while adhering the wallpaper to the top of the wall, *"Jennifer Ross."* I am so shocked at having a name come out of the blue, my hand slips on the wallpaper and it tumbles down covering my head and shoulders.

Not caring if anyone hears me or not, of course no one is around to hear me anyway. "Where did that come from? Who in the world is Jennifer Ross?" I try to pull the now crinkled wallpaper away from me and tear it. "Doggone it! Who's Jennifer Ross?"

"She's the realtor who is going to sell your house." I continue to try to untangle myself from the glue, water, and twisted wallpaper. "Okay. Just how am I going to find this Jennifer?" *"You'll see."*

Being told I'm going to sell my home that I've lived in for fifteen years doesn't seem to bother me right now. There's more important things to worry about, like getting out from under this sticky wallpaper without falling off the ladder!

"Do you think you're ready to move?" I throw the wet wallpaper on the floor and carefully climb down off the ladder, irritated. "Yes, well, I guess so." I've finally finished the living room with no further interruptions.

It's taken me five days to finish all that I started and I'm now able to relax and enjoy my newly decorated rooms. Furniture rearranged, newly potted plants placed strategically around the rooms, I'm content with my work.

For some reason the word, Wyoming, keeps coming to mind. "This is bugging me. Lord, why would Wyoming keep coming in my mind?" No answer. I am sitting on the swing out on the patio. "Wyoming? Cowboy? Dream!"

I stop the swing suddenly. "Wait a minute! Lord, are You telling me I'm going to move to Wyoming to marry some cowboy? I don't think so!" No reply, just a chuckle. Then the name Sage starts bugging me.

"Maybe it means something. I'll see if it's in the dictionary." I drag out the Webster's dictionary and flip through the pages. *"Sage, sage. Here it is."* "Hmmm, it means, 'A man, usually an older man, who is characterized, revered for his wisdom, experience, and justice.' "Oh thank you Lord! At least he isn't a bum."

Having told my daughter about the dream and the Lord asking me if I'm ready to move, I dial the phone. "Hello."

"Sharon! I've figured out where the Lord's moving me."

"I've prayed about it and He has confirmed I'll be moving to Wyoming. But He isn't telling me where in Wyoming. The thing is when I look at the map my eyes keep going to a town called Kemmerer."

"I'll get my map and see what's there. Hold on." During the time she's getting her map, my eyes continue to be led to Kemmerer. "Mom. I have my map. I'll look and see where it's at on my map."

I wait a few seconds while she's looking. "Oh my gosh! Mom, there's a little tiny town named Sage. It's just a little speck on the map."

"You're kidding!"

"No, it's near that town you keep seeing, Kemmerer?"

"That makes sense. Me marrying a man named Mr. Sage." I close the map on my table. "Are you still coming next week?"

"Yes, I'll fly into Idaho Falls. Are you still able to pick me up?"

"Sure."

13

There's a saying in Christianity, that the Lord will "check you." Meaning I'll get a caution in my spirit. It's as though the Lord touches my spirit saying, "No, no, not right."

I'm "checked" as Sharon and I are focusing on the small town called Sage.

Ignoring it I'm convinced this is where the Lord is going to move me. It's the only thing that makes sense out of all this. Why else would He give me the name Sage in the dream?

As I walk to the small baggage area in the Idaho Falls airport, Sharon is waiting with a big smile on her face. "Hi Mom. How was your flight?"

"It was okay."

She takes my bags and walks to the car.

"You know, Sharon, maybe we should just forget about this Sage business."

"If that's what you want."

For the past three days we've visited and I've taken her and my granddaughter, Ginny, for dinner and shopping. We're no longer focusing on the Mr. Sage stuff. We've decided we've blown everything out of proportion and let it go.

I am sitting on the steps of her wooden deck in the sun. *Go to Wyoming.* I jump up, and run into the house. "Sharon, Sharon. Where are you?"

She walks out from the bedroom. "What? What's going on?"

"The Lord just told me to go to Wyoming."

"Oh my gosh! We were right after all." Sharon rushes over to the shelf and pulls out the map. She drags her finger along a line drawn on the map. "Here it is. If we take highway 15 down to highway 30, we'll go right to Sage."

"It looks like it's about a three hour drive like I thought. Can we leave early in the morning after I get Ginny off to school?"

"Well, let's go check it out."

Going south on highway fifteen we've found the turnoff to highway thirty.

Driving down the two lane highway we're winding our way through mountains, rolling hills and open fields. Every few miles we see a sign, Antelope crossing. Then farther down the road there's one, Elk crossing.

Being used to all the greenery and trees in Georgia I'm surprised these mountains don't have any. The sides of the hills and fields are barren, covered in brown grass. "This place sure is barren. Where's the trees?"

Sharon keeps driving and finally there's a small square sign, "Sage." We pull onto the side of the road. "This is Sage?"

"That's what the sign says, Mom."

The only thing we can see is a railroad track running parallel to the highway and a small old deserted ramshackle small house.

Putting the car in gear, Sharon slowly drives over the railroad track. Hardly clearing the railroad track, on our left are four rusted out junk cars. "This must be the way to Sage. Let's go a little farther and see if the town is down there."

About three quarters of a mile down the narrow black topped road a house sits off to the left. Slowly driving past the modern, nicely kept home, following the road about five more miles, not another house is in sight.

The pavement suddenly ends. Only a narrow dirt road is ahead. Stopping the car, we're both confused. Twisting around in my seat, looking all around I say, "There isn't anything out here! The only house we've seen is that one."

"Maybe we should turn around, Mom. It doesn't look like there's anything out here."

A sinking feeling comes over me. *"I can't believe the Lord wants me to live out here. This place is desolate! There isn't even a tree!"* As Sharon turns the car around, tears well up in my eyes. *"You can't mean for me to live out here in this God forsaken place!"*

My emotions are going rampant. *"You're doing this to punish me, aren't You! Well, if this is where You want me to live then I will!"* Looking out my side window to hide the tears, an overwhelming sense of confusion and fear settle in.

She glances over at me. "Are you okay, Mom?"

Not looking at her, the pain in my voice is evident. "If this is where He wants me to live then I will."

"Go to Kemmerer." So caught up in the array of emotions I ignore the Lord's words. *"Go to Kemmerer!"*

We drive back the five miles and approach the modern style house. "Mom, there's a lady in the yard. Let's stop and ask her where the town is." Saying nothing, tears streaming down my face, not losing control is difficult.

As we pull the car near the yard the lady in her shorts and sleeveless blouse lays the hose down that's in her hand and walks toward the car. Sharon leans her head out the car window. "Hi, can you tell us where the town of Sage is?"

"There is no town Sage any more."

I can't even look up. *"He putting me out here and there's not even a town!"*

"There used to be a town many, many years ago. It was a train stop."

Sharon glances over at me then back at the lady. "Thank you."

Pulling away, we're slowly going back to the main road. Before arriving back at the railroad track, on the right is a side area where bulldozers have piled a mountain of dirt.

Pulling over she's parked next to the pile of dirt. Sharon shuts the ignition off and looks over at me. "Now what do we do?"

I get out of the car, lean against the fender, the tears stream down my face. *"Go to Kemmerer!"*

By now hurt and a sense of betrayal have set in along with a whole variety of emotions. My mind is reeling. *"I've done everything You've asked. Why? Why are You putting me out here all alone with nothing around but dirt and dry grass? I've trusted You and now this?"*

I want to yell and shake my fists. *"I don't understand You. Why way out here in the middle of nowhere? If this is where You want me it's where I'll live. I don't know how, but I will!"*

I look at Sharon through the tears. "I'm determined that if He wants me to live here, then I will! Even if I die out here in this horrible desolate place."

Sharon sees how upset I am. "Mom, it's going to be okay."

"No, it isn't! He's putting me out here to kill me!"

I'm sure she's biting her tongue to keep from laughing. She knows me well enough not to do that. She walks around the car. All rational reasoning has left me by now. Sharon walks over to the dirt pile and stands next to me. "Mom, we need to look at the map and see what's around here."

I'm sniffling. "Okay." We walk back to the car as I swipe at the tears on my cheeks. "I keep hearing, go to Kemmerer." Sharon walks to the drivers side of the car, reaches in and pulls out the map she has laying on the seat.

"Here's Kemmerer. It looks like it's only about twenty miles down the road." I walk up to the car, still so upset I

114

just want to sit in the dirt and cry. Screaming and kicking the crap out of the dirt would be good, too.

My mind is set on Sage being the place the Lord wants me to live. *"This is His way of punishing me for all the sarcasm and flippant things I've said. This is what I get for being such a smart ass to God!"*

Slowly pulling back onto the main highway and continuing to wind our way toward Kemmerer, both of us see the sign at the same time: "Kemmerer 20 miles." Sharon looks over at me. "How about we try to get some lunch? I'm getting hungry."

Nodding okay, my mind is still going crazy with the thoughts of living in Sage. A sign sits proudly along side the road; "Welcome to Kemmerer. Population 3005. Elevation, 8,012."

Pulling around a small curve we're suddenly on the main street of Kemmerer, Wyoming. *"At least it's a town."*

Passing slowly by homes on each side of the street, some look quite old with small fenced yards. Some are neatly kept but others need refurbishing and lawns manicured.

Going about two blocks a large brick home sits on a large corner lot. The front yard is long and narrow. Pointing to the home Sharon says, "Look Mom, that house is for sale." Looking back at the home, I'm disinterested because I'm still convinced I'm to live in Sage. I notice a cross in the window. "Yea, it has a cross in the window."

Driving slowly on we pass a small boarded-up sandwich stand. "Road Kill Sandwiches" is painted on a board hanging over the now boarded-up door.

"Sharon, look at that. No wonder it's boarded up. Yuck! Who would want to eat there?"

On the right is a small bank, across from it is the small town square. "It looks like a clean little town," I say.

"Yes it does."

A small J.C. Penny store sits on the corner. "See Mom, they even have a Penny's store. It won't be so bad living here."

Glancing around I'm not too thrilled. I've never lived in a small town. "*Go to that real estate up ahead.*" I see the real estate office just ahead on the left and being upset, tired and hungry, "*I'm hungry, I'm tired, and I'll do it later.*"

A small Mom and Pop style café, furniture store, second hand store, all small businesses line the narrow main thoroughfare. Passing an old gas station on the left Sharon says, "I need to fill up with gas."

"Let's see if there's another one with a convenience store. Maybe we can get a sandwich." We approach a small curve. "There's one. I'll get gas and you see if they have sandwiches. I'll be in, in a minute."

Picking out our sandwiches and a drink, I pay the clerk. "I don't want to eat in the car, let's see if there's some place we can sit outside to eat." Overhearing our conversation the clerk looks up from ringing up our items. "There's a park just around the corner. Just go one street over and it will be on your left."

"Thank you." Taking our lunch, we're glad to get out of the car for a while. It's only 11:00 when we sit down under a large oak tree, stretch out our legs and begin eating our sandwiches.

Sharon looks over at me. "Do you feel better? This doesn't look like too bad of a place to live." I look around. "I don't know why the Lord would want me someplace out in the middle of nowhere."

"I don't either, Mom. But He has His reasons."

"Oh, I'm sure He does! It would be nice if He'd clue me in though!" Neither one of us are anxious to get back in the car.

I force myself to stand. "I guess we better get to that real estate office the Lord said to go to."

"I didn't know He told you that."

"Yea, well that's what He wants us to do."

Driving back the way we came Sharon pulls into the parking lot of the small real estate office. Walking into the cool office, an older woman is sitting at a desk behind a counter that separates the small room.

She asks, "May I help you?" As Sharon glances at the pictures of homes and their descriptions on the wall I say, "I'd like to see one of your agents."

"We only have one agent and he's the owner. Are you interested in some property?"

I glance over my shoulder at Sharon, then back to the woman. "Yes, I'm looking for a home."

"He'll be back any minute if you'd like to wait. We have some listing books if you'd like to look through them."

I take the two albums she's handing me and hand one to Sharon, who sits down on the love seat against one wall and starts looking through the book. I take a seat on one of the two chairs across from her.

Sharon suddenly looks up. "Mom! Didn't you tell me the Lord asked you what kind of home you wanted?"

"Yes, so?"

"What did you tell Him?"

"I said I wanted a four bedroom, a whirlpool, large living room, and an attached garage. Why?"

"You're not going to believe this, but this is exactly what you described! It's that house we saw on the corner when we came into town. Do you want to go see it?"

"I suppose so. It won't hurt anything."

The front door swings open and a middle-aged man wearing khaki pants and a short sleeve shirt walks in. Looking surprised to see us sitting here he says, "Hello." Looking over at his secretary, she smiles up at him. "These ladies would like to see some property."

Looking back at us he says, "Now?"

"Yes if you have time."

Sharon chimes in, "We're only here for the day. I'm Sharon and this is my mother."

Reaching out his hand he says, "I'm Tom, and you're?"

"I'm Sue Cass. I'll be moving here and am interested in seeing some homes."

He notices we've been looking through the listing books. "Have you picked out any particular ones you'd like to see?"

Lifting the book where he can see it I say, "I think we want to see these three."

Looking at the three I'm pointing out he says, "I'll go give them a call if you'll just give me a minute." He comes back into the waiting area. "It will be fine. They're all willing to let us come now. My van is just outside."

As we step into the bright sunlight he asks, "Which house would you like to see first?"

Climbing into the large suburban, Sharon pops up before I can say anything. "The house on the corner lot."

I'm not anxious to start house hunting still being convinced I'm to live in Sage. As we leave the parking lot Tom looks at me in the rearview mirror. "So where are you from? I detect an accent."

"I'm from Georgia and Sharon lives in Idaho Falls."

"Georgia? You're a long way from home. What brings you out here?"

"The Lord."

"The who?"

"The Lord Jesus."

Giving me a look of, oh no, a nut he says, "Here we are."

Pulling up to the curb in front of the brick home and turning off the ignition, he says, "This is a newer home. It's only about six years old. The owner had it built to his specifications. It's a nice home and very well built."

Looking out my window I say, "It doesn't look like it has a back yard plus it's right on the main drag." I point to a very old building at the far end of the lot. "What's that old building?"

"It's an old one car garage. It's almost a hundred years old. It even has the heavy wooden door that slides to the side on a tract."

"The house looks nice on the outside but I think I'd like to see the other ones. I just don't like this being right here on the main road."

I point out my window. "Where does that road go?"

Leaning over to see what road I'm talking about he says, "That's the highway going to Big Piney."

"Oh."

Looking across the street where the road goes up the hill. I can see a river flowing through a lower section of land.

Along its banks are a few trees. They look more like shrubs than trees. "What's over there?" Sharon sits quietly while I ask all my questions.

"Just below the hill is a train track."

"A train track! Oh no. I'm not living next to a train track!"

He turns in his seat to look at me. "A train very seldom comes through here. I don't think it will be a problem."

"No, no! I won't live with a train running over my head. Let's go look at the others."

Leaning out the window he says, "Mr. Smith, we'll be back in a little bit if that's okay with you." The tall thin older man who's standing next to a car in the garage, waves an okay and leans over sticking his head under the car hood.

As we pull away from the curb I ask, "What churches do you have here?"

Looking at me again in the rearview mirror he replies, "There's several. There's a couple on Sage Avenue."

Sharon spins around in her seat. Looking at me she mouths, "Sage Avenue!" I nod, hardly able to keep quiet as Tom continues.

"We have a variety. Just about all denominations." Sharon slowly turns back around facing forward. Our surprised looks haven't escaped him. "Did I say something? You looked surprised."

Sharon glances over her shoulder at me then back at him. "No. Well, it's a long story. Can we ride down Sage Avenue?"

"Sure, it's the next street over."

He turns onto Sage Avenue and drives slowly down the street. As we pass a small church on the left, *"That's where you'll be going."*

Looking back at the church I don't acknowledge the Lord's comment. Tapping Sharon on the shoulder, she looks over her shoulder. Pointing to the church and then to my chest, she understands what I'm saying.

After looking at the other two houses we had on the list, Tom turns in the seat to look at me. "Well, that's all three you wanted to see."

Sharon pops up before I can say anything, "Let's go back to the first one."

Tom looks at me. *"That darn railroad track. If it wasn't there it might be alright."* "Yea, okay. We might as well."

Going back down the main street, Tom points to the J.C. Penny store on the corner. "That's the first J.C. Penny store ever built. J.C. and his wife Berta built it. After building this one, when it became a success, he branched out and began building stores all over the country. The rest is history."

120

As he continues slowly through town, "Their original home is that little white house back in the corner." The little store displays a coat, dress, a pair of shoes and other small items in its window.

"What else is famous in this town?"

Glancing back at me and laughing Tom says, "Nothing. That's our claim to fame."

Pulling up to the curb once again, the owner is still working on his car. Stepping out a side door his wife joins him in the garage. Tom steps out of the car. "Mrs. Smith? Is it alright if I show your home now?"

Noding her head yes, we approach the two steps leading up to the door. "You'll have to take your shoes off before entering." Looking at Tom surprised, Sharon and I untie our tennis shoes as Tom slips off his loafers.

Stepping into a small foyer, we're standing next to the living room. It's spacious with a large picture window covered with sheer drapes cascading down to the floor.

The window looks out over the narrow front yard and street. Soft thick salmon-colored carpet covers the floor. A large mahogany entertainment center takes up one wall. Matching end tables are sitting at the end of the sofa on the back wall.

Walking around the corner toward the kitchen we enter the dining area. A divider with marble counter tops separate the spacious kitchen from the dining rom. A small T.V. sits in the corner on the counter top.

Looking across the table are large windows facing the house behind this one. "*I can spit out this window and hit that house!*" I turn from the window, and walk around the divider. "Hey Mom, look. This stove is one of those flat top ones where there's no burners."

I walk over to it; a separate oven is inset in the wall on the left. A large microwave is recessed into the wall on the right. Walking over to another room off the kitchen and standing in the doorway I say, "Oh wow. I really like this big laundry room."

Along one wall a washer and dryer sit. Next to them is short white metal shelves holding detergent, softener, and an iron. A folding table sits across from the washer and dryer with an ironing board leaning against the wall.

Opening a door next to the washer and dryer I'm peeking out into the oversized two car garage. Mr. Smith glances up, Mrs. Smith smiles as I'm gently closing the door. Tom is standing with his hand on the knob of yet another door. "Shall we see the basement while we're right here?"

"Sure."

Opening the door Tom starts down the stairs. "These are pretty steep so be careful." Holding the railing, Sharon and I follow carefully, watching our steps as we descend.

As I step down off the last step I say, "Oh wow! I didn't expect it to be this big."

"Mom, look. There's a fireplace."

To the right is a fireplace with a blower, screen, and rock decorative wall behind, it is nestled into its own cove.

"The fireplace is thermostatically controlled." Tom is pointing out the control on the wall. Looking back into the room it looks like a large room all by itself. Windows line the top edge of the long cement walls.

One wall of windows looks out over the front yard. The other windows face the back yard of the neighbor. Stepping into a large storage area underneath the stairwell, a hot water heater and furnace is positioned in the corner of the back wall.

Walking around the wall that separates the stairs from both sides of the basement, Sharon calls, "Hey Mom. Come look."

I walk to the other end of the full basement where she is; there's a window lining the full length of the front wall. Sharon is standing in a doorway.

I look into the small room where she's standing. "Oh. It's another full bathroom." Tom is standing near the center of the room letting us explore without interference.

Moving back from the bathroom and taking a few steps beyond it, Sharon is grinning like a Cheshire cat. She is looking around the huge basement. "This sure isn't like any basement I've ever seen."

"Okay Sharon, what did you find now?"

I gently push her to the side so I can see in. "A bedroom!"

"Yea Mom. It even has a double closet."

A small twin bed sits in the middle of the room with a child-size chest of drawers against one wall.

Yet another window looks out over the main street. All windows have burgler bars on the outside due to being ground level. Grinning at me as I leave the room Sharon says, "Ginny and I can sleep down here when we come to visit. This is great!"

Looking around the large expanse as we walk back to the stairs, I'm beginning to think this might be where the Lord wants me after all. Climbing the stairs, Tom is coming up behind us. He turns off the light and we're once again in the dining room.

"The bedrooms are this way ladies." Sharon walks ahead of me with Tom trailing behind. Poking my head in a door on the left, it's a bedroom that's being used as an office.

Across the hall is yet another full bathroom.

"Mom! Come here."

"Okay, where are you?"

"I'm back here."

Following the sound of her voice and entering a large master bedroom, Sharon is standing in a doorway blocking entry. "*Gather around angels. Watch Sue's reaction to this.*"

Sharon's five foot ten "farm girl" body blocks the view. Walking up to her she suddenly steps back with one arm outstretched into the room, the other on her hip. "Taaaaaa-daaaa." Looking past her, "OHHHHHHHH, I DON'T BE-LIEVE THIS!"

Crossing the room and falling on my knees next to a large, four person whirlpool, Sharon is laughing. Tom is standing just outside the bathroom door. Rubbing my hand along the side of the tub I ask, "Tom, do you want to sell this whirly?"

He steps inside the bathroom. "What?"

"I said, do you want to sell this whirly?" Tom looks confused. "Huh?"

Sharon bursts out laughing.

I turn around to face Tom and cross my legs Indian style, one hand still touching the side of the tub. "Do you want to sell this whirlpool?"

"Are you saying you want to buy this house?"

"No. I asked if you want to sell this tub. If the house comes with it, oh well."

He walks backwards out of the master bathroom. "Oh," he says. Sharon and I are laughing as I'm trying to get off the floor. Sharon is offering me a helping hand. "*Buy it.*" "*This is the house You want me to have?*" "*Yes.*"

I hate to leave this bathroom with my cherished tub. "Look how big this bedroom is. I'll have no trouble getting my king-size furniture in here." Walking back out into the hall, there's yet another bedroom.

We walk outside, and put our shoes back on. "I'm going to walk around the house and check it out." The so-called back yard is a five-foot-wide strip of grass between the houses.

The neighbor has her yard fenced so there's only a small space to get past the back corner of the house. Between the house and the old garage is grass with a clothesline stretched between two poles.

I walk over to where Mrs. Smith is standing. "Mrs. Smith, you have a lovely home. I like the cross you have in the window."

Looking puzzled she says, "What cross? I don't have a cross in any window."

I look at Sharon. "Didn't you see the cross in the window when we first came into town?"

"No."

I look back at Mrs. Smith. "*I know I saw a cross!* Oh, I'm sorry. It must have been some other house. Thank you for letting us see your home. *I know I saw a cross!*"

Tom walks beside me back to the van. "Do you want to go to the office and write up an offer?"

I am still puzzled over no one seeing the cross but me. "Ahhh. There's no fence, the railroad tracks, being on the main drag, *"Buy the house!"* "Yes, okay."

We stand up, shaking hands after the contracts are completed. "Oh Sue. Do you have a phone number I can reach you at?"

"Yes." I give him Sharon's phone number. "I guess we'll have to come back tomorrow to sign the final papers."

"Okay, have a safe trip."

All the way back to Sharon's I'm trying to figure out why I saw the cross and nobody else did. "Sharon? Are you sure you didn't see that cross in the window?"

Looking over at me as she maneuvers the mountain road she replies, "No Mom. I didn't."

"But you had to. I even said when we were passing by the house, there's a cross in the window."

"I didn't see it. I must have been looking at the road or something else. I didn't hear you say it."

"I know I saw that cross! Maybe that was the way the Lord was showing me that this is the house He wants me to have."

"It could very well be. But I didn't see it. I wish I had."

Arriving back at Sharon's we're both exhausted. Laying down on my bed the impact of what I've done starts hitting me.

"Grandma, can we go have pizza tonight?"

"No Ginny, I don't think so. Mom and I are very tired."

Turning over with my face in the pillow the tears start. Feeling overwhelmed, "*What have I done? I just bought a house in Wyoming of all places.*" Crying into the pillow so as not to be heard, a knock on the door startled me.

"Come in."

"Mom, are you okay?"

"No Sharon. I must be nuts. I've just bought a house and I haven't even listed mine."

"You don't know if the offer is being accepted yet. We have to go back tomorrow."

"I know, but I just can't believe I'm doing this."

"Didn't the Lord tell you to do this?"

"Yes, but . . ." the tears stream down my face. It's a long night and I can't help but think I didn't really hear the Lord.

We're once again on our way to Kemmerer. The day is warm, bright sunshine, and a clear sky. Arriving in Kemmerer and entering the reality office, Tom is waiting for us.

We sit down in front of his desk. "Good morning, Tom. Was the offer accepted?"

"No Sue it wasn't. They've made a counteroffer so we need to go over that. Are you going to be in town all day?"

"That depends. How long do you think all this is going to take?"

"If we can get it written up I can take it over and see what happens."

Smith has rejected my offer once again. Two

r ck and forth between Kemmerer and
I otally wiped out.

last trip to Kemmerer, we're yet
a e mountains. "Well, Mom, you
l I would imagine it does here."

nd cold weather! The Lord knows
end me here where I'm going to

be that bad."

he weariness is evident on our
"

er counter."

now?"

pt your offer but he wants it
r house in Georgia."

e to sell my house?"

tract will be null and void."

ves me a little over a month! He
ouse in a month!"

want to keep his off the market for

the papers and we return to Idaho Falls. Laying on the bed the tears start again. "Mom, I forgot to ask you . . ." I'm bawling like crazy now.

Walking over to the bed Sharon asks, "What's wrong?"

"Sharon, I'm crazy! I just bought a house in a town I've never heard of, in a state that I didn't even know where it was. Will you please call the white coats? I've really lost it now."

"Mom, you aren't crazy."

"God's sending me here to kill me! You heard Tom. It gets below zero! He even said they have blizzards. I don't know how to live in snow country!"

Sharon gently strokes my back. "You'll get used to it."

"No I won't!" He's sending me here to freeze to death! I'm completely off my rocker! You just don't buy a house without selling your own first! This is the craziest damn thing I've ever done! It makes no sense at all."

Sharon can tell I'm not going to accept reasoning and walks out of the room as I beat my fist against the pillow.

"Grandma, are you crying?"

"Ginny, I just don't feel good. Let Grandma rest."

"Lord, please. Tell me this isn't what You want. I don't know anyone here, it's a little dinky town, I'll freeze to death here. Please tell me not to do this." "Trust Me. You'll be fine, I'll be with you."

My flight being this afternoon I'm able to pack between crying spells. Sharon drives me to the airport. Still upset and thinking I'm really off my rocker, the flight home is not pleasant.

14

All the way home I can't convince myself that I've made the right decision. "*Lord, what are You doing to me? You know I hate cold weather? What am I going to do when I get there?*"

"*You'll be fine. Just do what I say. You're not crazy.*" "*That's easy for You to say. What if my house doesn't sell and then I lose the other one?*" "*Trust Me.*" I arrive home and pull my clothes out of the suitcase. "*Oh, here's that little information newspaper Tom gave me that tells about Kemmerer.*"

I set it aside and finish my unpacking. "*I'm tired, I think I'll go to bed.*" Waking early, fixing a pot of coffee, and noticing the little newspaper laying on the table I pick it up to read with my coffee.

The first thing I see at the top, "Kemmerer, Wyoming. The Cowboy state."

"I don't believe this! The Cowboy State? The cowboy in my dream! You knew this all along, didn't You?" No reply, just a chuckle. "I don't think this is a bit funny!" I'm a bit put out with the Lord's little joke. I see no humor in it at all.

When I arrive at church the word has gotten out that I'm going to sell my house. As I walk out to my car after the service I hear, "Sue, wait up."

"Oh hi Greg."

"I heard you were going to sell your house."

"Yes."

"Have you listed it yet?"

"No."

"I know a really good realtor. I used to work with her and she's fantastic. A really nice lady."

"What's her name?"

"Jennifer Ross. She's right down on Highway five."

I feel the blood draining from my face. "Jennifer Ross?" Greg reaches out and touches my arm. "Yes. Are you okay? You look faint."

"Greg, you aren't going to believe this." I tell him how the Lord gave me that name while wallpapering my living room.

"You have got to be kidding! That's just unreal. He gave Jennifer's name? Wow!"

Going home feeling flabbergasted I can only shake my head in wonder. *Call the realtor and set up an appointment.* "Do You realize that only gives me six weeks to get everything packed and sell this house?" *"Yes."* "I'm sorry Lord but I don't think I'm the only one crazy around here." A chuckle is the only reply.

"Is Jennifer Ross there?"

"Yes, hold on."

"This is Jennifer, can I help you?"

"Yes, my name is Sue Cass and I'd like to list my house."

"Oh, okay. When would you like for me to come out? Where do you live?"

"I live off one sixty-six. How would Wednesday be?"

"Wednesday is okay but are you sure you don't want me to come sooner?"

"No."

"Start sorting through your things. You'll need to get rid of a lot."

Feeling overwhelmed I can't even think straight. "Lord, what are You thinking? I have three weeks to sell this house before the contract on the Wyoming house expires."

"Trust Me."

Beginning to sort through a few drawers and closets I'm realizing this is going to be a huge task. One, there's no way I can do by myself. Picking up the phone, I call my sister-in-law in Nebraska. "Hello Michelle."

"Hi Sue."

"I told you about the Lord moving me to Wyoming and that I've bought a house there."

"Yes, the Lord told me that I'm to help you move."

"Oh praise God! That's what I was calling about. I wanted to know if you could come out and help me with all this."

"Yes, just let me know when you're ready."

Jennifer arrives. She walks through the house, out in the yard, asking questions, and re-enters the house.

"Have a seat, Jennifer. Can I get you a cup of coffee?"

"No thanks, I'm fine."

She places her legal pad on her lap. "How did you get my name? Did someone refer you?"

"Oh Lord, what do I tell her? She'll think I'm nuts if I tell her You gave me her name."

"Ahhhh, Greg Mathis. He said he worked with you."

"Oh yes. I'll be sure to thank him for referring you to me. Now let's start on the particulars."

"Before I list this, you need to know it has to be sold in three weeks."

The shock on Jennifer's face is well worth taking a picture of.

"What? Why that soon? If that's even possible. Do you already have someone who wants to buy it?"

"I've bought a house in Wyoming and if this one doesn't sell in three weeks I lose that one."

Shock is written all over her face. "No I don't have a buyer. You'll really have to bust your butt to earn your commission on this one."

"I can't promise anything, but I'll do my best. Three weeks?"

"Yes, do you want the listing?"

"Yes. But like I said I can't promise anything."

I step outside to watch her take the pictures. "Would you like a glass of ice tea? It's hot out here."

"Yes, thank you. There's a couple of things I'd like to ask you about."

We sit in the living room with our tea. "Jennifer, I need to tell you something. I hope you don't think I'm crazy."

"Yes? Is it something to do with the house?"

"Yes and no. Well, yes." Looking even more puzzled she's sitting here staring at me. "When I told you that Greg recommended you, he did. But that's not all." Taking a sip of her tea and saying nothing, she waits for me to continue.

I take a deep breath. *"Tell her."* "I was wallpapering this living room and the Lord told me I was going to sell this house." Watching for do, do, do, do, do, do, do, do expression, she's showing no sign of locking me up or calling the paddy wagon.

"Then when I was doing that wall, He gave me your name." I'm fully expecting the "she's nuts" look now.

Jennifer reaches her arms out in front of her and looks at them. "Oooh, that just sends chill bumps all over my arms. This is incredible."

"You don't think I'm nuts?"

She laughs and rubs her arms. "No! Not by any means."

"So you'll still sell my house?"

"Of course but I'm going to have to get cracking. I sure don't want the Lord mad at me."

She places a sign at the front of the yard and leaves.

"Lord, are You sure this is what I'm supposed to do?" *"Yes."* Five days, then ten days go by. Not one prospective buyer has looked at the house.

I am frantically dialing the phone. "Jennifer? What's going on? Nobody has been out here!"

"No other agents have shown it?"

"No. We don't have much time."

"I'm really pushing people here in the office to show it."

Two and a half weeks have passed. Still no one has come to look at the house. I'm panicking now. "Jennifer, this house has to be sold! What are we going to do?"

"Don't get discouraged, we still have a couple of days. Something will turn up."

The Wyoming contract expires at midnight tonight. Suddenly the phone rings. I grab it. "Hello."

"Sue, we have a couple that would like to see your house. Can they come over?"

"Of course! Just make sure they buy it."

I leave the prospective buyers to go through the house while I'm walking around outside pretending to be busy with the flower beds. "*Oh Lord, if they don't like the house I'm sunk.*"

As I show them the creek, the markers for the land boundaries, the separate garage, "*Please Lord, make them buy the house.*" As they walk over to the realtor's car their agent turns to me. "We'll let your agent know what we decide."

I pace the floor most of the afternoon. The phone finally rings. "Jennifer? Have you heard anything?"

"No, not yet."

"This is the last day! The Wyoming contract runs out at midnight tonight!"

"I'll call the agent and see what's going on."

"Oh thank you! Call me right back, please."

"I will."

Pacing the floor my heart is doing flip flops. "Lord You better do something!"

Thirty minutes have passed. "Dear Lord, what's taking so long?" Suddenly the phone is ringing. I grab it like my life depends on it. "Hello!"

"Sue, this is Jennifer. I just talked to the other agent and they're writing up the contract now. They have no problem with the price."

"Thank you, Jesus!"

"The agent is trying to talk them into making a mid-September closing date."

"Close on August twenty."

"They're going F.H.A. and there's no way they can get approved before then."

"Jennifer, the Lord is saying August twenty."

"Oh my. That's only three weeks. F.H.A. takes at least six weeks. Hold on, I have another call. Maybe it's them."

Coming back on the line with me, "This is just too much! I can't believe this."

"What? What?"

"The buyers told Lorie they want August twenty for the closing date."

"Did you tell them August twenty?"

Jennifer is laughing. "No! The agent is insisting they can't get approved for the loan in that short time but the buyers are insisting on August twenty."

"Oh wow! So when are they bringing the contract over?"

"She's faxing it to me now. Can you come to the office?"

"I'm on my way!"

I grab my purse and run to the car. *"Oh thank you, thank you, thank you, Lord."*

Running into her office I don't even stop at the reception desk. "Jennifer? Did you get it?"

"I have it right here. All you have to do is sign it and we're all set."

"Where do I sign?"

"Aren't you going to read it first?"

I quickly read it and take the pen from Jennifer's hand and sign the contract. "I have to call Tom in Wyoming and let him know we have a contract."

"You can call him from here."

I dial Tom's number. "Hello. Mountain Real Estate, can I help you?"

"Is Tom there? This is Sue Cass in Georgia."

"Hi Sue. How are things going? The Smiths called a while ago and wanted to know if you've sold the house."

"Yes! Yes, I have. We just completed a signed contract on it just a few minutes ago."

"That's great. It is an accepted, signed, sealed, and delivered contract?"

"It sure is! We're closing August 20."

"Fax me a copy so I can show it to the Smiths. You have my fax number, don't you?"

"Yes. I'm at the realtors now and we'll fax it to you right now."

Jennifer faxes a copy to Tom and as I'm standing here beside her the tears of relief come.

"You'll be in Wyoming the first of September. Start packing."

Jennifer looks at me with the same expression of relief on her face. "This just has to be God doing this! I never dreamed we'd sell your house so fast. It's a first for me."

"Oh it's definitely God and He's giving me a heart attack!"

I am laughing and give Jennifer a hug. "I'll talk to you later. I need to start packing."

"Sue, they still have to be approved."

"The Lord just told me I'll be in Wyoming September first. They'll be approved."

"Somehow, after what has happened, I think you're right."

"Thank you again. Call me."

"*I can't believe You pulled it off, Lord. You're just too awesome.*"

I get up early. "*I need to go find some boxes.*" Riding from one dumpster to the next, I've filled the back of the car with boxes. Arriving home the answering machine light is flashing.

"Sue, it's Jennifer. Will you call me when you come in? I'll be in the office until three."

I pick up the phone and dial. "*Oh Lord please don't let her tell me they've changed their mind.*" I try to sound confident. "Hi Jennifer, this is Sue. What's up?" I can hear typing in the background.

"How are you?"

"I'm a nervous wreck!"

"I just talked to Lorie. She has all the paperwork filled out and is ready to submit it to the F.H.A. office in Douglasville."

"Okay."

"I told her everything, even how you got my name. She agrees this has to be a God thing."

As she continues I'm holding my breath. "I know the head of that office personally as well as having taken many applications to him, so I'm going to take it over there myself this afternoon."

"Okay. Do you think there will be a problem?"

"I don't know. It always takes at least six weeks for an approval. Sometimes even longer. So we'll see."

"We better start praying."

"I have another call. I'll call when I hear anything."

"Okay. Bye."

It's six o'clock, and I am sitting with a plate of food in front of me. *"I have no idea how we're going to pack all this stuff, Lord. I had no idea there was this much stuff. Fifteen years worth of God only knows what."* "You'll do it. Trust Me."

I reach for the phone and dial. "Hi Michelle. I sold the house and have started packing. The Lord said I'd be in Wyoming September first."

"Yea, I know. He told me the same thing."

"We need to get your flight schedule planned. When do you want to come out?"

"How about I come a week in advance and help you finish up the last minute packing."

"That will be great!"

I walk out to the garage and open the door. *"Lord how am I going to do this? Brian had all this woodworking equipment. Look at all the wood stacked up against the wall! I don't even know where to start."*

I close the garage door, feeling overwhelmed with all that has to be done in such a short time. I walk back in the house; boxes are scattered everywhere. *"I can't do this!"*

"Go to the Chevrolet car lot on Thornton Road." *"Why? My car is perfectly good."* *"You'll see."* I put down the items in my arms, go to the car and drive the fifteen miles.

I pull into the dealership lot and park near the showcase with new cars shining through the window. A salesman walks up as I'm barely out of the car. "Can I help you find something?"

"I'm not sure." *"I'll show you which one."* I stroll around through the lines of cars. "Is there anything in particular you're looking for?"

"Four wheel drive." *"I don't need a four wheel drive! Why a four wheel drive?"* *"You'll see."*

"Do you have any four wheel drives?"

"We only have two left, they go pretty fast. They're right over here." Leading the way the salesman approaches a white Blazer.

"*I don't need a four wheel drive, Lord. Why do I need this?*" No answer. "My brother had a four wheel drive pick-up."

"I'm not going to have to get out and do whatever on the wheel to change to four wheel drive, am I?"

"Oh no. Those are long gone. These have buttons on the dash that you just push to change into four wheel drive."

Opening the door he sticks his head in and points to three buttons. "Each is a different power level for setting the traction you want to drive in." I get out of the truck. He points to another truck. "This green one is the same thing."

He opens the door and steps aside so I can see in. "The price is a little higher because it's fully loaded."

"I don't want the white one for sure. I'm moving to Wyoming and that's all I need. If I get stuck in a blizzard they'll never find me."

I inspect the green one, then walk into the office and discuss the price and trade in value of my little station wagon." "You've got to be kidding! That's all I can get for my car?"

"That's the best we can do."

"My car is worth more than that." "I don't think so!" I stand up to leave, shaking his hand. "Thanks for your help but I can't accept that little amount for my car."

"Well, if you change your mind, come back. The four wheelers go pretty fast."

I leave the lot fuming all the way. I walk into the house and set my purse on the counter. "*Go back and buy the green one.*" "Looord Why?" "*You'll see.*" I get back into the car and drive back to the lot. The same salesman greets me as I'm getting out of the car. "You changed your mind?"

"Let me see the green one again. *Lord what are You doing?*" "*Buy it!*" We go back into the office and sit down where we sat at his desk before. "So what made you change your mind?"

"The Lord did."

"The who?"

"I said the Lord, L-O-R-D." "Oh."

We finalize the deal and I drive the Blazer home. "*I still don't think I need this.*" "*You'll see.*" Pulling into the church parking lot, Ben is just getting out of his car. "Sue? What's that you're driving?"

"A four wheel drive Blazer. The Lord told me to buy it but I don't know why."

He runs his hand alongside the truck. "You're moving to Wyoming. You'll need it." As he's talking he's crawling in behind the wheel looking at the various instruments.

I lean in, reaching across him. "Those are the buttons for the four wheel drive, but I still don't think I'll need it."

"Sure you will! You'll be in snow country."

"I'm not even going to leave the house! I don't know how to drive in snow. Plus I'm not going out in it anyway, I have no intention of freezing to death."

Several people approach me telling me they've heard I'm moving to Wyoming. I'm getting the same questions and I keep giving the same answers to each one.

"That's what the Lord said to do."

"Are you sure it's the Lord?"

"Yes it's the Lord."

"Are you going by yourself?"

"Yes."

"Do you have family there?"

"No."

"Do you know anyone there?"

"No."

139

"You can't move clear across the country and not even know anyone there!"

"This is what the Lord wants me to do so that's what I'm doing."

I walk into the Sunday school class. "Hi Sue. We heard you're moving to Wyoming."

I sit down at the long table. "Okay everyone. Listen up. I'm moving to Wyoming the end of August."

I open my Bible. "The Lord is sending me there. I don't know anyone there, I don't know why or what I'll be doing there when I get there. He wants me to move and that's what I'm doing. It's called being obedient and stepping out in faith."

Several are concerned that I'll be driving across the country. "Look. The Lord is telling me to move. Since the Lord is telling me to do this I'm sure He's going to keep us safe."

Geraldine pops up, "God isn't moving you! I don't believe it for a minute!"

Patsy flips open her Bible.

"I think we should start the lesson."

"*Lord what are You getting me into?*" I return to the garage, and open the door. "Lord, I just can't do this!"

As the door drops closed and I re-enter the house, my eyes well up with tears. Picking up yet another box I think, "*What am I going to do when I get there? What kind of ministry are You going to have me doing out there in the middle of nowhere?*" "*You'll see.*"

Feeling more and more pressured each day to get everything done, my tears come and go. "Lord I can't do this. Brian will have no one to visit his grave. I can't just leave and never visit it again." "*He's not there.*"

"But You don't understand! If I leave it's like he never existed. There's no one to put flowers on his grave or anything." "*He's not there.*" Throwing the blanket I'm folding on the floor I throw myself across the bed. "I just can't leave him here alone!" *"He's not there."*

I've spent the last couple of days trying to argue my way out of this move, out of having to sort through and pack all this stuff, and having to leave Brian behind. As creepy as it sounds, had I had Brian cremated I could be carrying my beloved husband with me. Well, his remains.

15

Sleep doesn't come easily. When Ben arrives to help me clear out the garage I'm barely awake. Going along each wall Ben helps me sort through, throw away, and clean. Ben stands at the open door. "What else do you have to do?"

I throw my hands in the air. "I still have to sell the boat. I don't know what I'm going to do with that whole wall full of wood that's stacked up."

Turning to look at the wood he says, "It's going to work out."

As Ben leaves I enter the house and the phone is ringing. "Hello."

"Hi Sue. This is Jennifer."

"Hi Jennifer."

"So how's it going?"

"Okay, I guess."

"I took the application in."

"Oh?"

"He looked at it and said it would take about six to eight weeks to get back."

I am frustrated with all this. "It can't take that long! You know what the Lord said. I'll be moved in the Wyoming house September first."

"Yes I know but you haven't heard the best part."

"And that would be?"

"I sat down at his desk and put the fear of God in him."

"What do you mean, put the fear of God in him?"

"I told him the whole story of how you got my name and so on. Then I told him that if he doesn't want to get hit by lightning he better get crackin'."

"And?"

"He listened and when I said this is a God thing, he looked at me and said, 'I think you're right and I'm not going to get the big guy on my case.' He said he's going to rush it through."

As I sigh a sigh of relief she continues. "I don't think we'll have any trouble. Lorie did a preliminary financial statement before they looked at the house."

"So how long before we know for sure that they get the loan?"

"I don't think it will take that long. He really believed me when I said this is a God thing and he sounded very serious when he said he didn't want to mess with God."

"It sounds good to me. He better not mess with God."

I hear a knock at the door and open it. "I'm here about the saws and woodworking equipment."

"Oh hi. They're out in the garage. I'll meet you out there."

I meet him at the garage. "My husband did a lot of woodworking." There's all kinds of saws and stuff as you can see."

He steps in beside me and looks around. "My son and I do a lot of woodworking, too. It's a hobby that's turned into a business."

I step back out of his way. "Feel free to look around and there's an outlet plug right here if you want to turn something on." *Lord, I really need to sell this stuff.*

He turns on one saw after another, then sanders, and mills through the tools. "If I take all this off your hands would you accept fifteen hundred dollars?"

"*Take it.*"

"That sounds fair enough."

He lays a tool on the bench and points to the wall with the various kinds of wood stacked to the ceiling. "What are you going to do with this?"

"I don't know. Are you interested in buying it? It's all kinds of exotic wood as well as the regular stuff."

He walks over to the wood and fingering several pieces. "Where in the world did he get this? This is fantastic! This one is from Africa. You just can't get this kind of wood."

Explaining how Brian had acquired all the wood, the man looks like a kid that's just entered a candy store. "How much will you take for it if I buy all of it?"

"You want all of it?"

"Yes."

"*Lord? Help me out here.*" "*Take seven-fifty.*" "*Seven hundred fifty?*" "*Yes.*"

"How does seven hundred fifty dollars sound?" Still running his fingers along the edge of the wood he replies, "I can't argue with that. I can't get this wood anywhere else and I'm sure not going to pass it up. Deal!"

"I'm so glad you decided to buy it. I thought I was going to have to have the firemen come over while I have a huge bon fire."

"You wouldn't!" The poor man looks like he's going to faint.

We walk out of the garage and stop. "Is this john boat for sale?"

"Yes."

"How much do you want for that?"

"Fifteen hundred for the boat, motor, and trailer. Since you're buying everything I'll let you have it for twelve hundred. You wanna' buy that Blazer, too?"

He glances over at it and laughs. "No, but I'll take the boat."

"Is there anything else I can sell you? Anything except the motor home."

"I'll be back this afternoon to get everything if that's okay. I'll bring you a cashiers check for everything."

I wanted to jump up and down. "I'll be here all afternoon."

I close the garage door and run into the house after the man leaves, dancing around in circles in the middle of the living room.

"Oh, God, thank you. I didn't know what I was going to do with all that stuff."

I stop twirling. "*You have to trust Me, Sue.*" "*I know. That isn't always easy and You know it.*" All I can do is plop down on the couch in relief. "*Thank you.*"

Ben stops me just outside the office door. "How are you doing with all this? When is Michelle coming?"

"Next week. I'm exhausted but okay. Thanks."

"Good."

I go home to continue packing. The phone is ringing as I enter.

I run to the phone. "Hello."

"Sue, Jennifer. I just wanted to let you know the buyers have been approved. We'll close August twenty right on schedule."

"Ohhhhhh, thank you Jesus. What a relief!"

Having already made the arrangements for the movers to arrive August twenty I still have a lot of packing to do. Boxes are everywhere. I can barely move through the rooms.

16

Driving to the airport my mind is in a whirl thinking about all the things left to be done. I park in the parking garage as close to the entrance as possible and run into the baggage claim area. Michelle is waiting.

Arriving home I'm showing her what is left to be done. "We'll have to tear down these beds the last day before the movers get here."

Looking at me as though I've lost my mind she says, "You aren't tearing anything down! The movers will do that."

"Suits me."

"How long are you going to stay once we get to Wyoming?"

"I plan on staying two weeks so I can help you get everything unpacked and situated."

Giving her a big hug, I say, "Oh thank you! I don't know what I'd do without you."

As she's opening the map she says, "I've mapped out our route. Come and see what you think."

"Oh no. I'm the one who travels by air. You're the ground traveler. I'll just follow the little green truck."

We've spent the last five days packing the last of the boxes. "Tomorrow is the last day I'll be at this church. Ben and everyone want to say good-bye so I guess we should go."

"That's fine. I'd like that."

"I'm so tired I really don't feel like it but I'd hate to leave without giving them the pleasure of hugging me once more."

"Well Sue, then I think we should go."

Arriving at church I find the morning to be bittersweet. I've been worshipping at this church since day one. Leaving it is scary yet a part of me is excited to see what the Lord has up His sleeve for me.

After singing praise and worship songs to the Lord and announcements were made, Kathy stands before the congregation. "As some of you know, Sue has been called by the Lord to move to Wyoming."

My head jerks up from looking at the bulletin. "Today is her last day at this church." Michelle and I are sitting quietly. "Sue, we have a special farewell for you."

"*Oh God, now what?*" Michelle looks over at me and whispers, "How nice."

One person after another comes forward and gives all sorts of compliments, telling cute stories about various experiences with me. Melinda gets up and goes forward. "Sue, I need to ask your forgiveness."

I look at her and mouth "Why?"

She continues, "You have walked around this church for all this time saying, The Lord said this, the Lord said to do, The Lord told me . . ."

I'm looking at her puzzled. "I got so sick of hearing you saying the Lord said, did, will do, told me and so on." Laughter ripples through the congregation. "I went home mad a couple of weeks ago."

I am sitting here totally puzzled. "*Why would she be mad?*"

Michelle turns and grins at me. "I went home and asked the Lord, 'Why do You talk to her all the time and You don't me?' "

Now I'm really interested!

"You know what He said?"

I look at her and shake my head no. "He said, Because she listens!"

I can't help it, "OUCH!" just pops out of my mouth.

"Will you please forgive me? You being true to the truth and speaking openly has made me wake up. Thank you."

I leave my seat and rush forward, hugging her. "I didn't mean to make you mad." Releasing her and grinning I say, "But I'm glad I did."

As the tribute goes on, I lean over to Michelle and whisper, "I feel like I'm at my own funeral." Looking back at the podium again Ben is standing grinning at me. *"Oh Lord, I'm in trouble now!"*

"Some of you don't know Sue quite as well as I do." *"God, here it comes."* "She's stubborn. She's independent, she won't take no for an answer and she's been faithful to the Lord to a fault."

I can't even look at Ben for fear of bawling. I've grown to love him and Carol and they're the ones I'll miss the most. "I've watched Sue grow over these past few years." He looks down at me. "It's amazing what the Lord has done in her."

I don't want to look at him as he continues. "Now she's being called to yet another step in this journey and Sue, you're greatly loved and we wish God's blessings on you."

"Okay, stop bawling!" Leaving the podium Ben walks past me and pats me on the shoulder. As he's taking his seat, Kathy returns to the podium. "Sue, would you like to say anything?"

Swiping at the tears and walking forward I say, "Thanks Kathy. You sure caught me by surprise." I look out over the congregation. "I started out as an egg here. A new Christian."

My words seem like they're coming from somewhere else. "You helped me to hatch and continued to grow me. You helped me through the teen-age years of Christianity." Chuckles ripple around the room. "Thank you for being my brothers and sisters in Christ and helping me to grow into a big chicken. Now what do I do?"

Applause bursts out as everyone stands smiling at me as I'm stepping away from the podium. "Sue, not just yet. We have this plaque that we all want to present to you."

As I'm approaching Kathy she's handing me a beautiful wooden plaque with a cross, praying hands and a Bible on it. "Read it out loud so everyone can hear what's on it."

I hold the plaque up at an angle and fight to keep from crying. "I don't know what to say, Kathy."

I read aloud. "Dear Sue. Take heart daughter, He said. Your faith has healed you Matthew 9:22 With Love, Your brothers and sisters in Christ.

Teary-eyed I'm stepping down hugging my plaque close to my heart. Pastor Kirk steps to the podium. "Sue, if you'll stand down front everyone who wants to can pass by and say goodbye. Now if you'll hold out your hands we'll close with the blessing."

I get in the truck to drive home; I'm sitting here without turning the ignition on.

"Sue? Are you alright?"

Looking over at Michelle a few tears trickle down my cheeks. "I've never felt so loved in my whole life."

Michelle leans over and hugs me. "You deserve it. We better get home and finish up. The movers will be here tomorrow."

"I don't want to go home right now. To heck with the packing. Let's go have some lunch somewhere."

We sit in the both at the restaurant. "That was really nice, Sue. Did you know they were going to do that?"

"No. If I had I probably wouldn't have gone."

"Why?"

"I'm not used to that kind of attention and all I do is cry anymore."

"So?"

"Michelle, when I was a kid I made a vow I would never let anyone ever see me cry again. Since I've been a Christian it seems like that's all I do!"

Grinning at me she says, "Gee, do you think the Lord softened that old hard heart of yours?"

Rising early we've stacked as many boxes as we can. I start nervously pacing the floor. "Where the heck are the movers? They were supposed to be here at noon!"

"They'll be here, just settle down."

Finally we hear the sounds of a big truck coming down the road.

"That's them, that's them. Hallelujah, they're finally here."

The truck is parked at the entrance of the long narrow driveway. The driver is walking toward us. I meet him half-way. "Are you Mrs. Cass?"

"Yes. You were supposed to be here four and a half hours ago."

"We were told we were supposed to be here tomorrow and didn't find out until an hour ago that there was a mix-up."

I turn back to Michelle. "Can you believe the size of that truck? Daddy worked on some big rigs but I've never seen one that big!"

"For sure."

The movers start hauling furniture and boxes out to the truck. As the first room is emptied Michelle says, "Sue, if you'll vacuum, I'll steam clean behind you."

We load the last piece of furniture and sit down on the front steps.

"Well, we're all loaded up."

"So when will you have my furniture and stuff in Wyoming?"

Looking at the date on his watch he says, "This is the twentieth? We have three more houses to load and deliver on the way to Wyoming."

I'm not sure where he's going with this.

"They're big houses so it's going to be after Labor Day before we can get yours there. That's why we put yours way in the back.

"After Labor Day! That's two weeks away!"

"Yes Ma'am but like I said, we have three huge houses to load and deliver. We're going all over the country to do it."

Looking at Michelle I say, "Well, we'll just live in the Angel Buggy until they get there."

Locking up the house, Michelle gets in the Blazer, me in the Angel Buggy. Rocky and Jacob are sound asleep on their favorite spots. The driver walks over to Michelle.

"Do you want us to pull out first?" he asks.

He burst out laughing. "Well, that was a dumb question. You can't get out unless we move."

Michelle smiles a tired smile. "I'll follow behind you and then Sue can follow me in the motor home."

The huge moving truck roars into action. Michelle pulls slowly down the driveway.

Driving the motor home slowly around the circle drive, down the long driveway, I'm on my way to what the Lord called, "A new way of life" without looking back.

17

Our long journey has officially begun. The darkness surrounds us and we're both exhausted from the long day of packing, loading, and cleaning. Michelle and I are both hesitant to drive at night but she's determined to reach Chattanooga before we stop for the night.

Since Michelle has done much traveling by car she is the one in charge of the route we take and knows pretty much how long it takes to get to certain destinations. I just follow the little green truck.

There is a limit to just how many hours I can stay behind the wheel of a car. Especially driving a twenty-eight-foot motor home. It takes much more concentration. "Michelle, there's no way I can drive ten or twelve hours a day. You know I can't handle that with my back."

"Yea, I know. The Lord has already told me I'm not going to do that on this trip."

"Thank you Jesus! I knew You'd look after me."

The first day of travel is behind us. As we continue on our journey we stop several times when the dogs indicate they need out.

Roadside rests, pulls off on the highways, and even a cow pasture on occasion are taken advantage of. Not just for the dogs but for us to stretch our legs. We have a signal if I need to stop: Flashing my headlights. I tried blowing my horn but she couldn't hear it over the radio blasting Christian songs in the truck.

Each morning we pray for safe travel and guidance. At night we're thanking Him for a safe trip. Tears begin to well up in my eyes every darn time we pray. I think the Lord has made mush out of my heart!

Rocky has his head on his favorite pillow at one end of the couch stretched out like a little kid taking a nap. Jacob is stretched out across the end of my bed letting the air conditioning blow on him. It's obvious these two are very much at home.

As we pass through Nashville, Tennessee there's no stopping for souvenirs. In each state we do stop at truck stops to buy a refrigerator magnet of that state to place on the motor home refrigerator door.

The dogs love it when they can wander around and sniff out the new area. Jacob, being half Collie and half German Shepherd, is larger than Rocky. Rocky is a small Beagle and sixteen years old. Jacob is two years old and is like any two-year-old, frisky.

Rocky tends to meander along while Jacob wants to bounce and jump everywhere in excitement to see what's there. At times, he'll tug on the leash until he almost pulls me off my feet.

"Jacob, wait up!" He has learned to slow down when I tell him that. Other times, when we need to get across a parking lot in a hurry, "Hurry, hurry, hurry" tells them we need to rush across.

They're both wonderful traveling companions and when they aren't sleeping, and I'm not talking to the Lord, I talk to them as we buzz along the highway. One would think there's three people having a conversation.

Clipping the southwest corner of Kentucky and into Missouri the miles are piling up behind us. Neither one of us want to go through large cities so we take the highways that bypass them when we can.

It certainly makes maneuvering the motor home much easier not having to wiggle through streets filled with stop lights, vehicles, and pedestrians.

The days are long and tiring but at least Michelle stops late in the afternoon so we can get a good night's sleep before heading out early each morning. The time we use to worship gives us renewed strength to face the miles ahead.

The August heat is almost overwhelming. The air conditioning runs day and night. That's the only way the dogs can survive and me, too, for that matter. Michelle has the air running in the truck all day, too.

Most mornings we're up before dawn or soon after so we can try to beat the heat. We also want to try to get through the cities before the heavy morning traffic hits the roads.

As we sit having our coffee before heading out on the road, Michelle is looking at the map, mapping out our route for the day. As a navigator she's pretty darn good. We haven't gotten lost even once.

Sitting across from her this morning as she's looking at the map, I don't bother her so she can concentrate without my interference. She's the lead and I just follow the little green truck. She isn't as driven to get from point A to point B in breakneck speed like she was the first day or so. She does try to push it occasionally though.

Because the roadside rest stops are pretty far apart much of the time we do stop at many of them for lunch, letting the dogs run, and to stretch our legs. We've passed St. Louis, Missouri. The "Gateway to the West" large arch stands majestically along the Mississippi river.

I have no idea how high the arch is but its brilliant lights shining in the darkness can be seen for many miles. It represents entering the west. Leaving the southern states and stepping over an imaginary line that places one in the western states.

Most of our meals have consisted of fast food along the way or small meals prepared in the motor home. Letting the dogs roam on the grassy area of the roadside rest pet area,

Michelle is standing nearby with Jacob sniffing the tree. "Michelle, how about we find a good restaurant and have a nice leisurely meal?"

She looks at her watch. "We'll waste a lot of time and we need to get back on the road." Glancing over at me while Jacob tugs on his leash she says, "We can eat here and not waste so much time."

I look at her exasperated, "Oh for crying out loud. What the heck is the rush? If we're going to make it with any sanity left we better take it easy. Lord, tell her to cool it! Never mind. We can do it later."

We're both tired and emotions are getting a little tight. We've been friends for thirty something years. She's my sister-in-law but more like my sister. We always get along great and enjoy being together as well as traveling together. It's a real treat for both of us.

We've decided to spend a little more time here so returning to the motor home we're listening to soft inspirational music. As I'm stretched out on the couch Michelle looks over at me from the table. "What do you see when you see an angel?"

I look across the aisle at her. "Well, sometimes I see them in long beautiful gowns. The gowns are always white. At least the ones I've seen are. I haven't seen any polka dotted ones yet."

She isn't laughing. Now I know she's serious. I scoot up to where I'm still laying down but not flat. "Other times I see them as what I call twinkles. It's like a dot of bright light. Brilliant light."

She reaches up to scratch her ear and does not let me finish what I was about to say.

"What do you mean a twinkle?"

Now I can tell she's getting excited. "Just what I said. I see a very bright spot. Sometimes they're very small and other times they're bigger."

I sit straight up on the couch with my feet stretched out. "Some are like a big sudden splash of light. It will have blue, green, sometimes yellow hues all combined. It's really pretty but doesn't last but a split second. Why?"

A shocked expression crosses her face and is gone as quickly as it appeared. "Oh my gosh! I was sitting here when we stopped the last time and saw a twinkle, as you call it. I didn't think it was anything. Do you think it was an angel?"

Laughing at her excitement, she looks like she's going to bubble over.

"Did it have any bluish green color to it?"

"I'm not sure. I think it was just a clear bright dot."

"Well old girl, I think you may have seen your first angel. Ask the Lord to confirm to you if it was an angel."

Before she bows her head I say, "I've seen them in churches. In people's homes. What's really cool is when there's several and they're flying in a big circle up near the roof in church. I could watch them all day."

I throw my feet over the edge of the couch. "Ask the Lord to show you what He wants you to see. Be it angels or anything else. Ask Him to open your spiritual eyes." Bowing her head I can hear her softly talking to the Lord.

As she prays I check on the dogs who are sitting outside by the door. We're parked where the door of the motor home is almost on the edge of the grass. Of course they're on their leashes.

Turning, I see she's still talking to the Lord. As I sit back down she raises her head and her eyes are filled with tears. Looking at her I know she's gotten an answer. As she sits humbly there my eyes want to tear up but I blink them back.

Wiping her eyes on a napkin she says, "He said it was an angel and I will see more and more of them." She blows her nose. "He said I will see a lot of things I haven't seen before because He is opening my spiritual eyes for me to see His wonders."

Doggone it! I can't help it. My eyes flood with tears. I know what a miraculous and wonderful gift it is to be able to see angels, to have visions, and even see the Lord Jesus as He wants us to see Him.

Many times I have seen Him hanging on the cross. I'm not talking about a picture in a book. I'm talking about the mental image He places there. It's His way of reminding me what He did for me.

Michelle jumps up and gives me a hug. "Michelle, the Lord is opening up a gift that you didn't know was there. As you grow closer to Him He'll reveal gifts when He knows we can deal with them what He wants us to do. Don't EVER abuse a gift."

Releasing each other she looks at me and then upward toward heaven. "Thank you Jesus. Thank you, Sue. I can't wait to see some more of them."

While I am laughing and not able to resist lightening the atmosphere a little I say, "There's an angel right over there sitting on the hood of the truck!"

She spins around. "Where? Where? I don't see it."

I have to sit down I'm laughing so hard. Just call me a prankster.

She slaps me lightly on the arm. "Darn you, Sue! That's not funny."

18

We're about halfway to Kansas City when I notice a very large billboard advertising a large gift shop with curios, Indian artifacts and several other items for sale. Michelle has started slowing down. I know she's going to pull into the gift shop parking lot.

We seldom stop for things like this but it's nice to be able to today, plus Rocky and Jacob need to get out. A look of anticipation comes on their faces as I pull into the large paved parking lot and stop.

If we're travelling along and haven't made a stop for a while and Rocky needs to go out, he'll sit by the door to let me know he needs to go. I'll signal Michelle and as soon as she can pull into a safe area she will.

At times I think I can see Rocky crossing his legs and doing a little dance with an expression on his face saying, "Pleeeeease Mama I have to go!" Jacob being larger, must have a larger bladder because he very seldom sits at the door while traveling to be let out.

Snapping the leashes in place and opening the door the dogs are more than happy to head for the few small shrubs on the edge of the parking lot. Michelle steps around the motor home. "I saw this place advertised back there and thought I'd stop. It looks pretty neat."

Pulling the big wooden door open with large deer antlers fastened above it, the cool air conditioning inside hits us in the face. Just inside the door we see rows and rows of shelves and tables filled with souvenirs. "Michelle! In case we get separated I'll meet you here in two days."

Laughing, she wanders toward some leather goods hanging on the wall. Standing still, trying to decide what to look at first, Christmas comes to mind. *I'm always looking for unique gifts for Christmas presents.*

With that in mind I begin meandering along the many tables and shelves. After picking out a few items for gifts I notice a display of angels against one wall. *"Oh Angels!"* and head straight for them.

I don't worship angels. I worship God through His Son Jesus Christ. But having had the Angel Ministry I collect unique angel figurines. It's like I have radar that beams in on angels.

I stand before them. *"Get one for Michelle."* *"That's right! She saw her first angel."* I can't talk to the Lord out loud now in case someone hears me and thinks I'm some kind of weirdo.

I pick up one after another and set them back down. *"I don't know which to get her."* Suddenly in the middle of all the various angels my eyes are led to one with a beautiful robe.

There's tinges of purple here and there and her wings are spread with gold speckles lightly sprinkled on them. It's very elegant and Michelle's favorite color is purple.

Michelle walks up beside me. "I thought I'd find you over here." Having not heard her walk up, I'm a little startled. Plus I don't want to give her a clue as to what I have in mind.

"Yea, but I can't think of anyone I'd like to get one for, for Christmas."

Taking the angel out of my hand she says, "This is really pretty! Maybe I'll get it for myself."

"Michelle, where are you going to put it? You know Anthony doesn't like a bunch of stuff sitting around. He'll probably knock it off a table or a shelf."

I'm talking as fast as I can without giving away my intentions. I'm so glad she really likes it because I've already decided that's the one I want to get for her. "Well, Anthony will just have to be careful!"

Now I'm really racking my brain to come up with something to detour her from buying this angel. "Now just how are you going to get it home? You know it's going to get broken if you put it in your suitcase."

Placing the angel back on the shelf she says, "I guess you're right." *"Thank you, thank you, thank you, Lord!"* Michelle wanders off in another direction. Quickly grabbing up the angel, checking my surroundings like I'm about to shoplift, I'm rushing over to the checkout counter.

Four people are ahead of me in line to make their purchases. *"Please Lord, make them hurry up so Michelle won't see me buying this."* Stepping up to the counter and sliding the angel toward the check out lady I say, "Could you please hide this behind the counter as you ring it up. It's a gift and I don't want her to see me buying it."

Grinning broadly the lady says, "I sure will." Handing her the other items I've chosen, she rings them up and slips the angel into a box while stooped behind the counter. I hand her my credit card.

"Oh thank you."

My gifts are wrapped in tissue paper and have been placed in a paper bag with a handle for easy carrying.

"Oh, have you found everything you're going to buy?"

Spinning around I say, "Michelle, I wish you wouldn't do that. You're like some ghost sneaking around."

"Lord please don't let her have seen what I was buying." *"She didn't. You're safe."*

Michelle nudges me, laughing. "I'll be out in a minute. I'll have to wait in the line to check out.

I take my bag. "I'll meet you at the motor home. I'll take the guys out once more."

She steps behind a woman in line. "Okay. I think I have everything I want."

After about fifteen minutes and Michelle still hadn't returned. "*I wonder what's taking her so long? The line wasn't that long.*"

Finally Michelle arrives. "What took you so long?"

"I decided I wanted to get that angel. When I went back over there someone else had already bought it."

Having to bite my tongue to keep from laughing I say, "Well store your stuff and let's get out of here."

She looks at me with a shocked expression. "That's my line!" Placing her bag in the corner of a cabinet she gets a bottle of Pepsi to take with her. Michelle leans out her window singing, "On the road again." Laughing, I give her a thumbs up sign.

Again the questions are plaguing me. "What am I going to do when I get to Wyoming?" "*You'll see.*" "Why won't You tell me? What's the big secret?" "*Trust Me.*"

"How long am I going to live there? Is this the rest of my life thing? You know I'll never survive the freezing weather." "*You're going to have to lean on Me, Sue. If you don't you'll never survive. You'll be there a year and a half.*"

I am feeling relieved. "At least it isn't for the rest of my life?" "*You have to trust Me! You have to do everything I say or you can not survive it.*" This statement sends chills down my arms. "What are You doing to me?" "*Not TO you, FOR you.*" "Yea, right."

I know the Lord knows my thoughts and He must be chuckling because my thoughts are going all over the place. "What's He doing? Why the big secret? Why can't He just tell me what I'll be doing?"

Michelle has warned me to stay close when we do have to go through large cities. "You know I just follow the little green truck so don't lose me." Because she has the map and is leading the way I could easily get lost if we get separated.

The Lord continually encourages and reassures me: *"You're going to be alright. I'm with you."*

We are parked at a roadside rest, letting the dogs meander on the grassy area for pets.

"You know, Sue, we never did stop for that nice dinner. Let's see if there's something nearby and do it."

"Okay. That sounds good. I could use the break and a good meal. I'm getting tired of spaghetti and salads. Well, those pork chops weren't too bad the other night."

"If you'll take Rocky I'll go in to the information desk and see if they know of any place near here."

Walking over to her and taking Rocky's leash she walks to the small building that has restrooms, an information desk, maps, and concession machines. Letting the guys wander, *"I hope there's one close by and we don't have to go very far."*

Michelle walks out and coming across the parking lot she gives me a thumbs up sign. "There's a restaurant called 'The Cattleman's Cove' four miles back at the exit we passed. She said it's a steak place but also has seafood and regular dinners."

"Ohhhhhh, a bit fat steak sounds good! My mouth is watering already."

"I don't want fish either. I want a T-bone!"

Finding the ramp leading us back the direction we came I can hardly wait to sink my teeth in a beautiful steak.

I turn to the guys. "Hey guys, maybe we'll have a good bone for each of you. That would be a real treat for you, too." At the word, bone, all ears perk up. Big dark eyes are looking at me. Glancing at the road and then back at them. I have to laugh. They know what I'm talking about.

Taking the exit and driving down the road I can see a large sign. "The Cattleman's Cove." The small meals we've been having along the road are fine but the thought of a big ole steak, baked potato with lots of butter, green vegetables, and garlic bread on the side is testing my taste buds.

We enter the big heavy doors and are led to a table. "Your server will be right with you. Enjoy your meal." Looking around the room there's old cowboy boots hanging in a corner.

Silver spurs hang next to a framed picture of the Sundance Kid. An old wagon wheel hangs off to the side with a saddle hanging near by. Country music plays softly over the speaker system.

As we take our first bite of our steaks we both look at each other. "Mmmmmm. Oh that's good!" Taking our time savoring each bite, few words are spoken. We're too busy enjoying this rare treat.

Looking over at Michelle, she looks like she'd died and gone to steak heaven. "Save some meat on the bone for the guys."

"The guys hell! I'm going to suck every ounce of this meat off the bone."

Laughing, I can see she's already cut around the bone and left meat on it for the guys. She loves them almost as much as I do and has no intention of depriving them of their treat.

We ask the server to wrap the bones in tin foil to take to the guys. We get up to leave as soon as she's returned with the bones.

Michells says, "Sue? Do you have wheelchair to carry me out of here with?"

Glancing over my shoulder I say, "I was going to ask you if you had a stretcher for me."

Handing the dogs their bones, each finds a place away from the other one to savor their treat. It's been a while since they had a nice juicy bone. I can hear the crunching and slurping as I sit down holding my stomach.

We've decided to stop at the first R.V. park we come to and spend the night even though it's still fairly early. Hopefully it isn't far. It isn't. We've only had to drive ten miles when we pull in to the park for the night.

19

Even on the short layovers we listen to Christian music that soothes our tired bodies, minds, and spirits. Stretching out on the couch Michelle closes her eyes and is humming to the music.

Leaning against the wall on one side of the table with my legs stretched out across the cushioned seat, eyes closed, I'm also softly singing along with the music. As the music plays we are drawn into serious worshipping.

We're no longer just sitting back and taking in the music. We're both on the couch holding hands and in deep prayer. *"Lay hands on Michelle's shoulder."* Reaching over I lay my hand on Michelle. Praying a prayer for healing tears begin to form.

It is so awesome to watch and feel the power of the Lord flow through me. At times my hand will feel hot. Other times I can actually feel His power flowing down my arm into my hand.

There's no question it's the Lord's healing flowing through into the painful area where my hands are. To watch the expression of relief as the healing comes is awesome to say the least.

Removing my hand as I sense the Lord is leading me to do, Michelle flexes her shoulder slightly. "Thank you Lord for healing my pain. Thanks Sue." We continue to worship Him.

Rocky and Jacob are stretched out on my bed savoring the cool air from the air conditioner. At home the guys would sleep with me. The king-size bed had more than enough room.

When Brian and I shared the bed, as Barnie, a German shepherd we had, grew from the tiny puppy to full grown, he took up more and more of the bed space. One night as Brian was trying to get in under the covers Barnie wouldn't move.

Brian sat there looking at Barnie. Then he looked at me. "I'm sure glad you don't love horses!" Since Brian's death a big ole bed can get mighty lonesome. I love snuggling up to the guys and have a sense of love and safety. It's like being a sandwich. They're the bread and I'm the meat.

Laying in bed about to fall asleep, thoughts of my brother Anthony come to mind. As a child I thought the sun rose and set in my brother. He was a rock to me, the knight in shining armor that would come to my rescue.

As I would sit on the porch crying he was there to comfort me even though he didn't know why I was crying. I was told to never tell "the secret." Anthony always treated me like a person.

Letting me ride his bike even though my feet hardly reached the pedals. Riding behind him on his self-made cart that would speed down the hill with blackberry vines threatening alongside the pavement.

When he'd go to the end of the country road to shoot at beer cans he'd let me go with him and shoot the gun. Anthony was a lifeline to me in a world that made no sense to me.

Our stop in Omaha, Nebraska was not what I expected. In fact it was a big disappointment. Instead of getting to visit with Anthony I found myself basically being ignored because a co-worker of his came with him to the motor home. I hardly got to visit.

Leaving with thoughts that Anthony didn't want to see me or visit with me brought a day of great pain, sadness, and disappointment. Thoughts of "he doesn't love me any more" plagued me all day.

The miles behind us are less than those now ahead of us. We'll soon be in Wyoming and the past four days have been more and more tiring. The weariness of sitting, focusing on the road, and long hours behind the wheel have taken their toll.

20

As we drive through the plains the dry fields and few trees whiz past. I'm still wondering what has happened that Anthony and I aren't close any more. I reach for the box of tissues that's sitting on floor between the seats. "Why didn't You just leave me in Georgia?"

I am wiping my tears. "Everything was fine there. Now You're sending me off somewhere out in the middle of nowhere." "*You'll be fine.*" "No I won't! I'm going to freeze to death, I don't know anyone, and now my brother hates me. I wanna go home and forget this whole stinkin' mess."

"*Trust Me Sue. You'll see you're going to be fine.*" "That's easy for You to say. Every stinkin' thing is a big mystery and You won't tell me anything." Having to wipe the tears constantly I'm surprised I haven't run off the road.

Michelle has slowed down. I have no idea how far we've traveled. The questions keep filling my mind. I'm not only hurt and disappointed about the events in Omaha but now frustrated because I can't get any answers.

Hurt usually transforms itself into anger. Frustration can do the same thing and I have both. Now I'm angry at God for this "crazy, stupid, move." Angry at Anthony for his rejection and angry at Michelle for having us go to Omaha in the first place.

Stopping at a roadside rest, I'm having trouble keeping my patience even with the guys. "Come on! We need to go. We don't have all day."

Michelle looks at me. "What's going on, Sue?"

"Nothing! Let's go."

Returning to the motor home I know Michelle's trying to figure out what's wrong with me. "Sue, do you want to talk about what's bothering you?"

Tears almost choke the words from coming out. "I'm just tired. I didn't sleep good last night." I know she doesn't believe me.

"Okay. We have a long drive ahead."

She's standing at the door with her hand on the handle. "I'd like to make it to the other side of North Platte before we stop."

Having no idea she's talking about driving another three hundred-fifty to four hundred miles I say, "Fine. Let's go."

Before flipping the lock and closing the door, she smiles. "On the road again."

I don't join in. I am driving in an almost trance-like state. "This is all Your fault! If You hadn't gotten this half-brained idea to move me I wouldn't be in this mess!"

The Lord is silent. He knows it will come to a head and all the pent up emotions will flood out. He's always there to give me His comfort. Right now I just want to sock something, pull nails out of the walls with my teeth.

I'm sure the Lord is sitting back tapping His foot and cleaning His fingernails, as He looks around at the beauty of heaven waiting for me to wear myself out and break down, reaching for Him.

Before going to bed for the night, I sit down across from Michelle. I've put the walls up around me but Michelle's sympathetic look is about to drive me nuts. The walls are high and quite thick. Only the Lord can bring those walls down but He won't make them come crashing down like they've been bombed.

It's a healing process we go through and some walls are more difficult to bring down than others. We want those walls. They keep us safe from being vulnerable. But there's a double side; when we keep the walls up we are closing out the love of others and keeping ourselves in a prison of inner isolation.

That isn't the will of God for our lives but as long as we refuse to let Him tear them down, we'll continue to hide behind them. Right now I'd prefer to keep my wall up.

I remember a time I was pretty angry about something while driving. The Lord said to me, "Are you going to stay angry or do you want Me to take it?" I didn't hesitate for a second. "Oh I think I'll wallow in it for a while." "Okay."

That wasn't His will for me right then; anger gets in His way of communicating with us. Within minutes the Lord lifted that anger. Like any parent there's only so much He'll put up with. Unlike us, He can do something about it, immediately!

Sitting down Michelle says a prayer of thanksgiving. "Sue, I know something's wrong."

Before she can finish the dam of emotions breaks. "Why did you have us go to Omaha? Anthony hates me and wouldn't even talk to me." Taking a breath, the sobs continue.

"If the Lord hadn't come up with this stupid idea of me moving I would be home playing in the dirt or something. The Lord won't tell me what I'm going to do when I get there, I'm going to freeze to death, and I just want to go home!"

As I run to the bathroom Michelle lowers her head in prayer. Raising her head as I return Michelle scoots to the edge of the seat. Reaching across the aisle to touch my hand, I pull back for fear another outburst will come.

Sniffling, wiping tears, Michelle leans a little closer to me. "Sue, I know Anthony loves you. He just doesn't know how to show it." I say nothing while I toy with the wadded up tissue in my hand.

The longer we talk the better I feel about the whole situation. But I'm exhausted!

We survivors may give the appearance of having a heart of stone—no emotions other than anger—but on the inside we're like many other people. We have fears, love, compassion. All the emotions. We just don't show them.

I step across the aisle and sit back down at the table. "He really hurt me."

"I know. He says and does hurtful things to me all the time but he doesn't realize it at the time."

Reaching over to the ledge and retrieving the map she slides her drink aside. "We still have a few hundred miles to go to get on the other side of North Platte. I really want to cover the miles today if we can. We'll see how far we can get."

If we're ever going to get to Wyoming we have to keep pushing forward. "Lord, are we *ever* going to get there?" *"Sue, listen to Me. You are going to HAVE to listen and follow my directions when you're there. If you don't, you won't survive!"*

"What are You doing to me? What am I going to do when I'm there? You're putting me in the middle of nowhere!" *"You have to trust Me."*

"That's the third or fourth time You said I can't survive." *"I didn't say you can't. I said you will if you lean on Me. Signal Michelle. The dogs need to stretch and so do you."*

The road is hypnotizing me so I'm having to look in different directions. I have no idea how many miles we've covered but we've been driving for what seems like forever. I think we've crossed the United States in one day. At least that's what it feels like.

We've been on highway eighty and as we bypass North Platte we're connecting with highway thirty. "I remember this! This is the highway Sharon and I got on to go to Kemmerer."

It's late afternoon and we've finally pulled into an R.V. park off the highway. There is absolutely nothing out here. A small office and a power hook up and septic connection sit at various places along a line that indicate the camper spaces.

There isn't even a cement pad. Stopping and dragging myself into the office to register, I'm so tired I can barely walk. My body feels like I'm still in the drivers seat and the motion of the motor home is still vibrating through me.

Filling out the registration card and pulling into the space assigned, the dogs are ready to get out again. Opening the door and stepping out I can't believe the desolation. There's absolute nothing for the dogs to get into so I don't even put their leashes on them.

Only two or three campers are parked here and they're a good ways from us. I think the dogs are as shocked as I am. They're out running with their noses to the dirt. We've carried my potted Ficus tree that my mother and sister gave me when Brian died, in the shower stall.

Each night we've had to take it out and set it beside the motor home. Going inside to get the Ficus tree and carrying it out, setting it beside the motor home, I look at Michelle. "It's good thing we brought this tree. Otherwise the dogs would have nothing to pee on."

Laughing she pulls out the chairs from the compartment on the side of the motor home. Having been able to run and sniff to their heart's content without the bothersome leashes, I can see they do not want to be confined again.

Looking at Michelle I can tell she's tired but nothing like I am. My neck, my back, my legs hurt and throb. I don't dare stretch out or I'll never get up. I've camped several places since I've had the Angel Buggy but never as desolate as this.

I look out over the open land. "The desert has more than this place, at least there's cactus."

"See, we covered some good miles today and you haven't died from it."

"That's what you think! I died two hundred miles back."

"Well, we'll get some rest tonight and you'll feel better tomorrow. I'm tired too."

"You'd never know it the way you just keep on truckin'."

She looks over at me with a serious expression. "Sue, I don't think living out here is going to be as bad as you think."

"Have you ever been to Kemmerer?"

"No."

"Then you have no idea what He's getting me in for."

"Anthony and I have been several places in Wyoming. It gets cold but there are interesting places in Wyoming."

"Yea, there are in Georgia, too. And I wish I was there right now."

"You're being obedient to the Lord. Are you ready to go in for the night?"

"Are you kidding? I was ready last week!"

Michelle stands up laughing. "Oh it isn't that bad."

Laying in bed I say, "Thank you Lord for Your angels. I need them." "*You have to lean on Me. You won't survive.*"

I pull the covers tightly up under my chin. "You're scaring me telling me that all the time." "*You're beginning a whole new way of life. If you don't pay attention you won't survive.*" "Okay, okay. I hear you! Do You want to tell me why I'm moving here?" "*Trust Me.*"

During the long days and many miles we've stopped for gas, stopped for hamburgers, spent time at rest stops. Now I feel that's all behind us except for the gas requirements.

When we first left Douglasville I went back and forth between excitement and being scared of the unknown. Now I'm dreading another day on the road. Let's just get there and get off the road!

Kirk gave a sermon once about the milestones we have in life. We all have them. They're significant or important events in our lives. Turning twenty-one, graduating from college, getting married, getting saved and becoming a Christian.

This is one of those milestones for me. Others have been losing my husband, selling my home of fifteen years and the biggest one, giving my life to Christ. This has not been what I would call, "a fun journey."

Having been doing what I want to do for all those years and now being "under God's thumb" as I often refer to it as, has been the hardest thing I've ever done. So many think that because we're suddenly a Christian that things get easier, nothing bad is going to happen, and all is hunky dory. NOT!

If we truly give our life to Christ some things are easier. There's peace where there was none. There's direction and guidance. Joy seems to fill us. I'm not talking about being happy.

That's different from joy. Being happy depends on our circumstances. That can change dramatically. I'm not really happy about this move and not knowing why but my joy comes from the assurance that God is in control and knows what He's doing.

Michelle is almost as exhausted as I am. In these last days of the trip I feel like if I have to drive another mile I'll never enter another vehicle as long as I live. For now though I have to pay close attention to my driving.

Traveling toward Cheyenne the wind is beginning to pick up. The sun is bright but I guess out here the prairie has nothing to hinder the wind. I have to slow down a little because of the headwinds.

Suddenly a blast of wind against the side of the motor home almost knocks me off the road. These conditions cause us to have to slow down. Which means it's going to take longer than we thought to the next stop over.

21

The two hundred something miles to Cheyenne seems to take forever. As I'm driving I'm still bugging Christ to tell me why I'm moving here, what am I going to do once I'm settled in, why won't He tell me anything. The answer is always "Trust Me" or "you'll see."

The "Lean on Me or you won't survive" still is spoken but less often now. I'm so tired I really don't care. He has promised to take care of me. He's the One that came up with this whole business of moving, so as far as I'm concerned, He better follow through.

He says that He lays the path before us and will go ahead of us, so that's what I fully expect Him to do. He called me to this "mission" and I'm trusting Him to be right in front of me leading the way and watching over us.

Coming down a slight hill on the two lane highway there's a large sign, Welcome to Wyoming. The Cowboy State." Suddenly I'm bursting out in tears. "Oh God, we have finally made it. We're in Wyoming."

I never thought we'd ever get here but now that I've seen the welcome sign it's like I have renewed energy. *"You're starting a whole new way of life, Sue."* The tears stream down my face. They're tears of exhaustion and relief. "What do You mean, starting a whole new way of life?"

"You'll see." "You know Lord, I'm really getting sick of hearing that!" There's no stopping us now. Our tunnel vision is pointed straight to Kemmerer, Wyoming. We've already been on the road about four hours today.

Normally we try to drive five hours a day sometimes six. Depending on where we're at and how exhausted we are. It already feels like we've done that. Michelle's determination to get as close to Kemmerer as possible I think is driven by exhaustion.

The Lord said I'll be moved in September first. We're not deliberately trying to make that come true. It if happens, it happens. We're just trying to get there without killing ourselves.

There hasn't been any sleep in late mornings any more. We're up early and on the road. Pulling into a roadside rest between Rawlings and Cheyenne I'm more than happy to stretch. The guys are happily resuming their usual adventure in being in yet another strange location.

I look out over the land. "Is all of Wyoming this barren? There's absolutely nothing out here. I don't think I've seen a tree for miles and miles."

"Sue, you're in the southern part of Wyoming. This is considered Wyoming's desert."

"How much farther do we have to go?"

"We don't have that much farther to go to get on the other side of Rawlings. If I remember right there's a park not far on the other side. We can stay there."

"You didn't answer my question. How far?"

"It's about one hundred fifty miles more. But that's not that far."

"Not that far?! My back is killing me."

"I know Sue. Just hang in there. I'm tired too. But we'll be able to rest tonight."

Yawning she continues. "Kemmerer isn't very far after that. I expect we'll be able to be there tomorrow. If we get past Rollins we're home free."

"That sounds better. At least you're not talking about five or six hundred miles."

It's three-thirty as we finally pull into an R.V. park. It's another one that is in the middle of nowhere. No trees, no cement patio. Just power and septic are available. I set the Ficus tree out beside the door. "Enjoy it guys. That's the only tree for miles!"

Thanking the Lord for our safe travel and His protection, the tears well up in my eyes. "Thank you Lord, we're almost there." Amen.

22

Stopping one more time to let the dogs out, we've been jokingly arguing about who gets to get in the whirly first. It's settled when I staunchly point out I'm making the house payments so I get to go first.

Our discussion changes. We're talking about how sad it is about people not believing there's a hell. I take my Bible off the shelf and open it. "Jesus Himself tells there's a hell! For example in Matthew 5:22 Jesus said, 'But whoever says, You fool! shall be in danger of *hell fire.*' " (emphasis mine)

"Here in Acts 2:27, 'For You will not leave my soul in Hades.' "Isaiah 14:15, 'Yet you shall be brought down to Shoel, to the lowest of the pit.' "

I lay my Bible on the table. "Jesus refers to and speaks of hell throughout the Bible. It's real and I don't understand why people say there isn't a hell!"

"Some people don't believe God would send them to hell if He's a loving God," says Michelle.

"But that's just it. He doesn't send them to hell. It's their choice. He gives them every opportunity and *they* choose to go. Even when I wasn't a Christian I still knew there was a hell. I just didn't care at the time."

Closing the Bible we both agree it's a shame more people don't know God's truth. We sit outside for a little while before packing it in for the night."

"It's cool out here."

"Yea, it is."

"Let's go in."

I've already called Tom notifying him we'll be there tomorrow and to be sure the power and everything is turned on for our arrival. Crawling under the warm blankets, I say, *"Oh Lord, I can't believe this nightmare is almost over. Thank you for getting us here. Are you going to tell me what I'm going to be doing now?" "You'll see."*

Remembering the ceramic angel I'd gotten for her, *"This is a good time to give Michelle her angel." "Oh that's right'!"* Jumping out of bed I retrieve the angel from its hiding place.

She's making her bed. I hide it behind my back like a kid that's going to ask, "Which hand do you choose?" I walk up to her. She straightens up when she hears me beside her. "Sit down for a second Michelle."

Looking at me curiously, she sits down on the edge of the couch. She can see I'm hiding something behind my back. Grinning like a Cheshire cat I pull the box out from behind my back.

I reach it out in front of her. "I want you to have this. I think now is a good time to give it to you." She reaches out and gently takes the box. "What?"

"Just open it."

Opening the box and removing the tissue her eyes suddenly widen and tears form.

"It's my angel!"

"Yea. I'm the one that bought it right under your nose."

Examining it carefully, she reaches up and dries a tear.

"Michelle, I bought it because I want you to remember seeing your very first angel when you look at it."

She's barely able to get any words out. Jumping up off the couch she throws her arms around my neck. That does it! We're both bawling. So much for getting to bed early.

I think the guys know this is our last leg. Each is standing looking out the windows. Rocky on the couch and Jacob on the seat at the table. Sticking my head out the drivers side window. Michelle stops as she's opening the truck's door.

Not caring if others hear us or not, and there aren't but a few in the park, we loudly sing, "On the road again." Laughing and feeling like I could swing on a cloud we start our final leg of this journey.

As the miles roll by I'm no longer angry at God. At least for now. "Michelle sure liked her angel." "*I knew she would.*" "I'm just glad she came over and saw it and liked it."

"We sure pulled one on her that time!" This leg of the trip, with spirits high, we pass over the Continental Divide. The roads have turned into good highway and we're clipping right along.

We have less than a hundred miles to go but in order to let the dogs out and stretch a little ourselves we stop in Rock Springs. Both of us are in much better humor and even though we're tired the excitement is evident.

23

"There's the turn off to Kemmerer, Yes!" Michelle has taken the turn and we only have about 30 miles to go. "Hey guys, we're almost there." Each of the dogs stand up and look out the window as though to say, "Yeaaaaah."

They're my "kids" but thank God they aren't asking, how much farther? every five miles. The relief of being so close washes over me. The road is a two lane highway with rolling hills on one side and flat land on the other.

Suddenly three antelope appear near the road. "It's antelope! Oh man, look at that. I've never seen a real antelope. I hope Michelle got to see them." Driving on my excitement is rising.

I'm a nature lover and get excited about seeing wildlife. To see real antelope has made my day. I'm surprised at how small they are. Their slick tan and white coats, two horns protruding from some of their heads. Grace, just absolute grace, as they scamper off in the other direction.

It's August 27th and I'm pulling up in front of the house I'm to occupy for the next year and a half. Michelle had pulled into the driveway in front of me. "Praise God we're here!"

Tears fill my eyes. Leaning over I plant a big kiss on the hood of the Angel Buggy. Patting the hood, "You did good! Thank you Lord."

Michelle laughs. "I should be kissing the truck, too. I'm just glad we're finally here."

Hooking the dogs to their long leashes at the back corner of the motor home, Tom pulls up. "Well, I see you made it.

I wasn't sure if you were here yet but I thought I'd come and unlock the door.'

"Hi Tom. Yes, we finally made it. I don't want to do that again. Michelle, Tom is the realtor that sold this house. Well, I told him I only wanted to buy the whirly but he insisted the house goes with it."

Laughing, Tom points at me. "Yea, you really got me on that one."

"Can we go in?"

"Sure. The Smiths said you could go ahead and move in as soon as you got here even though we don't close until the 29th."

Tom leaves and after showing Michelle the house Michelle runs the faucet to wash her hands. Turning the faucet off she says, "I have bad news, Sue."

"What? What?"

"There's no hot water. No hot water, no whirly."

Running over to the sink I flip the hot water faucet back on. "WHAT? What do you mean there's no hot water? Tom turned all this stuff on!"

"There better be hot water! I've waited three thousand miles to get in that whirly. I'll kill him!" Running the water for at least three minutes I feel like crying. I finally turn the faucet off. "I'll go call him. I can't believe this!"

I'm trying very hard not to scream at him when he comes on the line. With a very controlled tone of voice, "We have no hot water! I've waited for three thousand miles to get in that whirly and there's no hot water. I thought you turned everything on."

"Oh my gosh! I forgot about the gas. The hot water heater is gas. I'll call right now. I'm so sorry."

"Thanks but that doesn't give me a whirly tonight."

By now it's getting late. We're both tired from the long hours and days on the road. As evening comes the gas has not yet been turned on so we aren't able to relax our weary bones in the whirly. I feel like the bottom has dropped out from under me.

If I didn't know better I think I've aged twenty years. All the miles, the heat, the long days, have suddenly crashed down upon me. The miles are now showing very distinctly on our faces.

Laying in bed, closing my eyes as my head rests on my arms, tears begin to fill my eyes. *"You're going to be okay, Sue."* All the years as a Flight Attendant I spent many nights in hotels. Eating in restaurants all over the country. But I always went home.

"I don't have a home any more. I don't belong here and now I don't belong there." *"You're going to be fine. Trust me."* The tears trickle dampening the pillow. I'm scared, I'm confused, and I just want to go home.

"Lord? What am I going to do when Michelle leaves?" *"You'll be fine."* Flipping over onto my side with my knees folded against my belly, fetal position, I've given up trying to get any answers.

Dreams flicker through my sleep. The one that jars me awake is so vivid it seems real. I've left the dogs at home. I'm out in the countryside along the side of the road. The truck has broken down and I'm buried under tons and tons of snow.

I'm banging on the window trying to get out and screaming for help. The fear, the cold, and the screams jerk me awake. Startled and sitting up in the bed, the dogs jump from my sudden movement.

Laying back down my heart slows from its rapid fear-filled beat. *"Lord, I can't do this."* Snuggling close to Jacob with my face buried in his soft fur, I fall back asleep.

The gas man arrives and you'd think we were going to hug him to death. We have both looked so forward to taking a long relaxing whirly to ease the aches and pains from our weary bodies.

We've had to wait several hours to make sure the water is really hot before diving into the tub. Before we even think about cooking supper, Michelle is laughing. "I thought I got to go first."

Without a bit of hesitation, "Dream on woman! You can go first AFTER me." Laying back in the tub, "Ohhhhh God, I've died and gone to heaven!" I hear the Lord chuckle.

Fifteen minutes of swirling, bubbling, soothing hot water I need to get out before I can't. Stepping out my legs will barely hold me up. They feel like cooked noodles and I have to hold onto the wall for a minute.

I dry off. *"As cold as it gets here I'll bet I'll be in that all the time. Just to thaw out."* *"You're going to be fine."* I'm still very much worried about the winter months here and what it's going to be like.

"Lord. You promised You'll take care of me here." *"Yes Sue. You'll be okay."* "Oh Lord. Thank you for this whirly." Going back to the Angel Buggy Michelle has cooked dinner while I was in bliss in the tub.

I stretch out on the couch so I don't fall. "I don't think I've felt this good since we left." Michelle sets the hot meal on the table. "How long before the water's hot again?"

Grinning like a Cheshire cat I say, "Oh it may not get hot until tomorrow night."

Her head spins around looking at me with a surprised look on her face. "You BETTER be joking!" "Not to be mean, but I've already had mine."

Reaching over she bops me on the head. "Yea. So you don't care if I get to have one. Dinner's ready."

I feel so good yet very weak from the bath that I barely eat anything. I just want to pile into the bed and sleep through until morning. Forcing myself up from the table I say, "You cooked, I'll clean up. Why don't you go see if the water's hot yet." By now it's seven o'clock so the water should have heated up.

Michelle steps out of the Angel Buggy grinning from ear to ear, singing, "I'm going to get a whirly. I'm going to get a whirly."

"You go right ahead. Enjoy it immensely."

Forty-five minutes have passed since she went into the house. Just as I'm about to go in to check on her she steps into the motor home holding her dirty clothes in her arms. "Ohhhhh Sue. That was out of this world! I didn't realize how sore my muscles have been until I got in there."

"I know. I was just getting ready to come check on you."

24

People don't understand my relationship with the Lord. He's my friend. He's my husband. I talk to Him like I'm talking to anyone else. Without the cuss words, which He took right out of my mouth.

Except for "Damn and hell." Then He'll get on me for using those two. Many times we'll joke around. The Lord has such a wonderful sense of humor. I've heard so many sermons and have read so many places how the Lord wants a completely honest and close relationship with His children.

Sitting beside the motor home we're watching the dogs as they struggle on their leashes. They hate them and I hate having to put them on them. "I still wish the Lord would tell me why I'm here."

"He will! Just be patient. All in His good time."

"I just can't imagine why He'd choose Wyoming?"

"Maybe you're going to marry that cowboy." Michelle laughs and picks up her glass of tea. "He might be getting that guy ready to ask you."

"Will you quit! I'm not marrying some cowboy?"

"There's lots of them out here. You'd have your pick."

"Like I want a bowlegged cowboy that smells like horses."

"You could do worse."

"I've already had the best now why would I choose less."

"Yea, Brian was a sweetheart. Anthony and I both loved him."

I haven't gotten homesick yet but I can't help but wonder what this "new way of life" is going to be. Sighing deeply and getting up, the dogs are ready to go in, too. It's already started getting chilly in the evenings.

I'm constantly trying to figure out why I'm here, what am I going to do while here, why Wyoming? Is this real? Getting no answers is about to drive me nuts. *"What am I going to do when it snows? What about blizzards?"* *"You'll be fine. Lean on Me."*

It's only nine o'clock and I'm usually up later than this, but not tonight. Laying in bed I feel like the only thing I have to look forward to is unpacking a whole house full of boxes and trying to make this place my home.

"Home. I don't have a home anymore. The Lord said I'm here for a year and a half. What kind of home is that? I'm just passing through and I have no idea where next."

Turning onto my side the tears wet my pillows. *"Sue, You're going to be fine. Trust Me."* This new place is scary. Laying here, the inner fear creeps in but I push it back. *"Maybe the furniture will get here tomorrow and I can start that chore."*

I haven't gotten used to the two hour time change so I wake early. Bending over to start making my bed, the dogs start barking. Michelle yells, "Sue, they're here! The movers are here!"

Running to the motor home door, I almost knock Michelle out the door. Both of us run out into the yard with our hands raised high in the air we're dancing around, singing, "They're here, they're here."

The huge moving truck has parked next to the curb in front of the house. The driver walks around the front of the truck and starts across the grass. He's the same driver that loaded everything at home.

Walking up to us, he looks tired. "You're Ms. Cass aren't you?"

"Oh yes. You made it."

Looking around he says, "I don't know how we did it this fast. We weren't supposed to be here for another four days."

Laughing and doing a little dance, Michelle and I look at each other with grins clear across our face. At the same time, "We do!"

Looking at us like we're some kind of nuts he says, "I need to turn the truck around. This is a dead end street isn't it?"

It takes less time to unload and set up the beds, washer and dryer, than it did to load everything for the trip out here. As they're pulling away *"I guess I really am going to live here."*

September 1, 1999 I am completely moved in. Just like the Lord said.

25

The two weeks Michelle stayed to help me unpack has been yet another blessing. We've gotten the kitchen put together, clothes and linens put in their proper places, and most boxes emptied.

We made previous arrangements for her to fly out of the small Rock Springs airport. I would have to drive six hours round trip for her to leave from the Salt Lake City airport.

The drive to Rock Springs is a quiet drive. We both are sad at her leaving and say little. The hugs and tears as she boards the small airplane leave me feeling abandoned. Not by her but because the Lord has chosen to leave me here alone.

Driving home I feel the loneliness seeping in. I hardly notice the few deer grazing along a stream or the bald eagle sitting on a fence post only to spread its expansive wings and glide off into the distance.

Placing several wooden shelves along one wall in the basement to store my many craft supplies, putting knick-knacks on shelves and end tables only take up some of my time as I continue to question why I'm here only to be given the same answers.

Having come from a very controlled environment growing up I rebel against being controlled by anyone. Having to ask, "Can I go to the grocery store?" only to be told, "Not now" is driving me nuts.

"Can I go to Fontenelle Lake?"

"*No*." "When are You going to tell me why I'm here?" "*Soon*." Now I know how the guys feel having to be on their leashes when they've been used to running free.

My leash is very short and in my opinion, totally unnecessary. After all, I'm a big girl. The frustration causes even more frustration and I feel like I'm going to explode if I don't start getting some answers.

The days are cold and the nights are even colder. Store clerks laugh when I want to buy heavy clothes. "It doesn't get cold until another month or so." "Excuse me, but I'm freezing now. Where's the heavy socks?"

I've managed to get heavy wool socks, boots that are warm in sub-zero temperatures. Hats and gloves, long john underwear isn't that difficult to get. Being told I'll need a snow blower I've driven to Rock Springs and now have one sitting in the garage along with a snow shovel.

I'm already wearing two layers of clothes and the whirly feels like a life saver to me. Laying back in the water so hot it would cook a lobster, "Thank you Lord. This is the best part of being here."

I've met my neighbor, Mary. She's in her early eighties, short, and exhibits a rough and tough woman that has lived here all her life. I respect the elderly for their wisdom and knowledge and being in this harsh land, I have learned to listen to her advice.

It hasn't taken me long to see beyond the tough persona. She has a heart of gold. We've become friends and she's quick to set me straight on things I do in ignorance. Sitting in my living room Rocky begins barking.

Jacob looks toward the front window and is growling as the hair on his neck stands up. Getting up and walking to the window to see what the fuss is about, I pull back the sheer curtain. I'm shocked to see a huge animal standing underneath the window grazing on the short grass.

The long gnarled arthritic-looking legs look as though they'll collapse right out from under its massive gray and black body. Its head is long and narrow, looking disproportionate to its body.

The huge scooping antlers look like upturned partially cupped hands with fingers spread wide. The moose raises its head and suddenly I'm staring into big black eyes. This monster of an animal is so ugly it could almost be considered cute. Well, that's stretching it.

I whisper, "Hush Rocky, you'll scare it away." The moose slowly meanders off toward the old garage and disappears into the narrow alley. I run to the phone to call Mary. "Mary! Did you see the moose?"

I'm so excited I can hardly contain the thrill I feel at witnessing a wild animal. Especially a massive moose in my front yard. "Sue Cass, don't you dare go outside with that moose. Where is it now?"

Shocked at the sternness of her voice I say, "It went behind the old garage and is in the alley someplace."

"Don't go anywhere near it! They'll kill you in an instant."

"I didn't go outside. I was watching it through the window."

Mary explains that moose not only kick with their hind feet but also will lash out with the front ones. They won't rear up like a horse but lash out hitting their target with deadly accuracy.

I've seen some antelope wandering through town but to witness my first moose right in my front yard is beyond anything I can imagine. The thrill stays with me and I'm always anxious to go see them grazing by the river in Frontier.

Kemmerer's population is made up of three small towns rubbing elbows with each other. Kemmerer is sandwiched in between Diamondville and Frontier. All are old mining towns and most of the men work in the coal mines scattered about the state. Most of the women are teachers at the elementary, middle, and high school in town.

I am sitting in Mary's small dining room sipping the hot tea she's prepared. "Do you think there's any moose down at the river?"

"I don't know, we can go see."

"*Not today.*"

I've told Mary about how the Lord brought me here and how I do what He tells me.

Exasperated at being told I can't do something again, I put the cup of tea down and stand up. "The Lord just said not today." She's accepted my statements of hearing the Lord tell me something. Whether she thinks I'm nuts or not she's given no indication.

The first snowfall has rendered me under the covers in my bed wishing it would go away. It isn't a big snowfall, only a half inch of snow covers the ground but it's an indication of worse things to come as far as I'm concerned.

Reading the instructions of how to operate the snow blower I'm not taking any chances of being caught off guard. The warm clothes, heavy coat, and boots are ready to be donned. Extra blankets are on the bed.

Mary has told me that I must carry a flashlight, blankets, flares, and water in the Blazer in case I get caught in a blizzard while out on the road. This doesn't help my insecurity about the winter months.

Others are excited about skiing and riding snowmobiles. No thank you, I'm perfectly content to be "swirled" in the whirly and remain indoors with the thermostat set on high.

Sharon and Ginny have visited and are thrilled to have me so close to Idaho. It doesn't bother her in the least to drive the snow-covered roads. I've ventured out to the bank or J.C. Penny's but I stay in town rather than go farther away in case one of the dreaded blizzards blow in.

Mary has shown me around Evanston, fifty-two miles away. The only Walmart anywhere near is in Evanston. We ride together to go grocery shopping as the grocery store there is much bigger, cleaner, and cheaper in prices than in Kemmerer.

Burger King, McDonald's, and Wendy's are all there and I've been shocked to learn Mary has never had fast food. She has now. I talk her into having a "whopper" with me when we go into Evanston.

She and I look after each other. I'll call to make sure she's okay if I don't see a light on in her kitchen. We ride together looking for moose, antelope, and elk. Our outings are an adventure to me and I love enjoying them with her.

She's become an asset to me. The Lord is using her to teach me "the ropes" of living here and using me as an outlet for her spiritual gifts that she's hidden from others for fear of being considered senile or crazy.

We have like interests and love seeing the wild animals. Binoculars in hand, camera set and ready to snap pictures, we'll ride along the roads looking for any wild animals we can find.

She'll call me asking if I want to go over to the river; moose have been spotted there. Or tell me there's elk on the hillsides, do I want to go see them. Excitement courses through my body and loading the dogs up so they can go for a ride, we'll drive the short distance.

Each time we park a good ways from the moose yet we're able to watch them. If I step out of the truck to take pictures Mary always warns me sternly to stay clear of them. I don't fear the moose but I do have a very healthy respect for them.

According to Mary they are extremely mean and danger-ous if mama moose has calves at her heels. She'll charge even if we are at a safe distance. We're far enough away that Rocky and Jacob merely sit quietly watching through the window.

I think I've used a whole roll of film taking pictures of the moose. The elk I have to use a telephoto lens and then they appear as dots on the picture. They roam the hillsides high up along the ridges and occasionally come down closer to where we can see them more clearly.

Antelope is quite common to see. I still get a thrill watching them. When the Lord will allow me I drive toward Big Piney to watch them. Heavy snow hasn't started yet but will soon.

Making sure the roads are perfectly clear I've started venturing out a little farther from home. I don't feel completely comfortable but cabin fever sets in and I need to get out.

Patches of snow dot the roadside filling ditches making them look like a part of the road. Coming back from viewing Fontenelle Lake I've pulled over to take pictures of a herd of antelope and learn a valuable lesson.

The back tires slide off into a ditch. The front of the Blazer is veered upward along the bank of the ditch. Knowing not to spin the wheels I try edging the truck forward and backwards.

It doesn't work, I'm stuck. I've seen no other cars on the road since I left and I'm still sitting here. "Now what Lord?" My eyes are led to the three buttons on the dash. "Oh wow! I forgot I have four wheel drive," and push the lowest gear button.

Pressing the gas pedal slightly the wheels take hold of the icy snow and pull out of the ditch at an angle with no problem. "Thank you, thank you, thank you Lord. Now I know why you had me buy four wheel drive." I hear his soft chuckle.

I've started attending the small church the Lord pointed out for me to worship at. I'm finding that being an outsider isn't readily accepted. A couple of the women have befriended me but most tolerate my presence.

Thanksgiving is just around the corner and it's been announced that the churches in the area all gather together for a Thanksgiving service. Mary tells me this is a yearly tradition here and I'm excited to attend. *"Ask the pastor if you can give a testimony."* "Okay. What am I going to give this testimony about?" *You'll see."*

The pastor gets approval from the other pastors that will attend the community service and I find myself standing before priests, pastors, and people from all denominations of churches.

Standing before them I'm telling how the Lord told me to move to Kemmerer. How He gave me the name of the agent that sold my house, the closing date, and when I'd be moved in here.

The testimony is well taken except for one women. Leaning over to her friend, she whispers, "God doesn't do that!" Mary overhears her. A priest walks up to me after the service and places his hand gently on my shoulder.

"Miss Cass, I want to thank you for your testimony. I have cancer and am dying. When you said that we are to trust and obey whether we understand or not, I now understand I'm to trust and that's all I need to do."

Tears have welled up in his eyes and for me, just this one man was worth standing and speaking to these people. Looking over at him as he walks away, my heart goes out to him as I tell Mary what he said.

She mentions the woman that made the comment to her friend. "Well Mary. Some people just need to give God a bigger box. The one she has Him in is just too small!"

Mary and I spend Thanksgiving together. She's cooked a nice meal consisting of a turkey breast and side dishes. The usual cranberry sauce, sweet potatoes, and some dishes of which I have never heard of.

I've been here three months. It's my first Thanksgiving in Wyoming and slowly I'm adjusting but I'm still questioning the Lord as to why I'm here and what I'm supposed to be doing.

26

"Do everything without complaining or arguing" is what Philippians 2:14 says for us to do. That's easier said than done for me. While I've been here I've been on a roller coaster of emotions.

I'm praising the Lord and worshipping His Majesty with tears rolling down my cheeks. Praising Him and thanking Him for keeping me safe and warm. Thanking Him for my whirly. I do that every time I get in it.

The next thing I know I'm so angry I can spit. Stomping to the front door, throwing it wide open the cold air blasts me in the face. I want to scream as loud as I can, "I hate this place!"

The rage continues until I'm totally confused about how it started and now I'm not able to stop it. Slamming the door against the freezing temperature I know I better do something to stop it.

Pacing the floor I'm trying to get control of my emotions without success. Going into my bathroom and turning on the faucet in the whirly I'm pacing and cussing as the tub fills up.

Climbing into the deep tub my rage has not subsided. Doubling my fists so tight my fingernails are cutting into my palms I begin to beat the water as hard as I can. Water is flying everywhere but I don't care.

Slam, the water flies. Thump, my hand hits the edge of the tub. I hardly feel it. Tears are streaming down my face as I viciously beat the water. Slamming my fists violently against the water, screaming, "GOD WHAT IS WRONG WITH ME?!"

My fist slams once more into the water when I hear one word, "Demons!" All rage, beating the water, anger, cussing, stops immediately. It's as though someone has blown the flame out on a burning candle.

I slide back and lay against the wall of the tub. "Demons!" I haven't learned a whole lot about the demonic world but I do know enough to know they can and will influence people's emotions.

I now know where the unexplained rage is coming from. "*Anoint this house.*" I look at the mess I've made all over the bathroom. "Okay Lord." Slowing crawling over the edge of the tub I feel like a dishrag that has been wrung out.

My energy is spent, my arms ache from the violent thrashing, my hand now hurts from hitting the edge of the tub. Drying off, mopping up the water from the walls and floor, I put on a nightgown and decide to do the anointing in the morning.

Crawling into bed my body feels like it's been in a war and I lost. Laying here quietly the word "demons" keeps coming to mind. I throw the blankets back and jump up from the bed. "I'm going to anoint this place right here and right now!" "*Use Hyssop.*"

Opening the sliding glass door on the cabinet with my Israel souvenirs and taking out the small bottle of anointing oil I'm armed to do battle. Praying, dedicating this house to the Lord I'm placing a cross made with Hyssop oil on each and every wall.

The spiritual significance of Hyssop is cleansing and purification. It's considered "Holy fire." Perfect! The Lord leads me in what to pray specifically for each room. Rest and comfort in the bedroom, feeding not only the body but the soul in the kitchen.

Every wall, every door frame, every window is anointed and prayed over. From the attic to the basement. Closets, anywhere the demonic might hide. At midnight I'm finally done. "Lord? Is there anywhere else I need to anoint?" *"You've done well. Go to bed."* I already feel His peace filling the house.

Ben has been like a lifeline for me since I've been here. He calls once a week, every week, to see how I'm doing. I've told him about the moose, the rage and anointing the house, and how Mary looks after me and threatens to throttle me if I go anywhere without telling someone where I'm going.

I've learned that to leave town without telling someone approximately what time I'll be back and where I'm going can be quite hazardous to my health. No wonder they carry emergency supplies in their cars. Blizzards!

I've talked to him about my emotional swings, how much trouble I had going through the process of getting a permit to install a fence for the guys. Now the tears flow as I'm telling him about the woman in the grocery store today who told me, "This is our town! We don't like outsiders, go back where you came from!"

"Ben, I want to come home! I'm not wanted here. Why am I here?" Sympathy is evident in his voice as he tells me to trust the Lord. He manages to get me calmed down and we're able to talk about something else.

Hanging up I'm still upset about what the woman said to me. I've felt like an outsider since the day I arrived and having her tell me I am only confirms what I already knew.

I lay in bed. "Lord, I just want to go home!" *"This is your home now."* "No it isn't! You said I'll be here for a year and a half. That's not home! It's just passing through." *"You'll be okay, I'm with you."*

"Why am I here? What am I supposed to be doing? All I'm doing is sitting on my butt watching it snow." *"You'll see, Trust Me."* "Why won't You tell me? I'm sick of this! I wanna go home NOW!" No comment. Obviously Philippians 2:14 hasn't had any lasting effect on me.

With the colder weather and now snow beginning to get heavier and heavier I want more than ever to go back to Georgia where I know how to survive. Where I can go to the church where I'm accepted, do my ministry, and live happily ever after.

27

Christmas Day is spent with Mary. A quiet day and surprisingly, it hasn't snowed. The ground is covered with snow and since learning how to use the snow blower I'm up every morning blowing snow off the driveway and sidewalk.

I'm sick of getting out in the freezing weather. I have long johns on, a pair of jeans, and sweat pants over those. Three layers of tops, gloves, hat, and a coat heavy enough to keep a bear warm. I'm still cold!

Mary has advised me to keep the snow and ice off the driveway. To never ever drive over it or it packs down and I'll never get it off. Between God, Mary, and Ben I don't know what I'd do.

It feels like the snow will never stop. The temperatures fall to below zero at night and days are barely above zero. Praise God I met a couple that is letting me store the Angel Buggy in their large warehouse.

On occasion they have to go out of town so I volunteer to keep an eye on their store. Making sure no one has broken in and feeding their dog. Once in a while I'll bring Chuckles home and let him visit with the guys.

In return they let me store the motor home for free. Which is a real blessing. They've been very helpful to me. Anytime I need something they help out if they can and I'm more than willing to reciprocate.

A neighbor three houses down and across the street is also willing to help. "Can you come over and help me move this couch? "That door is scraping against the carpet, does it need to be shortened?" He's always willing to help and is a good handyman.

There are some in this small town who accept me and want to be friendly and neighborly. I can count them on one hand though. Most are people who have lived here all their lives and it amazes me to learn many have never been out of the state.

So far I haven't had to experience drastic weather conditions but that doesn't last long. Waking to the sound of wind rattling the windows, I'm not sure if it's a tornado, hurricane, or what outside.

Listening closely, the wind is tremendous. The dogs are awake and listening intently, too. It sounds like the roof is going to fly right off the house! Dear Lord, please protect us." "*You'll be okay.*"

Laying, listening to the howling wind, I'm scared half out of my wits. The wind continues and there's no way I can go back to sleep. The dogs settle down. Not me! I'm laying there with covers jammed under my chin clinging to them like they'll save me from being blown to China.

Dawn finally peeks in and the wind has died down. Still buried under the covers, "Thank you Lord. What was that?" "*You're okay. I'm with you.*" I slowly crawl out of the bed and walk to the window. "Good grief!"

Snow is piled so high it's covering the bottom of the window. Closing the curtain and going to the front door, the dogs are waiting for me to remove the cover on their doggie door.

Lifting the cover slightly I can see the snow blocking any entrance or exit. Looking out the window all I see is snow. "Oh Lord, now what do I do? The dogs need to go out." "*Lift the garage door.*"

Walking into the garage and pressing the button the garage door begins rising, exposing a mountain of snow. "*Use your snow blower and make a path through the snow for them.*"

Both Rocky and Jacob have emptied their bladder on the edge of the snow without even stepping out of the garage. The joke, "Don't eat yellow snow" suddenly comes to mind and I can't help but laugh.

It's stopped snowing and taking the snow blower I start making a path through the deep snow. I wind it along the fence line, around the corner, back toward the front door. Standing on the porch it looks like a labyrinth.

The townspeople think I'm nuts. They continually are asking Mary what in the world is that woman doing? Why they don't come to me I have no idea other than I'm that crazy outsider.

Another blizzard blows through but this time I realize what it is. That doesn't mean I'm not scared but at least I feel a little more secure. The Lord has promised to protect me and so far He has.

The streets have been cleared. "Lord, can I ride out to the lake and see what it looks like?" "No." But the streets are clear." "Trust Me." "Soon," and "You'll see" have continued along with approval or disapproval of my plans. I feel trapped. Feel like a robot, a puppet and He's pulling the strings.

I can argue only to lose, I can stomp, cry, and beg but if it is not what He wants me to do He lets me know. Depression comes and goes. Frustration and anger at being "tied down" is prevalent.

My independence is being taken away and it's not setting well at all with me.

It's even become a chore for me to get out of bed and go to church. The services are different from what I'm used to and these seem mundane and boring to me. I'm flabbergasted when asking the women in the Sunday School class if we can pray for the pastor.

They look shocked at my request. "Why would we need to pray for him, he's the pastor!" I can't believe my ears. "He's the shepherd of this flock. He needs the Lord's guidance as much as we do. Even more."

Even more astonishing is that the pastor is uncomfortable with us praying for him. "I've never had people pray over me." Maybe that's why the Lord has put me here but I'm more than willing to leave. I feel no Holy Spirit dancing or blowing through this sanctuary. "Lord please move me somewhere else."

28

It's the end of January and the temperatures have fallen to twenty below. We almost never see above zero during the daytime. "Lord, is this freezing weather EVER going to end?" No answer.

The phone rings. "Hello."

"Hi Sue. It's Brenda."

"Oh hi. What are you up to these days?"

The conversation continues and finally, "Sue, I want to come visit. I miss you."

No matter how hard I try to convince her that February is not a good time to come, she won't listen. "I want to come February first." "*Lord, You need to divinely intervene here. If this isn't what she's supposed to do then close that door.*" "*Tell her to come on the fifth.*"

She's never flown before and is inundating me with questions on what to expect and do. "No the wings don't flap like a bird." "Yes you can get up and walk around." I know how gullible she is and I can't resist the temptation to really pull her leg.

"Is there a bathroom?"

"*Forgive me Lord but I can't keep quiet on this one.*" Very seriously. "Yes. They're usually in the back of the plane.

"Sue, is it true that the waste goes out into the air when you flush the toilet?"

"*Oh God this is too good.*"

I try to keep from laughing. "When you tinkle it evaporates before it hits the ground. If you can wait for the other, do, otherwise you'll be bombing the cities." I'm almost dying inside to keep from falling out of the chair laughing.

I'm the expert on flying, aren't I? Why would she not believe me?

"But what if I really have to go and can't wait?"

"Then go and when you flush the toilet holler bombs away."

My tongue is about to bleed I'm biting down so hard to keep from laughing. "*I can't believe this. She's really believing me!*" "How will I know if we're going to crash?"

I can hear a little fear in her voice. "Okay, I'll tell you what. If you see the flight attendants strapped in their seats and crying, you put your head down between your legs and kiss your butt goodbye. I gotta go."

Hanging up, I can't help it, I'm roaring with laughter. "*Shame on you, Sue Cass.*" My ribs hurt from laughing so hard. "Oh Lord, I couldn't help it. She's so gullible she believed it all."

She does believe all of it until in her excitement she's telling Susan about all the things I told her about flying. Calling me back with her flight schedule she tells me Susan said I'm lying. I burst out laughing.

For a full two days I have laughed until tears run down my cheeks every time I think of it. "You lied to me! The bathroom stuff does not go out of the plane." I'm laughing so hard I can't talk.

Most of the time she's here she has been bundled up in a heavy afghan on the couch. Her lupus and failing kidneys affect her circulation and she stays cold constantly. Looking at her as she's huddled under the afghan I say, "I really wish you had waited until the weather is warmer."

While she's been here the Lord has let us go for short drives when the roads were clear. Even with two pair of my wool socks on and sub-zero boots she's freezing to death. In the car with the heater blowing on her feet they're numb and she can't feel them.

In the house with the heat turned up on high she's still cold. I'm pretty concerned about her and when she wants to help me clear the snow off the driveway she insists she'll be okay.

Looking over at her as she shovels the snow off the front steps I can see her cheeks are bright pink. "Brenda, put the shovel away and get in the house!"

"I'm okay."

"No you aren't! Get in there and get in that whirly. You can't take this."

She finally agrees, puts the shovel back in the garage, and goes in the house. I breathe a sigh of relief. That's all I need is to try to get her to a hospital where the doctors won't have a clue about her medical needs.

The Lord doesn't allow us to leave the house much. It's been too cold, the roads are too slick or not cleared and she can't stand the sub-zero temperatures. For that matter, neither can I. I've realized the Lord knows best and don't put up a fight.

Walking into the living room, she's bundled up on the couch. Looking up at me, she says, "Would it hurt your feelings if I went home early?"

"No, but it's going to cost more to change your ticket."

"I know. I just want to go home." I need to change her return schedule, she's planning to leave tomorrow. Waking during the night to the familiar howling wind, I get up and walk to Brenda's room to see if she's awake and terrified. She's sound asleep. "*Thank you Lord. She doesn't have a clue what's going on outside.*"

I know we've had another blizzard. Looking out the window, snow is piled high. Lord, there's no way she'll be leaving today." "*I know.*" Walking into her room she's barely awake.

Looking down at her I know she's going to be really disappointed.

"Brenda?"

"Hmmmm."

"I hate to tell you this but you're not going to be able to leave today."

Her eyes fly open, "What? Why?"

"We're snowed in. We had a blizzard last night. We can't even get out of town much less to Salt Lake City." She's so disappointed she's stayed in bed crying most of the day.

Brenda is back home after spending another week with me. Once again the feeling of being alone settles in. The winter months seem to go forever. The longer the cold weather continues the more depressing it is for me.

29

Mary and I continue to share in each other's lives. I've told her some of my spiritual experiences and she's shared some of hers with me. The bond between us in growing stronger by the day.

She continues to advise me on the in's and out's of living in this cold, snowy country. To hear me talk one would think the cold is the only factor that I'm focused on. It isn't. Doing the Lord's will is uppermost in my mind. The cold, feelings of aloneness and depression get in the way at times. With God's help, I persevere.

One of the ladies in the Sunday School class has invited me to a Bible study in someone's home. Arriving, we're meeting in the living room and I'm introduced to a few people.

The pastor leading the group is wearing cowboy boots, black jeans, and a long sleeve shirt with a bolo tie. He's tall. I'll guess him to be at least six foot three or four inches tall. He presents himself as THE authority.

At the end of the Bible study we're chatting amongst ourselves and as I'm about to leave I'm standing in front of him. He's sitting on the hearth of the fireplace leaning back against the bricks. His long legs stretch out into the room.

I smile down at him. "I'm sorry, I didn't catch your name."

Looking up at me he hesitates. "You can call me pastor."

Without a beat, "Is that your first name or your last?"

His eyes flash with anger, sitting up he glares at me, then gives me his full name.

From that moment on he and I don't see eye to eye. The Lord has released me from the church on Sage Avenue and now has me worshipping in this church where this man is the pastor.

It's an eighty mile drive one way and I'm not a happy camper at having been given this "assignment." The upside is that I get to see an occasional moose, a few antelope, and bald eagles on the round trip drive.

Over the past few weeks I've learned that anyone who opposes this pastor is considered a "rebel and rebellious." We are not to question his knowledge of scripture, we are not to question his authority.

He does have a way of keeping the congregation's attention and they all seem to love this man. I, on the other hand, seem to be a thorn in his side that just won't go away. I do question.

He'll pull himself up to full height and stare down at me. I'm sure he's trying to intimidate me. There's only one problem, I don't get intimidated! I don't care how tall he is. If he does choose to answer me it's in curt tones.

After the long drive I'm standing to the side and back from the podium. The congregation are all standing. Some are dancing in the aisles. Several are speaking in tongues, other are running around the borders of the room shouting in tongues.

To me it's total pandemonium. Everyone is shouting at the same time while pastor eggs them on louder and louder. It reminds me of a high school pep rally. 1 Corinthians 14:26–40 speaks clearly about the order in church meetings. In my opinion this does not exemplify scripture.

During all the shouting and dancing he walks in front of me and stops. Leaning over close to my face he says, "You aren't too old to get on fire. Worship, woman, worship!"

Surprised at his command I respond, "Don't tell me how to worship!"

The chasm grows wider. During a private conversation with him in his office he's letting it be known he despises denominational churches. I ask him, "Pastor, why are you so angry?" He denies it and stomps out of the room.

In church he's standing before the congregation and announces very loudly, "Sue believes I am a very angry man!" Everyone turns to look at me. So much for pastor, parishioner confidentiality.

"Lord please get me out of this church." "Soon." "Is that Your soon or mine?" Once again rejection and alienation is my cross to bear. I'm shunned by many of his followers.

The Lord has kept me here for the past four months. Maybe I'm supposed to be a thorn in this pastor's side. Maybe I'm supposed to be here to wake up some people to God's truth. I don't have the answer but I want out!

When someone gives the devil the credit for what the Lord is doing, it's called blasphemy. "My soon" comes very quickly and the Lord moves me to yet another church. This one is very small.

The pastor has recently been ordained. He's one that insists on being called pastor. Telling him, "That isn't who you are. It's your job" is a wakeup call for him. He's knowledgeable, and interesting. All eight of us enjoy his sermons. Testimonies are welcomed. Fellowship, and covered dish gatherings are a joy.

I've never been in a small congregation, well not this small. It's nice. But once again, I'm the outsider regardless of how small the congregation. Small town folks are family and no matter how friendly they can be, you're just not family.

Winter has finally come and gone. Praise God. The snow shovel is set aside. The snow blower is covered and sitting in a corner of the garage out of the way, waiting for the next bout of snow and ice.

The weather has slowly been warming up although I am told we can still have snow in July. Disheartening news and lots of prayers that it won't happen while I'm here. I feel like it will take me all summer to thaw out.

Brenda has called and once again wants to come visit. It's okay now. Hopefully she won't freeze to death on this visit. We're able to wear shorts if so desired. I'm not ready for that quite yet.

Taking the motor home out of storage I'm able to go camping at a small campground just below the Fontenelle Dam. There's no hook-ups but it sits next to the river that flows from the dam.

Across the river is a high bluff. Water from above seeps through the jagged rocks and down into the river. Mary has told me this place is called "Weeping Rock" and it's obvious how it got its name.

With few campers I don't have to put the dogs on their leashes and they love roaming around the area. Each will stand knee high in the water on the edge of the river but go no farther because the water is ice cold.

The lake has thawed but the cold water hasn't warmed as yet. Mary once again warns me, "Sue, don't go there by yourself. Some of the local men go out there for a few nights of drinking and partying. It can be dangerous for you."

I don't have people to go with me so I listen but loving the outdoors I can't resist getting out in the motor home. I have found that each time I go there's usually a family camping so I don't have to worry about being out in the middle of nowhere alone.

It's a pleasure to take Brenda with me since she's arrived. The temperature has risen into the low eighties and for me that's a heat wave. Having survived the winter anything above zero is now considered a heat wave.

Brenda, the dogs, and I head for Weeping Rock for a three day outing. Pulling into the camp ground I've noticed a van parked into a space next to the river. Mary's warning quickly comes to mind but I say nothing to Brenda.

A man is sitting in the driver's seat watching us park in my favorite campsite under a large oak tree next to the river. Having a bad feeling about this situation I don't set up camp as I normally would.

The man sits in the van watching us as we are playing Yatzee at the table. Brenda has noticed him by now and is getting quite nervous about his constant watching us. I'm not too thrilled about it myself.

We've been here about three hours and the man hasn't left. He's only gotten out of his van once and went around to the back of it to retrieve something. I can't see what. My "antennas" to danger begin to zero in on this van with the man.

Suddenly his engine roars into play and he slowly pulls out of the campsite all the while looking directly at us. Feeling a sense of relief we resume playing our game of Yatzee. But not for long.

Stretching the awning out and feeling sure other campers will arrive soon, I'm taking the carpet out of its compartment. "*I want you to pack up and go home.*" "But Lord, he's gone and others will be here." "*Go home!*"

"Doggone it. We're going to be okay, he's gone." "*Pack up and leave. He'll be back. It isn't safe.*" Hearing "he'll be back" sends chills down my spine. Going into the motor home Brenda is bundled up on the couch under my afghan. "We have to leave."

She looks up at me. "Why? I thought we were staying three days."

I glance out the window, hoping the man hasn't already returned without my seeing him. "Brenda, the Lord said that man is coming back and we aren't safe staying here. Help me with the awning."

As we're rolling the awning up Brenda says, "Sue, I'm glad we're leaving! I was hoping we would. The guy gave me the willies."

A shiver passes through me. "Yea me, too. The Lord is looking after us."

There's no going home early for Brenda this time. She isn't able to wear shorts but praise God she's enjoying the warmer weather as much as I am. After her statement, "I'll never leave Georgia again" when she arrived home the last time, I'm glad she's enjoying this visit.

Driving out in the country we're enjoying being out of the house. The dogs are also enjoying being out and able to play in the open fields. As we're driving Brenda sees a large snow fence.

They look similar to bleachers at a sporting event and keep the blowing snow and snowdrifts off the roads. She's looking out her window as I'm watching for antelope hoping she'll get to see one.

Brenda points to the fence. "Sue, what's that?"

"Oh it's bleachers."

"Bleachers? Why would there be bleachers way out here?"

"*Forgive me Lord but I can't resist.* You know the song that says, where the deer and the antelope play?"

"Yes."

"There's nothing around for the locals to do so they come out here, sit on the bleachers, and watch the deer and the antelope play."

"Oh."

I have to turn my head away to keep from laughing.

Sitting at the table playing Scrabble I ask, "How would you like to go to Yellowstone National Park? It's not that far from here and we can stay a couple of days if you want."

"Can we do that? I've never been and that would be cool!"

"I'll call and see if we can rent a cabin. It's more fun in a cabin than the hotel."

She's putting the Scrabble pieces back in the box, excited to be able to go some place she's only heard of.

As we carry our luggage into the cabin the view is perfect. We're surrounded on three sides with tall trees. The front looks out over an open area where buffalo wander through.

Mary has shown me an article in the newspaper that is telling how someone staying in a cabin here heard knocks on the cabin door and opened it only to be staring into the face of a large bear.

Without telling Brenda the story I say, "Brenda, no matter what, do not open the door if you hear someone knocking. Got it?"

"Okay. Why?"

"We don't know who will be there. There's lots of weirdos out there."

Our two days are a real treat for both of us. Sharon, Ginny, and I came some time back so I'm familiar with what to expect. Elk roam the fields, a few moose meander by. The buffalo are the biggest attraction.

Driving very slowly along the winding road through the park a small herd of buffalo with young calves slowly walk beside the truck. Cars are lined up for miles behind us as the buffalo cross in front of us. We've all had to stop as they walk beside and across the road.

Both of us are taking pictures. I have the video camera aimed and following the buffalo being sure to capture the babies as they clumsily follow mama. We've gotten to get a glimpse of a bear strolling through some trees but aren't able to get a clear view of it.

The park rangers have given explicit instructions about feeding the animals, remaining in our cars, and don't get close to the buffalo. We're careful about following those instructions but some aren't.

Standing on a slope watching the buffalo just down the hill but at a safe distance, everyone gasps as a man and a child walk out onto the open field and approach the buffalo.

Someone hollers, "Come back." He ignores it and continues to draw closer and closer to the buffalo to take a close up picture of them. A mama buffalo, with her baby beside her, looks up and gives a snort.

Snapping his picture he turns and walks toward the gathered crowd. Sighs of relief echo through the crowd. One person yells, "You damn fool. You endanger your child for a damn picture." He ignores all of it.

Getting up early we have breakfast in the hotel restaurant and walk over to Old Faithful. A man walks over to the geyser and pores a "magic potent" into the blow hole announcing loudly that the "potent" helps the fountain of water to rise. "Sure it does."

Suddenly water begins spouting out of the hole. Just a little at first and gradually climbs in height until a sudden whoosh and water is shooting sky high making a beautiful fountain effect. Everyone ooh's and awh's while clapping.

The spouting water lasts for a few minutes then gradually decreases in its height until it disappears only to repeat the same performance some thirty minutes later. It isn't a trick. This is one of nature's marvelous wonders. Along with sulfur ponds that stink to high heaven and beautiful waterfalls.

While picking out souvenirs in the gift shop I say, "Brenda, I think we need to head home after we get what we want in here. Have you seen everything you want in the park?"

"Yes. We toured it twice didn't we?"

"We sure did."

Leaving Yellowstone we have to pass through Jackson Hole. Deciding to stop we enter just about every souvenir shop as we roam through the town. Being summer the streets are filled with people from all over the country.

Stuffed bears stand tall on their hind legs as we enter one store. Antlers piled high make an archway to the entrance of the busy streets. Shops of every kind line the streets elbow to elbow.

Spending a few hours we're ready to continue toward home. The Grand Tetons line one side of the road and we decide to drive along their baseline. The expanse of this mountain range with its rocky, jutting cliffs and crevices is awesome to see. We've had a great trip and Brenda is ready to return home.

It's late summer and Brenda has returned home with her stuffed buffalo, Yellowstone sweatshirt, several items for friends, and souvenirs. I've lived alone for some time but it seems when someone visits, then leaves, it leaves me feeling alone more so that usual.

I've noticed some changes taking place in Jacob. Disturbing changes. He's begun to attack Rocky. Rocky will be asleep on the couch, Jacob asleep on the chair across the room.

Suddenly Jacob will wake, jump off the chair, look menacingly at Rocky. His ears will go back and suddenly he's attacking Rocky. Rocky is totally unaware of what's coming.

Being old and smaller than Jacob he's almost defenseless. This is no game Jacob is playing. At times he's actually drawn blood. When I see that menacing stare I quickly grab Jacob by his collar to prevent the attack.

I don't understand this change occurring in him. He and Rocky have been friends, brothers. Rocky has become terrified of Jacob. He peeks around the corners of the walls before entering the room to make sure the coast is clear.

I've learned that as I hold Jacob back from attacking if I hum, or sing "Amazing Grace" he calms down and returns to his normal sweet self. I'm becoming aware that something isn't right. When I sing it stops the attack.

"What's going on?" Before I figure it out, Jacob once again attacks Rocky as he's sleeping on the couch. This time it's more vicious and Rocky yelps, blood dripping from his head.

Grabbing Jacob by the collar he suddenly turns on me. Before I realize it he has his teeth sunk in my wrist. I won't let go of his collar as tears stream down my face. He's trying to get to Rocky but I'm preventing it.

I start to sing "Amazing Grace" as blood drips off my arm; he begins to settle down. Sitting on the floor he looks up at me as though to say, "I'm sorry, Mama. I don't know how that happened."

Bandaging my arm and putting him outside with the doggie door closed so he can't come in, I call my friend. She says, "I had a cat that was aggressive like that. The vet gave him a shot and it stopped all the aggressive behavior. Maybe he needs a shot."

It's late evening and I am still crying, holding my bandaged arm, in disbelief that my beautiful "baby" would attack me. I call the vet in Big Piney.

Sobbing, I tell the answering machine my dog has attacked me and I'll bring him first thing in the morning. It's sixty miles to Big Piney from Kemmerer. The two lane road winds past Fontelle Lake up through the mountains.

The vet's office opens at seven in the morning and because I haven't slept I'm awake to make the trip. I've closed the bedroom door keeping Rocky in bed with me and Jacob outside the bedroom.

Some of the attacks would happen in the middle of the night with Jacob flying across my body to get to Rocky on the other side. It isn't fun having my lip ripped accidentally by a growling dog as he passes over my head.

Leaving Rocky at home Jacob is sitting in the passenger seat next to me. "It's okay, baby. The doctor will give you a shot and you'll be okay." His beautiful black eyes look up at me as I pet his head.

I'm convinced the doctor will give him a shot and we'll be able to go home and be the happy "family" as we were before this nightmare started. Unknowingly, the real nightmare is just beginning.

With Jacob sitting at my feet I explain to the vet what happened and show him my bandaged arm. "Mrs. Cass. When a dog turns on its owner there's nothing that can be done but to put it down."

I fall to my knees beside Jacob with my arms wrapped protectively around his neck sobbing. "But you can give him a shot and it stops the aggression!"

"I'm sorry. That's cats, we can't do that for dogs."

I bury my face in Jacob's soft furry neck. "NOOOOOOOOOOO."

"Are you alright, Mrs. Cass?"

Without looking up I say, "What if we give him to a good home with no other dogs?"

I can barely speak for sobbing uncontrollably, my mind is reeling. I never dreamed it would come to this. "If a dog attacks its owner it can't be placed somewhere else."

I hug Jacob tighter. "But he didn't mean to!"

"Maybe you can keep him and the other dog separated."

"No. There's no way to do that."

"Then you have no choice."

The receptionist has tears in her eyes as she watches me go into hysterical sobbing.

I can't stand it. I stand up on wobbly legs. "I'll be back in a minute," and lead Jacob outside walking around the gravel parking lot and along the bushes in front of the building.

"Looooord, please! I can't do this. I can't kill my baby." *"It's going to be okay. You must. He's dangerous."* "NOOOOOOOOOOO." I want to scream, I want to run, I can't stand knowing what has to be done. There's no escaping it. I can't take him home, I can't give him to someone else, and I can't bear the thought of what has to be done.

Jacob is very much aware of my emotions and leans in against my leg. Kneeling down beside him all I can do is sob and hug him. His soft hair is comforting in a crazy kind of way. I love this dog almost more than my own life. Rocky, too.

"What have you decided, Mrs. Cass?" I can see the sympathy in his eyes through my tears. I can't speak, I nod and the doctor gives my precious Jacob a shot. He takes Jacob to a rear room holding him in his arms.

In my mind I'm screaming, sobbing hysterically, I know the exact second Jacob takes his last breath. My face is swollen, I can barely see out of my swollen red eyes, and gasping for breath I feel like I'm going to pass out.

My spiritual eyes see Jacob slowly walking down the long hallway. He turns his head looking at me with an expression in his eyes that seems to be saying, "I'm so sorry, Mama."

Collapsing on the floor I can't stop the sobbing. It's uncontrollable. The vet and the receptionist are beside me.

Kneeling down he says, "Mrs. Cass, I'm sorry. You did the right thing. Are you going to be able to drive home?"

I can't speak, I can't stop crying. They leave me sitting here for a few minutes and I'm finally able to stumble out to the truck. He's told his receptionist to bill me. It's more than obvious I can't write a check if my life depended on it.

Sitting in the truck with my head resting on the steering wheel the crying continues. I sense the doctor looking out the window with a worried expression even though I don't see him.

I'm in a trance-like state barely aware the truck is being driven home by unseen hands. Slowly maneuvering around each curve, slowing down on each steep downgrade, the steering wheel and gas pedal have a mind of their own.

As the truck approaches the lake I find myself fighting the steering wheel. Something is making it want to turn so it will fly off the bank into the freezing waters of the lake.

I'm aware of the cliff, the water down below, the struggle of going straight along the road or veering toward the cliff. Someone takes control of the steering wheel. The truck drives on down the winding road past the lake.

I find myself stopped in a wide pull off on the side of the road. Between the sobs and tears I see a woman standing in a field. She's standing perfectly still. Her feet are spread giving her a semi-wide stance.

With her hands at her sides clenched into tight fists, she is screaming, screaming, screaming. Her head is thrown back and screams rip through her. There is no echo. Screams that would send chills down anyone's spine do not disturb the quiet of the field.

Blinking I'm suddenly aware I'm in the truck and coming through my mouth are the ripping screams coming up from my very soul. My head is thrown back, my hands clenched in fists, and screams, bloodcurdling screams rip through me.

It's been six weeks since Jacob died and I'm still grieving. Rocky has gradually realized he is no longer in danger but is terrified of large dogs. I've stopped bringing Chuckles to visit because Rocky falls back into the old pattern of peeking around corners.

I've sobbed my heart out to Ben and his concern for me is evident. The summer months are over and with a chill returning in the air I have yet another winter to survive. Laying in bed with tears once again soaking the pillow, a vision appears.

In the vision a blanket is lain out on a carpeted floor. A small baby, barely at the crawling age, is laying in the center of it on its belly. Her head is raised, smiling, she's looking at Jacob. He's crouched in an attack mode at the end of the blanket baring his teeth.

The Lord says, "That is why he had to die. He would have killed a child." The vision disappears leaving me crying even harder but understanding why it had to end as it did.

The first snow has now fallen. Sitting on the floor next to my bed, leaning against the night stand, the phone rings. Immediately I recognize Ben's voice. "Give me one good reason why I shouldn't pull this trigger."

Ben's voice suddenly changes from a cheerful hello to his serious "counseling voice." "What's going on, Sue? What's happened?"

I sob into the phone and lay the three fifty-seven magnum gun on the floor. "I can't do this anymore."

The months of freezing weather are here once again. Sub-zero temperatures, snow, snow, and more snow. Depression has set in and gradually I don't want to get out of bed.

I don't want to go to church, I don't want to shovel snow, blow it far off the driveway or walkways. Mary and I still enjoy each other's company and go to Evanston on occasion but I'm hiding the turmoil within me.

Aren't we Christians supposed to be happy? Aren't we supposed to have peace beyond all understanding? No worries because we've cast them on the Lord's shoulder? I mean come on.

Aren't I serving the Lord? I'm filled with His Holy Spirit, have His strength to lean on, He's guiding me and protecting me so why am I having such difficulties? Simple! I'm human!

In the honeymoon stage He calls us to small simple things to test us. As He sees our faithfulness He'll add more and more as we gradually grow in Him. As maturity comes in our walk with Him—the tasks, if you want to call them that—gets more difficult.

This "assignment" as I like to call it, is not an easy one. It has stretched me, tested my faith, ripped me out of my comfort zone. On the outside I appear to be dealing with the circumstances I've been called into.

But on the inside my world is dark, lonely, and in turmoil. Suicidal thoughts flicker in and out. *"I'm going to kill you, bitch"* is stated more than once. This voice is not the Lord's by any stretch of the imagination.

The enemy does not like what the Lord is doing in me, through me, or for me. "Go talk to Jesus about that and leave me alone!" He does for a little while and the taunting continues.

In my Christian journey I've learned that the more we walk in the ways of the Lord, the closer we become in our relationship with Him, the more the satanic attacks will increase.

It's enough to make us want to turn and run but that isn't what the Lord says we are to do. "Put on the whole armor of God, that you may be able to stand against the wiles of the devil. For we do not wrestle against flesh and blood, but against principalities, against powers, against rulers of the darkness of this age, against spiritual hosts of wickedness in the heavenly realms." Ephesians 6:6–12. Also see verses 13–20.

I put the armor of God, I stand firm against the wiles of this world, but there are many times that I fall into a state of mind where I just don't give a damn any more. It's in those times I call on the Lord and ask Him to do the battle in the heavenlies for me. I just can't fight any more.

Louise, Ralph, and Chuckles are standing in the yard. I'm bundled up in my usual three layers of clothes with the snow blower idling. Rocky is laying in the open garage staying clear of Chuckles.

Ralph reaches down and pats Chuckles on the head. "We're going ice fishing. Do you want to come?"

I look at him like he's lost his mind. "Ralph, I'm freezing my butt off out here. Now why would I want to go sit on solid ice, with a little hole in the ice, just for a small fish?"

"No, no. We have a little shack we sit on the ice. It's warm and we fish in there through a hole in the ice."

"No way! I don't care how warm you say it is. And beside, if it's so warm it will melt the ice and my butt will end up in the water. I don't think so."

Louise is laughing. "You'll enjoy it, Sue."

"I don't enjoy ANYTHING about this cold and I'm not about to go sit on ice!"

As they turn to leave, "Suit yourself but you don't get any fish when we catch them."

The doorbell rings and Ralph is standing on the porch. "I thought I'd check that valve you told me about."

"Oh thanks, come on in."

As Ralph checks the water heater valve he says, "I'm glad you didn't go with us ice fishing the other day."

I look at him surprised. "Why?"

"The ice broke and we nearly lost the house with us in it."

I can feel the blood draining from my face. "Ohhhhh, I'm so glad I didn't go!"

"Yea, you would have been scared to death."

Anthony and Michelle are here for Thanksgiving and will stay a couple more days before they have to leave. The thoughts of them leaving haunt me and the feelings of aloneness start settling in before they've even left.

It's been a nice Thanksgiving but I know the bad weather will be moving in any time. Mary and I are driving back from Evanston. "Sue, do you see that bluff up there?"

I look over to the high bluff she's pointing at. "Yes."

Glancing over at me with a small smile on her face she says, "When I was a little girl my father worked in Evanston. My mother and us kids lived in Kemmerer and we'd go visit him sometimes on the weekends."

She's told me many stories about her life growing up here so I'm anxious to hear another one. "We were riding along in an old wagon. Mom driving the horses and us kids in the back."

She points to the bluff. "Right up there on the top of that bluff Indians were lined up watching us."

Shocked, I glance over at her and automatically slow the truck down. I'm looking more closely at the bluff as she continues.

"There were five of them, if I remember right. Mom started whipping those horses like you wouldn't believe. We took off in that old wagon and was flying down this road as fast as we could. It was dirt then."

Almost stopping in the middle of the road, I want to hear all her story before we get home. "What happened?"

"Oh, the Indians came barreling down that hill after us."

Now I have to pull over!

"They were chasing us lickity split but we outrun them. We left them in the dust. Made it home safe and sound."

"Are you serious? Indians really chased you down this road?"

"Yes! I was about seven years old. I can tell you we were all scared!"

I shake my head in amazement at this woman and the things she's lived through all these years. "You are one fascinating woman, Mary. I love your stories."

"I can tell you a lot of them. Wild Bill Hickok, Jessie James, all of them used to roam this country."

"Did you ever meet any of them?"

Her head snaps around looking at me. "For crying out loud, I'm not THAT old!"

I laugh as I pull back onto the road. "Sorry."

After hearing several of her stories I expect to see most anything out here. Who knows, I may come across a gun fight out in the middle of the Wyoming desert. Mary and I like to take rides. No particular place in mind, just ride.

Driving out in the open spaces, what am I talking about—everything is open spaces here. Looking out my window I see an old dilapidated small building sitting in the middle of nothing. Absolutely nothing around it for miles.

It's a one room shantie with an opening where a door may have hung at one time and a small window on the side. I point at it and look over at Mary. "What's that?"

"What?"

"That little building."

"I'll bet that's where Annie Oakley lived!"

Mary bursts out laughing. I love to hear her laugh. Her laughter bubbles up right from her toes and her face absolutely beams when she laughs one of her "belly laughs." I have grown to love this woman. I call her my surrogate mother.

The temperatures are once again below zero at night. On occasion the days will be thirty to thirty-five. Crawling out of bed, looking out the window I think, "*I'm not doing anything today. I'm not even going to fool with the darn driveway, either.*"

Padding around the house in my pajamas, boot style slippers, and a heavy bathrobe, I feel like if I have to shovel another shovel full of snow I'll scream. Actually I seldom have to use the shovel with having the snow blower. It's God's gift to people who live in these places.

I decide to get dressed after all. "I need to go to the bank. Phooey on clearing the driveway! There isn't much snow on it!" Ignoring Mary's warning about not clearing the driveway and driving over it, I back out and drive to the bank.

Sleeping in feels good today. There's a small new layer of snow on the driveway. The T.V. announces it will be twenty-eight today. "That's not too bad, I'll shovel that little bit of snow off the driveway. I won't even need the blower."

Opening the garage door I can see hints of my truck tracks from yesterday under the splattering of new snow. Scraping the snow shovel along to clear it, it keeps jamming against the hidden layer of ice.

Chipping, stomping up and down trying to break the ice, doesn't work. The sun is shining brightly, the temperature isn't that bad. "*I'll just use the hose and blast this darn stuff off here!*"

I hook the hose up and attach the adjustable sprayer on it. "*This has a pretty powerful stream. It will loosen the ice and I can scrape it with the shovel.*" Did someone say idiots are born every day?

Mary walks around the corner as I'm blasting the driveway ice with the hose. "What the hell are you doing?"

Shutting the water off I say, "I'm tired of shoveling this darn driveway. There's a layer of ice and I can't get it off so I'm breaking it up with the hose."

Mary leans against the fence and is laughing so hard I think she's going to have a heart attack.

"What's so funny?"

She can't speak for a minute and just points at me as she howls with laughter. I'm sure the whole town can hear her.

Finally she catches her breath. "You damn fool! You're only making a skating rink out here." She bursts into laughter again leaving me standing holding a dripping hose and a stupid look on my face. Oh the joys of being a Georgia peach in the wilds of Wyoming.

30

I am sitting on my couch. "*I want you to go see your niece in Phoenix.*" I sit up straighter and surprised. "I haven't seen her in years!" "*I know. Call her and tell her you'll be in town and want to stop by to say hello.*"

As usual the Lord loves to catch me off guard. "Okay Lord. I'll see if I have her phone number." That was a week ago. Sharon has agreed to drive to Phoenix with me. As we're driving along laughing and talking, we're halfway between Phoenix, Arizona and Wyoming.

We've turned the radio off so the familiar voice is quite clear. "*Oh, by the way. You'll be buying a house while you're there.*" Thank God Sharon is driving or I'd be running the Blazer right off in a ditch. "*Start packing.*" "*You don't have to tell me twice!*"

I tell Sharon what the Lord just said. "Lord! Phoenix has over a million people. Would You care to tell me how I'm supposed to find the house You want for me?" "*I'll show you. Trust Me.*"

After having a nice visit with my niece for the day the Lord leads me to a realtor in Peoria. Twenty-five miles north of Phoenix. "Ms. Cass. How did you get my name?"

"The Lord led me here."

"The who?"

"The Lord."

"Oh that's wonderful." Her expression doesn't reflect the same enthusiasm.

In Wyoming I looked at three houses only because "You just don't buy the first house you see." I've looked at two this time. I put a contract on the second one. I lay across the bed in the hotel room. *"You'll be here one year."*

Once again I get the "You'll see," "Trust Me," and "Soon" answers to the questions of why Phoenix? What will I be doing there? All the same questions I've asked for the last year and a half.

The Lord finally let me have a support group the last six months. The ladies and I gather in the basement for our meetings. The craft tables can be lined up on the one side where the bathroom and bedroom are.

When the craft tables are lined in a row we can enjoy the nights we do craft projects as a way to get away from the heavy issues at hand. I've lain carpet on the cement floors making the room so much more homey.

The new couch, recliner, and lamps give it the finishing touch and with the fireplace burning the room is toasty warm and quite inviting. It's comfortable, relaxing, and a feeling of safety is present as we discuss the issues at hand.

I'm thrilled beyond words to get to leave Wyoming but the women rely on support groups for support as well as the valuable insights into their wounded hearts. I hate leaving them but nothing is going to keep me from leaving.

The house the Lord has chosen for me in Peoria is an open floor plan. The living room is large with sliding glass doors leading out to a large brick walled-in yard. The three bedrooms are large with the hallway open to the living room with only a long short counter separating them.

The whole interior is sunny and bright. Lots of windows. An airy atmosphere runs throughout the house as well as the kitchen and dining room. The house sits on a large corner lot, which I like.

The houses in this part of the country are mostly stucco. Stucco is a type of material that keeps the houses cooler from the heat. It is typical for temperatures to rise well over one hundred degrees.

As is typical of Arizona landscaping, the front yard is graveled with a few varieties of cactus for decoration. The back yard hasn't been landscaped due to the house being newly built.

I love playing in the dirt, as I like to call my gardening, and look forward to landscaping it. Plus the dirt will be so hot Rocky will burn his feet just walking a few steps out the door.

Spending three days Sharon and I have enjoyed our stay even though it is a business trip. I haven't been able to visit with my niece due to her baby becoming sick. We've been busy with the realtor, signing papers.

Returning home to Wyoming the packing has once again begun. Michelle arrives to help me. This woman is an absolute blessing! Because the Arizona house is much smaller I'm having to sell and give away several pieces of furniture: The bedroom suite I bought for the fourth bedroom, the large dining room table and chairs, the large wooden shelves where I store my craft supplies. "*I want you to donate most of those supplies.*"

Oh this sets off a stomping fit. "I have thousands of dollars in those supplies! I do crafts all the time. You know that!" "*Donate them! You won't have time for that any more.*"

Begrudgingly I'm sorting through and as the Lord says "Get rid of that." "You don't need that." I'm furious. The several boxes I brought out here filled with the supplies has dwindled down to about half.

Instead of hiring a large moving company I've decided to rent a large U-Haul truck. Michelle will drive the U-Haul with my Blazer on a car carrier pulled behind. I'll drive the motor home.

Instead of following the little green truck, I'll be behind the largest truck U-Haul has. We've had to drive to Rock Springs to rent and pick up the truck. The attendant hooks up the car carrier to the truck. Michelle forces him to check and recheck to make sure it's fastened properly and secure.

Hiring three local men to load my belongings on the truck my mind is in a whirl. Leaving Mary is ripping my heart out. The pressures of packing and now loading, cleaning, and getting ready for another long trip has caused my blood pressure to go through the roof.

Yet another move is bad enough but leaving Mary, whom I've grown to love dearly, is making this move even more difficult. The house hasn't sold even though it's been on the market since the Lord said, "Start packing."

I'm worried about how I'm going to handle all the responsibilities of having two house payments, insurance coverage, and property taxes to pay until it does sell. I'm not happy about these circumstances.

I have to remind myself that when the Lord says to do something He's always faithful to follow through with His promises to meet our needs. I have to keep reminding myself daily.

Mary walks around the corner to see us off just as I'm placing the last few items in the motor home. Rocky is already on the couch waiting for the door to be closed and the engines started.

Mary is handing me a small gift and a card. I know I don't dare read the card right now or I'll break down and not be able to leave as planned. Looking at me the tears have welled up in her eyes.

Reaching out to hug this beautiful woman the tears flow down my cheeks. By the time we release each other we're both bawling. I'm not afraid of changing my mind about leaving. I love the Lord and want to remain in His will.

Pulling away from the curb I can see Mary standing in my driveway. Wiping the tears she waves one last time. I can almost feel the loneliness ebbing in as she walks slowly back to her house. She's told me several times I'm the best neighbor she's ever had. I'll truly miss this woman.

Michelle is leading the way as we climb the mountains and drop down into the flat lands of Utah. Miles and miles of road construction has slowed our progress by a couple of hours. Detours, one lane traffic, stop and go for signalmen waving one lane through and stopping the other.

Frustration sets in interrupting the sighs of relief and calm I've started feeling after the six weeks of packing. The trip ahead, thankfully, isn't going to be the long tiring trip like Georgia to Wyoming was.

Michelle is calculating three days at the most, maybe four. With the U-Haul loaded to an inch of its capacity plus pulling the carrier with my truck, the going is going to be slower.

Las Vegas is over five hundred miles away so we won't be making that today. We're exhausted and even though it's not noon yet we aren't even going to try to make it. We're just too tired.

Once we've maneuvered the maze going through Salt Lake City we're able to maintain a steady speed. Of course the normal stops at roadside rests will be taken but we're not having to meet a deadline to arrive in Peoria. The closing has been finalized through the mail and overnight deliveries.

Between Provo and Cedar City we've pulled into a campground for the night. We've been on the road long enough for today and getting a good night's rest is more than welcome.

Utah is hot! We've had to run the air conditioner all night and waking early we're ready to get on the road and hopefully beat the higher temperatures of the day. We hope to make it to Las Vegas today.

We're about thirty miles from Las Vegas when I recognize a casino, motel, and R.V. park off the highway. Sharon and I stopped here for the night and tried our luck at the slot machines and having a good meal in the casino restaurant.

"As for you, you were dead in your transgressions and sins, in which you used to live when you followed the ways of the world and of the ruler of the kingdom of air, the spirit who is now at work in those who are disobedient. All of us also lived among them at one time, gratifying the cravings of our sinful nature and following its desires and thoughts." (Ephesians 2:1–3)

Like anyone else I still sin. I'm human, or at least that's my excuse. The slot machines are calling. Signaling Michelle she pulls into the casino parking lot.

Walking back to the motor home, "Why are we stopping here? We can make Vegas. It isn't that far. Why don't we park here for the night, play some slots, and have a nice dinner? What do you think?"

I can see the thought of an evening of playing slots is just as enticing to her. Parking the motor home in back of the motel in a dirt parking lot we let Rocky sniff around for a while before checking in.

The registration office is in the front of the casino for both the motel and R.V. park. Entering the casino's back door the whistles and bells of the casino are almost more than we can resist as I zig-zag my way through the slots machines, poker tables, and roulette wheels.

I reach the desk. "I'm sorry, Ma'am. We have no spaces available."

"But you have to have! What about the motel?"

"I'm sorry, that's full, too. We have a computer software convention going on and we're full for the next three days."

Michelle is eagerly awaiting to start playing the slots. "Can we stay in the lot behind the motel? There's nothing there."

"I'm sorry. That's strictly for our guests."

"Michelle? They're full up."

"The R.V. park, too?"

"Yes."

My sinful nature isn't going to let go just yet. Looking around, I whisper to Michelle, "Maybe we can stay in the lot without them knowing it."

"No. We need to get going and find a place in Las Vegas."

We've been on the road almost nine hours and it's still early. We're tired and looking forward to stopping for the night. Las Vegas is "just down the road a piece" so we should make it easily.

How wrong we are! Once again we've encountered road construction. Having to wind through detours, side roads, stop and go. We've been led through a maze of bright orange barrels and are in a warehouse district.

Smoke suddenly boils out from under the U-Haul truck. Michelle sees it in the rear view mirror; before I can signal her she pulls into a dirt side road next to a warehouse.

Getting out and looking under the truck at the rear tires, the inside tire is the one smoking badly and we can't drive any farther. By the time the repairman we've called arrives, we've sat here for hours. It's now midnight.

In the process of changing the tire the repairman notices the hitch holding the trailer with my Blazer on it is broken and has been barely holding. It's an absolute miracle the trailer hasn't broken loose and come flying at me as I'm following behind.

If it had broken loose it probably would have killed us both. Jackknifing the truck, throwing the trailer all over the road, not to mention the Blazer breaking free and going who knows where.

The Lord promised Michelle and I that we would be alright on this trip. That He would be with us every inch of the way. Looking at each other with the thoughts of what could have happened we're both convinced the tire catching fire was the Lord's way of protecting us from an even worse disaster.

Michelle is so exhausted from having driven so many hours. I'm tired but nothing like she is. She's been driving a loaded truck with extra weight behind. I haven't. By the time the men return with a new trailer we can hardly stand up.

It takes another hour or so for the new trailer to arrive, load and unload and hook up everything. Michelle is staggering and I'm getting very concerned. She refuses to lay down in the motor home for fear of falling asleep and not being able to wake up.

The two men are very, very nice. Michelle steps over to the one that seems to be in charge. "Is there an R.V. park near here?"

"No. The closest one is about fifty miles south of here."

Michelle almost falls and grabs hold of the truck door. "We can't go that far! I'm so tired I can't stand up. Is there any place we can park for the night?"

He looks at me and then back at her. "There's a big casino about five miles from here that lets R.V.'s park overnight in their parking lot."

As only Michelle can do, she talks the man into driving the U-Haul. He has the other man drive the repair truck. Like a small wagon train we're winding through the narrow lanes of the road construction being careful not to knock down the darn orange barrels.

Finally a huge casino with its thousands of lights comes into view. Its huge parking lot already has several motor homes parked in marked spaces. "Praise God we're finally here!" I walk Rocky; Michelle has collapsed on the couch and is asleep without removing her clothes.

Crossing over Hoover Dam, into Arizona and passing through Kingman we're stopping in Flagstaff. The weather has been cooler as we've climbed in elevation. Flagstaff is cold. Coats are needed. There's still patches of snow on the ground.

Parking in a roadside picnic area we're planning on staying for a while. Having lunch, letting Rocky explore the area filled with large pine trees. It's nice to lay back and relax for a while.

Instead of the three days we expected to get to Peoria it's taken almost four. The time lost in Las Vegas cost us almost a day. We've slept in. The harrowing night has left us rattled and tired.

Flagstaff isn't but a little over a hundred and fifty miles from our destination. It's early in the day so we'll make our last leg of the trip and be at my new residence by late afternoon. Having called Ruby, she's lined up a couple of men to unload the truck for us.

Driving from the mountains into the valley presents more problems. Michelle has trouble getting up the high grades due to the weight of the truck and carrier. She's going so slow that I pass her and wait at the bottom until I see her coming down the hill.

She flashes her lights as she approaches and knowing it's a signal to stop, I stay alongside the road in a pull off for trucks. Smoke is billowing out from under the truck. Getting out of the truck Michelle is shaking.

Fear is written all over her face as she approaches the motor home. I can tell something is very wrong. We sit down on the couch.

"That was scary!"

"What happened? You look like you're going to faint."

Michelle gets up and gets a soda out of the fridge. "The brakes went out! I could barely keep the truck from doing a hundred miles an hour down the mountainside."

"Dear God what happened? How'd you do it?"

"I kept praying and praying and praying and the Lord was telling me what to do. I've never prayed so hard in my life. I thought I was going to be killed!"

I can tell she's still very shook up from the experience and I don't blame her.

"Sit there and get settled down. We're far enough off the road that we can wait."

Taking a sip of her Pepsi she says, "Yea. That really scared me. We'll have to wait for the brakes to cool down and see if I even have any."

Praise God the brakes had just gotten very hot and we're able to continue after sitting for thirty minutes or so. It's taken Michelle a little while to get calmed down and I'm almost afraid for us to try to drive any more but from here we're out of the mountains and flat land is ahead.

We chose U-Haul because they have a good reputation for safe and well-maintained trucks. This one has been a fluke. A really big fluke. We're both more than happy to know we will be in Peoria soon.

Looking out across the desert Saguaro cactus reach their arms skyward. I yell out the window, "Yippee! At least there's cactus!" The desert is welcoming because I know it won't be snowing where I'll be spending the next year.

Pulling up to the curb in front of the house, we're both happy to have the drive behind us. Now for the unpacking and starting all over once again. *Okay Lord, we're here. Now what? What am I suppose to do here?* No answer.

We've been unpacking, putting things in order. We've been praying and talking about a variety of topics. "*I want*

you to lay hands on her. Have her stand up and anoint her."
I'm not sure what the Lord is about to do.

I do know, without a shadow of a doubt, that when He
tells me to lay hands on someone something wonderful is
about to happen. I look at Michelle. "The Lord wants me to
lay hands on you. You need to stand up."

Getting the small bottle of anointing oil out of my purse,
Michelle stands waiting expectantly. Walking over to her I
ask the Lord to clear my mind so I can focus on Him. Praying
the prayers the Lord is leading me to pray, placing an oil
cross on her forehead, the Lord leads me in everything to do.

Anointing her hands, "These are the hands of the Lord.
They are to reach out in service to Him and others." Anoint-
ing her feet, "You will walk in boldness as you follow the
Lord Jesus Christ."

Her eyes are closed. Her head is tilted back slightly as I
place my hand over her eyes. "Open her spiritual eyes, Lord,
that she may see what You want to show her." Covering her
ears, "Let her hear Your voice."

Finally, anointing her lips and covering them with the
palm of my hand, the Lord gives me the words to tell her. A
special message for her. Part of the message is that she will
have a prayer language. She will pray in tongues. (See Acts
2:4 and Mark 16:17.)

Still being in the Spirit, I ask her to, "Ask the Holy Spirit
to come and Baptize you." (See Acts 1:5, Acts 8:12–19.)

The power of the Holy Spirit fills her and suddenly she
drops to the floor. We, as Christians, refer to this spiritual
experience as being "Slain in the Spirit." Why the word
"slain" is used I don't know.

Many have experienced the power of the Holy Spirit and
can't stand up under His power. Some denominations believe
this is of the devil or that it's fake. I can understand they may
think it's fake. The devil part? No!

I had witnessed others "hitting the floor" as I call it, and thought it was some fake thing to look "religious." The first time it happened to me I felt a weakening coming over my body.

I was determined I was NOT going to hit the floor like these other "religious nuts" do. Locking my knees, straightened my back, I stood as stiff as a stick. I thought, "No way! This business isn't going to happen to me!"

The Lord must have said, "Oh yea. Let's see who's boss here." I hit the floor like a ton of bricks and was out like a light. I have learned since then that some who "hit the floor" will still be aware of their surroundings in a surreal way.

Others, like me, are out cold. It isn't unconsciousness like hitting my head on a hard surface. I laughingly call it "my coma." Waking up leaves me with a feeling of coming out from under anesthesia. Groggy and a little disoriented.

Since that first time I have found myself hitting the floor as though my knees have been knocked out from under me with no warning. I usually go straight down to the floor. I've seen others fall straight backwards.

Michelle has fallen straight down hitting the floor as though I've kicked her feet out from under her. I've done no such thing. I haven't pushed her, either. I lightly touched the top of her head and down she goes. It isn't by any power I may have. It's totally and absolutely the power of the Holy Spirit.

I've heard a couple of preachers say that you are not Baptized in the Holy Spirit unless you speak in tongues. Hogwash! For me it was five years before praying in the tongues manifested itself. It's also called, "Praying in the Spirit."

Michelle began praying in tongues within two days. I know someone else, it was twenty-five years. Whenever the Holy Spirit decides it's time, a Word of knowledge, a prayer language will come forth. It is He who determines and gives this gift, not the individual! (see 1 Corinthians 12:4–11)

Michelle isn't staying as long this time so I still have plenty to do as she boards her flight for home. I don't feel the loneliness like I did in Wyoming as she leaves. The Phoenix area is familiar to me.

I spent my high school and college years living here. I was living here when I got hired by the airlines, so I don't feel so totally out of place. Familiar ground and all that. I'm definitely enjoying the warm weather.

From living here previously I know all too well the summer heat can reach above one hundred on a regular basis. The winters are absolutely wonderful. If one wants snow, Prescott and Flagstaff are close by for snowballs and skiing. This area is for "Sun bunnies."

I put dishes away out of the dishwasher. *"I want you to volunteer at the hospital."* I almost drop the plate in my hand. "I don't think so!" *"Go to the Chaplain's office, tell her I sent you."*

I can't believe this. I've barely gotten the house in order and already He's giving me an "assignment?" "No, Lord. I spent five years in the hospital with Brian. You know that. I won't do this!"

I've spent the last week stomping around fighting, arguing, bawling. All to no avail. *"Go see the chaplain."* "No! I won't do it!" I know I'm going to lose this battle but I'm going to give it my best shot.

Finally, after many sleepless nights and tear-soaked pillows, "Alright! If that's what You want. But don't blame me if I crack up and go nuts!" *"You'll be fine. Trust Me."*

The large hospital is a mere seven miles from my house. Driving to it I'm passing a church on the right side of the road. Glancing over at it, *"That's where you'll worship."*

Still upset about having to spend time in a hospital I say nothing. At this point I can care less about anything except trying to figure out how I'm going to survive being in a hospital day in and day out again.

Walking into the unfamiliar hospital I find myself standing in the doorway of the chaplain's office. A tall, slender woman turns. "Can I help you?" My mind is in a fog. I'm not sure what to say.

Not saying anything for a long moment she stands looking at me, waiting for my reply. In almost a whisper, "The Lord sent me here."

"The who?"

"I was praying and the Lord said I'm to come and see you. He wants me to volunteer."

I can tell, she's trying to decide if I've escaped the psychiatric ward upstairs.

After discussing my background Tania asks if we can sit and pray together. I comply and apparently the Holy Spirit has convinced her during the prayer that I'm not some nut case and she agrees to my helping her in ministering to the sick.

I've gone through three weeks of training, shots for T.B., flu shots, and being acquainted with hospital policy. I'm issued a blue jacket with "volunteer" embroidered on the lapel.

Tania begins giving me a variety of assignments. "Go to room 400 and pray with Mrs. Hall." "Go to Mr. Gardener and sit with him. He may let you pray and he may not." I'm so nervous about walking the halls of the hospital I continually want to run.

Tania has given me a clipboard filled with the room numbers and patients' names that I'm to visit. Walking into one room a middle-aged man lays in the bed. "Hello Mr. Harden. I'm Sue and I'm a volunteer with the Chaplain's office."

Looking up at me with a scowl he says, "I don't need any prayer!" This isn't the first time I've encountered hostility from a patient.

Smiling I reply, "That's okay. Is there anything I can get you? Magazines, a book?"

His scowl lessens and we begin talking about his family and kids. The conversation turns to religious beliefs. "I don't need God!" I don't push my beliefs on him.

I sit in the chair next to his bed. "It seems to me, that as sick as you are, this might be the time you really do need Him in a big way." He's confessed he's never asked Christ to be his Savior.

After more discussion he's shedding tears. He's invited the Lord Jesus into his heart. Leaving his room I know in my heart the Lord must have prepared his heart and He used me as His vessel to lead this man to the gift of salvation.

The patients have a variety of needs. Some will welcome prayer. Others want no part of it. There are some who desire prayer as well as someone to talk to. In this "assignment" the Lord has given me I fill some of those needs.

Walking into a room, Mrs. Baxter has asked me to visit each day. This is my third visit with her. She's middle-aged, has had major surgery, and no visitors. Sitting beside her bed I can tell by the expression on her face that something is pressing on her mind.

Touching her hand I say, "Is there something you'd like to discuss? You look as though you have something important you want to talk about?"

With a grimace of pain she scoots higher in the bed. "Yes, but I don't know how to start."

I wait for her to form her thoughts. "My father abused me as a kid. I hate him!" Sitting quietly beside her she continues to vent her anger. Looking at her as she lays on her sickbed I can definitely relate.

I tell her my own story of childhood abuse and about the support groups I've led. "Mrs. Baxter. The only way much of the pain and anger leaves is to forgive your father."

Her eyes flash with anger. "Forgive him? Forgive him? No way! Not after what he did to me!"

"I forgave my father and that anger has finally left."

Tears well up in her eyes. "How did you forgive him?"

For thirty minutes we've talked about forgiveness. I've suggested counseling, going to a support group. "I'm going home tomorrow. Thank you for coming each day." She's agreed to seek help. I'm not supposed to but I give her my phone number.

Tania is now having me help her plan a lay pastor program and training. Many times the pastors who visit patients aren't available when needed. I've told her about the lay pastor training I've had.

In between praying and visiting patients we're working together on a training schedule. Since being her assistant I'm surprised at myself. I'm usually the one in control. I'm the leader of the group. Now I'm submitting to the authority of someone else.

It must be the Lord at work in me because since I've been under her authority I submit like a little mouse. I'm not exuding the air of confidence around her. I'm not the "take charge" individual I usually am. I notice this in myself and think it's weird.

When I'm not with Tania the confidence and in control air is back. I'm comfortable praying with the patients, I'm more comfortable walking the halls of the hospital.

Suddenly the confidence is jerked out from under me. Walking along the hall looking down at my clipboard I walk into one of the units. Without realizing which unit I'm on I stop, looking up from my clipboard.

I freeze! My feet are glued to the floor yet I'm trying to run as fast as I can. *"You're not running this time. Go pray with the man in that room down there."* I feel like my feet are spinning like a car's wheel yet going nowhere. My hands are shaking. I'm standing in the middle of the intensive care unit.

I can't move. My mind is screaming, "Run!" *"Go pray for that man."* Looking toward the far end of the unit I see a woman sitting in a chair next to the glass wall of her husband's room. In my mind I'm seeing myself sitting next to Brian's room.

Walking ever so slowly I can see into the room. The front of the room is glass. The bed with the man in it sits in the center of the room. He has tubes going into and out of his body. The whoosh, whoosh, whoosh of the respirator brings tears to my eyes. *"Please God. Don't make me do this."*

Clinging to the clipboard like it's a lifeline for a drowning person. I'm standing in front of the woman. Blinking frantically to keep tears from overflowing I say, "I'm Sue. I'm a volunteer with the Chaplain's office. May I pray over your husband?"

Glancing through the window at her husband then back at me she says, "Yes. That would be nice." I was really hoping she'd say, "Get lost" but now I have no recourse but do it. Walking like I'm on the last ten steps to the death chamber, I enter the room.

Heart monitors with their beep, beep, beep, scream in my ears. Looking down at the elderly man with the large tube taped in his mouth I feel like I might vomit. Flashbacks of Brian, of the sounds, and the smells flood my mind.

I can almost feel Brian's doctor's hand on my shoulder as I look down at this dying man. Taking a deep breath I begin praying for this man. Tears stream down my face.

Thankfully the clipboard is made of strong material or it would crush under the pressure of my grip. My legs are beginning to feel like rubber and although we've been told not to touch or sit on a patient's bed, I have to grab the railing or fall.

My prayer becomes fervent. I want this man to live! I'm not sure how long I've stood beside his bed praying. Finally taking several deep breaths, wiping the tears, I'm able to turn and leave the room.

Saying a few reassuring words to the wife I want to run through the halls with flailing arms screaming. But I don't. Walking as quickly as I can without drawing attention to myself I leave the Intensive Care Unit.

The first door exiting to the outside world I slam through. Breathing as deeply as I can, I collapse on the grass under a tall palm tree. Sobs rip through me. I don't care that people are glancing over at me, I don't care that I have the blue volunteer jacket on.

Grief, loss, memories too vivid tear through me as though I had just left Brian's hospital room. The Lord lets me expel all that has built up yet again. The memories are flashing through my mind. Pictures of Brian, the vision where he's crossing the finish line, sitting beside his casket. All come flooding back.

Walking into the chaplain's office I feel like I've been hit by a train and backed over by a bus. Tania looks up from her desk. "Are you okay?"

Holding onto the door jam I say, "No. I'm going home."

The motor home has been in storage since I've been here. Desert, rattlesnakes, scorpions, no thank you. I know this country. In high school and college we used to go to Saguaro Lake for the day.

The Verde River isn't far from Phoenix so we'd often sit on the bank or play in the water. That was back then. My idea of camping is not parking beside a cactus and pretending I'm on some desert oasis. The motor home is tucked in for the year.

31

Brenda has called and wants to visit, laughing when she asks if she can come.

"What are you, my one woman groupie?" I know she's been deprived of seeing another wonder of nature, the Grand Canyon. Before she arrives I'm planning to take her there.

It's one hundred five degrees outside. I've had landscaping done in the back yard. A small oval lawn encased in its curb sits a few feet away from the cement patio I've installed myself.

Bougainvillea brighten the corner with its blooming arms reaching across the cement block wall. The Ficus tree I've carried across the country is now planted in one corner of the yard. An irrigation system has been installed.

Brenda is stretched out on the lounge chair in the scorching heat. I've warned her about getting heat stroke but she's determined to get a tan while she's here. Looking out the sliding glass doors at her I know the sprinklers are about to come on.

I can't help but laugh at the thought of what will happen when they come on with her chair sitting almost on top of one of the sprinkler heads. I notice she isn't moving. *"She must be asleep. Oh this is going to be worth watching."*

Suddenly there's a whoosh and the water shoots up from the sprinkler head. Screaming, she almost knocks the chair over as the water blasts against her backside. She jumps up and turns toward the door only to see me laughing so hard I'm crying.

I am sitting across from her at the table eating breakfast. "How would you like to go to the Grand Canyon?"

She almost drops her glass of juice. "Can we? I've never been."

"I know and yes we can. It isn't far from here."

Just south of the Grand Canyon we stop to visit the Fred Flinstone's park.

The park is small and depicts the characters from the television show, *The Flintstones*. It's a kids park. One can slide down the tail of the huge dinosaur, walk through the make-believe stone house, and ride the makeshift car from the stone age.

Spending the night in a local motel we're up early and enter the Grand Canyon Park. The view is breathtaking. The sun reflecting off the colorful walls that drop hundreds of feet are unbelievably beautiful.

The Colorado river snakes its way through the valley below looking like a thread winding its way between the cliffs. Brenda is sitting on a tree stump overlooking the canyon. I walk over to her. "Do you want to take the trip to the bottom?"

"I don't know. How do you get down there?"

"By donkey."

She steps off the stump. "I don't think so!"

The park also offers helicopter rides but with two house payments I don't dare spend the extra money. The helicopter ride isn't cheap. Walking along the edge of the cliffs is awesome enough. Driving from one overlook to the next we see a good bit of the canyon.

Spending time in the gift shop, Brenda buys gifts for herself as well as everyone under the sun at home. "Brenda? You're going to go broke in here."

"I'll never get to come back."

We've taken dozens of pictures and Brenda is so excited to be able to see this canyon that she's only seen in pictures.

For someone who has never left Georgia she's definitely taking advantage of every opportunity offered.

The church the Lord has me worshipping in has about three hundred people. I'm encountering the same "outsider" attitudes as before but not quite as bad. The pastor gives fairly good sermons but so far nothing that will make me stand up and take notice.

I've joined the ladies Bible study on Wednesday nights and that's proving to be interesting. One lady is feeling ill and I ask if it's okay if we lay hands on her. Everyone looks at me as though I'm from another planet.

I get up out of my chair and walk over to the sick lady. "Would you mind if we prayed over you?"

She looks up at me. "What are you going to do?"

I try to keep the shock from showing on my face. "I'll place my hand on your shoulder and we'll all pray for healing."

Signaling the others to get up, they cautiously get out of their seats and gather around the woman. It constantly amazes me that these women have all been Christians since childhood and have never prayed over someone for healing or laid hands on someone.

Once again, no one raises their hands in worship. I think someone has slipped into these churches and put glue on the seats. Gretchen, Connnie, and Helen have been in churches where this is an acceptable practice.

Sitting together like the three musketeers I'm the only one standing with raised hands in praise to Jesus as we sing. The others are afraid they will be out of place and rather than risk being "looked at funny" they remain seated.

The pastor gives a tremendous sermon on calling people to accept the gift of Salvation. Had I not already been saved I would be running up the aisle begging Jesus to be my Savior.

At the end of the service I'm waiting for the pastor to give an altar call. A time given for any who wish to pray or be prayed with to come forward. Nothing! The pastor steps down and walks away. People file out of the building.

I can't believe this! Standing beside an older woman that has been a member of this church for years I ask, "Why didn't he have an altar call? That sermon was begging people to come forward."

She shifts her Bible from one hand to the other. "He doesn't believe in them."

In a split second words fly out of my mouth. "Then what the hell is he doing as a preacher!?" Indignant she spins around and stomps off.

I walk into a room with a small fireplace, several free standing shelves line an entire wall. They're empty. "Donna? What are these shelves for?"

Setting her purse down on the round table in the center of the room she says, "We were going to have a library but no one donated any books."

I soon arrive home. "*I want you to go through your books. I'll show you which ones to donate.*" I don't even bother to argue or make a fuss. Since the Lord told me I'll only be here a year I've only unpacked the bare essentials.

Most of my belongings are still in the boxes stacked in the garage. I decided I was going to make this packing and unpacking as easy as possible. Several of the boxes are filled with books.

This is not going to be an easy task. Boxes filled with books are heavy! I'm not Hercules so moving boxes around is not going to be easy. I have no one to help this time. Struggling to move the boxes, it's taking me two days to accomplish.

I stop two men in the parking lot, they're willing to help me carry the books into the church. The library is now started with the fifty-five books I've lined up on the shelves.

All the books are hardback covers by well-known Christian authors. Tim LaHay's *Left Behind* series, *The Purpose Driven Life* by Rick Warren. Authors such as Jack Hayford, T. D. Jakes and many others.

After the announcement of the donation the shelves soon fill up as people bring more books. A system is set up for checking out books and it seems everyone is enjoying the new library.

Sharon has visited, another friend from home has come for a few days. Being here has been much easier than my year and a half in Wyoming. The Lord has let me make more choices. I'm not under His thumb as strongly as before. Which is wonderful!

That isn't to say I'm off the "leash." He still tells me what I can and can't do if I'm veering off the path. Mostly I'm at the hospital or home. Because of the heat Rocky and I don't venture out much. By now it's hit one hundred ten. Thank you Lord for air conditioning.

In the evenings Rocky will stretch out on the small lawn and I'll sit on the patio admiring the sunset. I don't think as a teenager I ever paid much attention to the sunsets. Now I'm in awe of them. They're the most beautiful sunsets I think I've ever seen.

I've overcome the anxiety of being at the hospital. Tania and I work together splendidly. I move from one room to the next, shock a few nurses and doctors with my "The Lord sent me" and have not had to revisit the Intensive Care Unit.

The Lord has told me that my next move is to northern California. Redding to be exact. I've lived there before. I have several not so pleasant memories from my teen years here in Arizona.

During this time here the Lord has put me in a variety of situations that make me confront the hurt from the past.

In doing that He has healed much of my wounded heart. But not all of it.

Redding is yet another story. I have fought, refused, and argued moving there for almost this entire year. I enter my home office and walk toward the computer. *"It's time you decide."*

Stopping dead in my tracks, I don't have to ask, "Decide what?" *"Are you going to move where I want or are you going to stay here? You have to decide right now!"* For this past year I've gone back and forth in trying to make that decision.

Not knowing fully the love of God and still equating Him with my father I'm terrified of what He'll do to me if I don't obey. Yet I don't want to go to California. My mind conjures up all sorts of horrible punishment He'll inflict on me if I disobey.

Standing, looking at my computer, tears stream down my face. *"Sue, What are you going to do?"* "I'LL GO!" I take a step then suddenly stop. "Oh Lord! I'm not going out of love, I'm going out of fear! I'm afraid of what You'll do to me if I don't go."

This revelation hits me smack between the eyes. "Oh Father forgive me. I want to go because I love You. Not because of fear. Forgive me for thinking You're like my Dad again."

I place dirty clothes in the washing machine. *"Start packing. Call Michelle to help you."* Closing the lid on the washer I call Michelle. Of course my traveling buddy will come to help.

32

Knowing I'm going to move to Redding I'm anxious to do it and get it over with. Tania has made my leaving the hospital difficult by creating a position for me on a permanent basis.

I've told her several times I'm only in Arizona for a year and I can't take the job. It's time for me to move. She continues to try to persuade me to stay. Finally, in tears, "Tania. The Lord said He wants me in California. You aren't making this any easier."

The time in Peoria has been a learning process as well as healing. The hot summer has been almost unbearable. Even Rocky has a hard time with it. Most of the time he stretches out on the air conditioning vent on the floor and gladly lets the cool air blow on his belly.

I've noticed he's been slowing down a lot. His age is showing and at times it worries me. He's still terrified of large dogs so I'm careful to walk him late in the evening when no other dogs are around.

The winter here has been marvelous! No snow! I've only had to wear a coat maybe a month out of the whole winter. Others walk around in shorts. But they're "snow birds." People who come to warmer climates for the winter then leave to escape the heat.

In contrast Redding is almost on the Oregon border. Mt. Shasta is fifty miles north of Redding and its fourteen thousand foot elevation towers into the blue skies. It's the tallest mountain in California and skiers love it.

Mt. Lassen is northeast of Redding and is a volcanic mountain. It hasn't erupted in years and can also be seen on a clear day. They aren't as majestic as the Grand Tetons in Wyoming but beautiful.

Michelle arrives and we've completed most of the packing. "Lord? What can't we leave now?" *"You'll see."* "We are already packed. Just let us go." *"You'll leave August tenth."* "Why that long?" *"Trust Me."*

We're both ready to hit the road, locate the house He wants for me, and get this move under way. Michelle plans to stay a month helping me and visiting with her son who lives in Redding.

Finally the long two week wait is over. We're driving to Redding; Rocky is happily looking out the back window of the Blazer. *"Call Northwest Reality and ask for Max."* We arrive in Redding on the second day of traveling. "Northwest Reality, this is Max, can I help you?"

One would think I'd be used to how the Lord operates. I almost drop the phone when I hear "Max." "This is Sue Cass. Would you like to sell me a house in the next four days?"

"Ahhh, yes. Sure. How'd you get my name?"

"The Lord."

"The who?"

Picking out a few homes to look at, the first one is in a nice neighborhood on a cul-de-sac. The house is ten years old. Three bedrooms with the usual kitchen, living room, and two baths. No whirly.

Stepping out the sliding glass doors onto a large covered patio, a roar fills the air. "No. No way! That's Highway five running right through this back yard. let's go. I don't like this house anyway." *"Buy it."*

Even though Mt. Shasta and Mt. Lassen is a panoramic view from the back yard it's totally unacceptable. Highway five is one of the busiest highways in California and spans from San Diego/Mexican border north into British Columbia.

I ignore His voice. "Where's the next house?" "*Buy it!*" Again I pretend I don't hear Him.

"Sue. The Lord just told me that you're to buy this house."

"Michelle! I didn't hear that and neither did you!" I wanted one with a pool because it gets hot here, too.

We drive less than a mile. "*You can't afford the houses with a pool. I'm putting you in a safe neighborhood and the only one you can afford. Go back and buy it!*" I look over at Max. "Stop the car and turn around. I'm going to buy that house."

"But you said you didn't like it!"

"I don't but the Lord said to buy it and I'm going to buy it. Now do you want to sell it or not?"

Turning the car around and driving back to the house he calls the listing agent and learns the house was just listed yesterday!

Michelle and I burst out laughing. "That's why He wouldn't let us leave when you wanted to. The house wasn't even on the market yet!" Max is standing looking at us like we've lost our minds.

Max has also learned someone else is writing up an offer on it so we rush back to his office, write up the contract for the amount the Lord has told me to offer and Max rushes it to the agent. The owner accepts it without hesitation.

We're spending three days in Redding so I can finalize the paperwork and Michelle can visit her son. On the way home Michelle starts laughing. She nudges me with her elbow. 'You're finally catching on, kid."

I glance at her and back at the road. "What are you talking about?"

Leaning over with a big grin she says, "In Wyoming you looked at three houses. Phoenix you looked at two. Here? Bingo! First one." I have to admit she's right. Maybe that "leash" is doing some good after all.

We're not using a rental truck this time. I've called a local moving company to move my belongings to Redding. Once again I'll be following the little green truck in the Angel Buggy.

The movers are loading the furniture as Michelle and I vacuum and steam clean the carpets. Everything is out of the house except for one free standing lamp I bought in Wyoming.

Its brass pole holds four glass flower pedal-shaped domes. Each is hand etched with the small bulbs lighting up and enhancing the etching. The gold trim on each dome elegantly gives the finishing touch. It's beautiful and I've never seen one like it.

The lamp is standing in the corner and I don't want to take any chances of it being broken in the move so we're taking it with us in the motor home. What happens next surprises both Michelle and myself.

Before I ever put the first piece of furniture in this house I anointed every inch of it. I certainly didn't want a repeat of the incident in Wyoming. I've experienced no demonic activity since being here or suicidal thoughts.

Michelle is standing in the middle of the living room wrapping the steam cleaner's cord around the handle. I'm setting the vacuum cleaner next to the door to be loaded on the truck.

We're both facing the lamp when it is suddenly thrown to the floor. It hasn't fallen. It's been <u>thrown</u> by unseen hands. It crashes to the floor breaking two of the beautiful pedal domes. We both sense anger in the air.

Michelle looks at me and I look at her. At first we say nothing then she shrugs. "Oh well. Someone isn't happy you're moving."

I'm not about to give the, whatever it is, the satisfaction of being upset. "Oh well, is right."

Once again we're on the road heading to another location the Lord has chosen for me. What I'll be doing, what church I'll worship in, or the purpose for this move, I have no idea. As to questioning why, I don't bother any more.

I've come to the conclusion that if He wants me to do something, whether buy a Bible for someone to selling my house, whether I lose money or not, which I did on the Wyoming house, I just do it whether I understand it or not.

This time the travel time is slower due to following the little green truck in the motor home. The movers have said it will take four days to deliver the furniture. That's okay with us.

The Lord has told me I'll be here for two years. The Peoria house hasn't sold so once again I have to trust Him for finances to cover the double house payments and expenses.

The stops at the roadside rest stops are scorchers. The pavement is so hot I try to park as close to the grassy pet areas as possible for Rocky. As has been the case in most of our traveling we've had to run the air conditioning constantly.

Michelle has once again led us through the various towns and onto highways where the going is steady.

I've had no problem following the little green truck and we're making good time. Except for one little goof. Just south of Sacramento is what we refer to as a "spaghetti junction" type intersection.

Overpasses, highways going in every direction, looking at it, it looks like a tangle of spaghetti. We're stopped at a roadside rest. "Sue, you need to stay close when we get to the interchanges."

"Okay, I'll be right behind you. Just don't lose me."

As we enter the tangled highways I can see Michelle a few cars ahead of me. We've cleared the tangle and enter on open road. Suddenly the little green truck takes off down the highway at a high rate of speed. "Michelle? What are you doing?"

In no time the truck is totally out of sight. Throwing my hands in the air I say, "What the heck is she doing?" As I continue on the truck is long gone. I've been driving for over thirty minutes and still can't see her.

I'm not about to drive the motor home seventy-five, eighty miles an hour. "Maybe she'll be beside the road up here." A highway sign appears along the side of the road, "Los Angeles 400 miles."

"LOS ANGELES! Oh for crying out loud. I'm going south, not north! How'd I do that?" I have to drive another ten miles to get turned around to go north. "I'll bet Michelle is not a happy camper right now. I can't believe I've followed the wrong little green truck!"

That's exactly what I've done. Michelle took one ramp and I followed another green Blazer just like mine going the opposite direction. Michelle is parked alongside the road under a line of Eucalyptus trees patiently waiting for me to return.

Seeing me she pulls out onto the highway. We only have about a three hour drive left and I'm not about to mess it up again so I'm almost kissing her bumper. Stopping at the Olive Gardens store, Michelle isn't happy with me.

"How in the world did you go the wrong direction? I saw you take the wrong ramp."

Laughing and a little embarrassed I say, "I have only one explanation, I followed the wrong little green truck!"

The movers arrived the night before and have been waiting on us. Tomorrow is Easter so we're all anxious to get unloaded and be able to spend a relaxing Easter. We've decided to go to the sunrise service being held at Shasta Dam. The service will overlook the dam at dawn.

Michelle cooks a large Easter meal and we enjoy it with her son and his wife. Easter has been a wonderful day but now it's time to continue the unpacking. Michelle visits with her son for a week as I unpack more boxes.

Thankfully I can park the Angel Buggy next to the house and not have to store it at some other location. This is beautiful mountainous country so I'll be able to get use of it. That is if the Lord lets me.

Michelle has returned to Nebraska and I have the house pretty much in order. The Lord still hasn't told me why I'm here or what I'll be doing. I'm sick of hearing, "You'll see" and "Trust me" so I wait until He decides to tell me.

He has told me to worship at a church just a mile from my house. I've noticed that He has placed me within five miles of each church He wants me in. Which is quite convenient.

The first moment I walk through the doors into the sanctuary I feel the Holy Spirit's presence very strongly. "Thank you Lord!" I'm welcomed by friendly people, not treated as an outsider. The praise band is awesome, and the preacher is so filled with the Holy Spirit I hang on every word.

I am so relieved to hear upbeat contemporary music, people swinging and swaying to the beat. Hands are raised in worship of the Lord, praying in the Spirit is acceptable.

Now this is my kind of church! It isn't a "pep rally" type service but Spirit-filled and honest worship without the disorder. A Word of knowledge is given on occasion and as the Bible tells us, an interpretation is given that is beneficial to the congregation.

I love worshipping here. The gifts of the Spirit that the Lord has given me are accepted with no hint of "she's weird." Visions are accepted. My telling of a dream that's interpreted by the Lord is accepted. When I say "The Lord sent me" there's no, "The who?"

Before marrying Brian I was living here and so were Anthony and Michelle. But it's been several years so I've forgotten about the various lakes other than Whiskytown Lake and Shasta Lake.

Michelle tells me about a lake at the foot of Mt. Shasta, Lake Siskiyou, and I've spent many days and nights camping next to it in a large R.V. park. I have my favorite R.V. slot with its full hook-ups.

Mt. Shasta looms across the lake and sitting in the Angel Buggy I can almost touch the mountain. Rocky gets to roam free, except when the tame deer meander past the motor home. They'll even eat out of my hand!

Sitting at the water's edge gazing at the mountain fills me with a peace that I haven't had since leaving Georgia. I spend as much time here as the Lord will allow me. I still consult Him on everything I do. Not because I have to now but because He has taught me that He knows best and has my best interests at heart.

My mother and I have not been on good terms for over ten years. Sharon wants to come from Idaho so I decide it's a good time for all of us to get together. Mom lives on the outskirts of Sacramento with my sister.

We all gather at my house for a day of visiting and have a Bar-B-Que. The day goes well after the initial anxiety of meeting after all these years. When Mom and my sister leave Sharon and Ginny stay for a few more days.

Before Brian got sick we had talked about flying out to Portland, Oregon, renting a motor home and driving the coast line all the way to San Diego. We never did get to do it.

I've decided I would like to take a coastal trip but go north into Oregon and Washington or wherever I decide to stop, turn around and come home. Looking out the sliding glass doors at the mountains, *"I want you to take your mother with you."*

I'm absolutely shocked. "WHAT? I haven't seen her but one day in the last ten years and you want me to be cooped up in a motor home with her for who knows how long?"

Turning from the windows, *"Take her with you. You haven't been able to talk to her about your childhood. You need to."* "Ohhh Lord. I hope You know what You're saying."

I've had tremendous anger about my childhood and have felt my mother never protected me. The same sex parent and child have stronger bonds than opposite sexes. Or so the psychiatrists say. I'm not sure she'll enjoy being in a closed environment with me.

My mother has always loved to travel. I know she'll agree to join me on this Angel Buggy adventure even though I have my doubts that this is a good idea. *"Buy a Bible for her and have her name put on it. Hide it in the motor home. She'll be saved on this trip."*

That's wonderful news and I believe the Lord but I don't want to put her name on it in case she doesn't want it. *"Put her name on it!"* That wasn't asking. That was telling, so I do. I've asked the people at church to pray for us while we're gone. They know what the Lord told me about Mom getting saved and quickly agree.

We're traveling up the California coast. We stop when we want, we shop, we spend the night on beaches, in R.V. parks, and visit every lighthouse we can.

At each overnight stop we've been discussing my childhood. I've had so much anger that the Lord has promised to do the confronting for me. It absolutely amazes me once again. Confronting my Dad, no anger. Mom? No anger.

We've driven the full length of Oregon's coastline and into Washington before deciding to head home. I would stay until I decided to go home but because of previous commitments Mom can only be gone for three weeks.

The entire trip has been phenomenal. We've had such a good time and our talks have brought about a tremendous healing in me. Parked on a sandy beach with the turbulent waves slapping at the sand the conversation turns toward Christianity.

Mom is sitting on one side of the table and me on the other. "Mom? Have you ever asked Christ to be your Savior?"

"No. Should I?"

"It's your decision but if we got in a wreck today and were killed, where would you go?"

Thinking for a moment she says, "I would think heaven."

Without wanting to get in a long Biblical discussion I say, "No Mom. Without Christ as your Savior you would go to hell. Being a good person doesn't put you in heaven when you die.

"Would you like for me to lead you in a prayer asking Him into your heart?"

"Yes."

After she's asked the Lord to forgive her of her sins and come into her heart I'm going to the closet in my bedroom and take the Bible out that I bought. It has her name printed in gold at the bottom.

"I have something for you." Taking the box with a surprised look on her face, she opens it. For the first time on this trip, tears come to her eyes. She's holding the Bible in front of her caressing the cover. "It even has my name on it."

Tears come to my eyes as I nod, yes. The tears aren't because she's happy with the Bible. They're because I know my mother will be with Jesus when the time comes. Tears flow as I walk to the water's edge. "Thank you Lord. You were right. She's in Your hands now."

Touring Long Beach, Washington, buying T-shirts and souvenirs we've decided to head south toward home. Mom has a longtime friend she'd like to visit so we stop for the day and visit with her.

I see the sign for the turn off to Lake Siskiyou. "Mom, we have four days before you need to be back. Do you want to camp at the lake for a couple of days?"

Her eyes brighten. The visit with her friend has left her feeling a sadness knowing she'll not ever see her again. Mom is in her early eighties and her friend is older than she is.

Looking over at me she says, "Yes! That will be fun."

"It sure will be. I camp here all the time and there's deer that come right up and eat out of your hand."

Our excitement is rising and as I park the Angel Buggy in my favorite spot Mom is thrilled to be here.

We've always loved camping and she and I have even gone on trips where we've camped on a river bank and slept in the back of the station wagon. Sitting by the lake, feeding and petting the deer, playing in the water and watching the chipmunks scamper around the motor home is the perfect ending to our wonderful trip.

33

My "one woman groupie" Brenda, has arrived. It's her first trip to California and like all the other places she's followed me to, she's excited to be in new territory. No snow fences to tease her with, no bears that might knock at the door.

The Lord has gifted Brenda with the beauty of sign language. She isn't deaf but worships using sign and works with children and adults who are deaf. At church she's been invited to sign before the congregation to the song, "Alabaster Box."

She's mesmerizing. There's no doubt in anyone's mind this woman is gifted and the Lord is showing Himself through her. She's been invited again to sign at a retreat but we decline. It's only when the Lord leads her to sign for various functions that she will.

We've decided to spend four days at the lake. It's been great fun and she's been able to pet and feed the deer. Something she's never been able to do before. We talked about going to Yosemite National Park but have decided against it since it's quite a distance from Redding.

She's spent two weeks with me and I've enjoyed every bit of it. But it's time to get on with the Lord's plans. I've started a support group through the church. The Lord has led me to call it "Healing Hearts."

I'm surprised at the age range of the women. The youngest is thirty-two with the oldest being eighty-four. One is seventy-three and the others vary in their forties and fifties.

We've been working on forgiveness issues. As with the other support groups I have had them write a letter to their abuser. And given each an opportunity to forgive whoever the Lord puts on their mind.

The eighty-four-year-old, Gretchen, breaks down sobbing. "I've never talked to my family about the abuse. I told my mother but she called me a liar. She never loved me from the first."

Gretchen is a very angry woman. Her tone when speaking is rough, brash, and angry. She doesn't mince words to anyone and says exactly what she thinks. To see this woman break down in tears. *"Thank you Lord. I know You've been working on her heart."* Leading her through prayers of forgiveness she leaves the room crying.

I wake early to the phone ringing. "Hello."

"What the hell did you do to me!?"

"Who is this?"

"It's Gretchen! What the hell did you do to me!?"

I don't know what she's talking about and stay silent for a moment.

"Well, what'd you do?"

I can tell she's upset. "Gretchen, I'm sorry I don't know what you're talking about. What do you mean, 'what I did to you?"

"Last night when you were talking about forgiveness I was so mad I could spit!"

I have a clue now as to what's going on. "And now?"

"I don't know what you did but I'm not mad anymore. I'm not mad at ANYONE!"

We talk for awhile and she's totally surprised that she's no longer angry at her abuser and family.

It's never too late to forgive. It's never to late to let the Lord heal our wounded hearts. This wonderful crusty old woman has been such an inspiration to me and many others.

She's not the only one changed in the support group, Bernice, the seventy-three-year-old has also been able to forgive her abuser and her past five husbands. The group is going wonderfully and lots of healing is taking place.

Rocky has come in from outside and is laying on the couch. He has slowed down considerably and I've noticed his lack of appetite, coughing, vomiting, and his joints seem to hurt him more.

As I'm picking up a pile of papers off the chair I hear a thud. Spinning around, Rocky has fallen off the couch and is laying stiff on the floor. Running to him and gently picking him up, he's unconscious.

I grab the phone and call the vet; I tell them I'm rushing him there. Rocky is still unconscious when the vet carries him to a room in the back. I'm pacing, I'm sitting, I'm pacing some more.

He's eighteen years old so I'm not surprised he'd get sick. What I don't expect is for the doctor to walk out with his eyes downcast. Rocky is gone. "I'm so sorry, Ms. Cass. His kidneys shut down. There wasn't anything I could do."

All I can do is sob. I knew I would lose him one day but not today. Not now. The doctor places his hand on my shoulder. Others in the waiting room walk outside so as to give me privacy for a few minutes.

Looking sympathetically at me he says, "Would you like cremation or." He doesn't finish. I've never had a pet cremated but this time it just feels right. "Yes." The sobbing continues and as I stagger to the truck, people hold their pet close and express their sympathy.

The house is silent. The walls seem to scream of emptiness. I've lost three dogs in five years. I can't do this anymore! My babies are gone and I can't go through losing anymore.

Walking into the vet's office the receptionist slides a small tin container toward me. On the lid is a paper, "Rocky Cass." My knees begin to buckle. I'm clinging to the counter with tears blurring my vision.

Someone steps behind me to catch me if I fall, I don't. Instead I cup the pretty little tin in my hand. My beautiful baby lays in this small container and it's almost more than I can bear.

I've painted "Rocky Gardens" on a rock and set it in the newly made garden in the yard in his memory. Rocky is tucked away in the corner of my closet. He's going home with me when I leave California.

The Lord has already told me I have one more move and that's the last of the moving. If He sends me back to Georgia, Rocky will go with me. Wherever the Lord sends me, Rocky will be there.

Rocky's been gone for three weeks and my grief continues. I continually thank the Lord for all my "babies" but losing Rocky has brought me to the point where I can't stand losing anything or anyone else.

Laying on a tear-soaked pillow the Lord gives me a vision. Dusty, looking like a new penny, and Rocky, looking healthy and refreshed, are happily playing together in a field filled with wild flowers. Just before the vision ends, they're side by side. Each is looking directly at me as though to say, "Thanks Mama, we're fine."

The past four years have been difficult. With any move there's the necessary changes that have to be done. Changing driver's licenses, car tags, new doctors, dentists, attorneys.

Knowing I'll be in some new location, new state, is wearing on me. Every new town I've been relocated to I know no one. I have to learn where the grocery stores are, drug stores, learning the streets. It adds to the anxiety of each move, not to mention the stress of not selling the last house.

The Lord hasn't told me where the next move will be. I quit asking. In the meantime I'm enjoying the Bible study and church services. For several Sundays we've been praying for a woman named Eve during our Bible study.

She's been in a women's prison around Los Angeles. Sitting down with the rest of the group to start our study, a woman walks in. Suddenly everyone is jumping up to give her hugs, "When did you arrive?"

She looks to be in her early fifties and has difficulty walking. Watching her as she sits down she appears quite tired. Her face is etched in lines of weariness and I sense a sadness within her.

After class she's talking to one of the men in the class. Picking up my Bible and purse I'm getting ready to leave. *"Go introduce yourself to her."* I'm not what I would call an outgoing person. I don't just bounce over to someone and say, "Hi. I'm Sue."

I don't question the Lord's request and walk over to where they're talking. I wait for them to finish their conversation. *"I'll just come back later and introduce myself."*

Suddenly I feel unseen hands on my shoulders turning me around and guiding me right back to where Eve and Henry are talking. Just as I step up to them Eve is telling Henry she has no place to go and doesn't know where she'll live. "I don't have a pillow to lay my head on tonight."

My mouth opens. "Yes you do! You're going to live with me!" I'm as surprised as she is. "Hi, I'm Sue Cass. I live a mile from here and you're welcome to stay with me."

She looks at Henry and he reassures her I'm not a nut case. "If you'll meet me after the service we can talk and see what you think. You are welcome to stay with me." I think she's still in shock. She nods yes and we go into the worship service.

Eve follows me home after church and as usual I show her what will be her room and bath. It's clear she's being very cautious but after we talk for a few minutes she says, "Do you mind if I go lay down? I'm just so tired."

"Sure. You know where your room is."

I can't help but wonder how she ever survived the two years while in prison. She is so sweet and has a heart of gold.

She's on parole for two years and has to check in with her parole officer frequently.

A knock at the door brings me out of the kitchen. Opening the door a giant of a man is towering in my doorway looking down at me. His posture is erect, arms slightly bent at his side. In his big gruff voice, "I'm Joe Fleming. I'm Eve's parole officer."

I bite my tongue to keep from laughing. His demeanor is another one of those that's supposed to make me quiver in my shoes. It doesn't work. My husband was a high-ranking marshal. "Well hello Mr. parole officer. Come on in."

One would think I suddenly deflated a balloon. "Ahhhh, yea. Ahhh, okay. Is Eve here?" Eve walks into the living room and suddenly stops when she sees him. She's terrified of this man. He has the power to send her back to prison.

After this initial visit to check out Eve's new living quarters we see little of him after that. At least at my door. Eve is the most amazing woman. The two years she's been in a hell hole the Lord has used her mightily.

Because of her medical problems and age some of the other women have protected her from the "bullies." She started a Bible study. She organized a prayer group. From the little she's told me the women are forbidden to leave their cells for any reason after a certain time at night.

The guards will wake her in the middle of the night and take her to someone in distress to pray with them. The women turn to her for God's comfort and peace. She reminds me of Paul in the Bible. In prison, horrible conditions, yet he converts the guards. How many she's led to Christ, I don't know. Plenty though.

The things she witnessed in prison, the ones she'll tell me about, make my hair stand on end. It's no wonder her eyes reflect fear and sadness. Two years of witnessing horrors that she can't, won't even talk about.

270

The Lord has told me I'll be moving in four months. I told Eve that when she moved in. This is a time for her to get on her feet, have a safe place to live, and work on the issues from her past.

That's the only reason the Lord brings these women to me. Eve being in prison hasn't bothered me. I know without a doubt when the Lord leads a woman to live with me, I don't have to worry. He'll take care of everything. Okay, I confess. I did make sure she hadn't committed murder.

The Lord telling me I'll be moving is six months earlier than He said I would. I have no idea why He's allowing me to leave early but I don't question it. Eve has been so hurt growing up. Her adult life hasn't been much better so we don't have long to work on her issues.

We've spent hours and hours working through her issues. Day in and day out confronting the pain of her past. Abuse, finding her dead daughter in a trunk at the end of her bed. The suicide gun laying on the floor. Cheating husbands, alcoholism. On and on.

The intensity is tremendous and I can't figure out why the Lord is having us pounding away at the issues with little rest in between. Normally I would never put someone through the grueling "therapy" like we've been doing.

Eve has some of the spiritual gifts that I have. The Lord reveals things to me about her that are pertinent. He also reveals things about me to her. It's hilarious at times when in fun we try to "out do" each other.

She's been able to find work, has gotten a car, and receives tremendous healing. Her physical condition is worsening. Collapsing in the recliner after coming home from work she says, "Sue, I know I don't have much longer. I'll be with my Jesus soon."

"My Jesus." Eve never calls Jesus, Lord. Not Father, it's always "My Jesus." Her eyes brighten, the lines of weariness seem to leave her face when she talks about, "My Jesus."

When sitting beside the lake looking up at Mt. Shasta, "Eve. You know I said I would be moving. The Lord is telling me to start packing. We need to find a place where you can live."

She looks down at her hands in her lap. "Where is He moving you?"

"I don't know yet."

"If it's back to Georgia can I come with you?"

"I thought you can't leave the state."

"Maybe I can talk my parole officer into letting me. I think he's got a thing for me."

Laughing, I poke her on the leg. "Way to go, woman!"

I wake early and make a pot of coffee. *"You can live anywhere you want. This is the last move. Where do you want to live?"* Hawaii? Nah. Stay here? I'm not sure. As the day continues my mind is in a whirl. I've decided I'm either going to stay here in Redding or go home to Georgia.

It's a mental tug of war. I like it here. I'm in a great church, I have the ministry the Lord's using me in, a beautiful lake nearby to camp at. I've gotten used to the roar of the traffic and grown to like my home. But!

Finally, "Lord, where do You want me?" *"Georgia."* "Okay." Eve is looking for a place to rent. Stretched out on the couch in the motor home having a quiet time with the Lord. *"I want you to fly to Atlanta."* "Lord. I lost money on the Peoria house. Where am I going to get the down payment for this one?" *"You'll see."*

Packing boxes, as much as I can, while helping Eve look for a place to live I get a letter in the mail. It's telling me about stock Brian had. I know nothing about this stock. Making calls and researching the company I find it's worth a good chunk of cash. "Lord, what am I suppose to do? Am I suppose to sell this?" *"Call the broker tomorrow and sell it."*

272

This mystery stock gives me exactly what I need for the down payment, air fare, car rental, motel expenses and all moving expenses. When the Lord promises He'll meet all of our needs, He isn't joking!

Closing my eyes, I'm assuming He will be sending me back to Douglasville. "Then where do I go?" "*I'll tell you when you get there.*" These past fifteen years have taught me one thing, if nothing else, just do it. He'll explain later. He gives me only the information as it's needed.

Driving to Sacramento and boarding a flight, I've already made arrangements to rent a car and stay with Brenda for the first night. Leaning my seat back to get comfortable for the five hour flight, I can't help but wonder where my next home will be.

Half asleep with the earphones playing soft music, "*You'll be living in Buford.*" Jerking the ear phones out of my ears, pressing the button, the seat flies forward. "BUFORD!"

I suddenly realize I've spoken out loud. Smiling sheepishly I lean back in my seat. "*Buford? Why Buford?*" "*You'll see.*" "*And of course You'll show me where the house is?*" "*Of course.*"

Ben has kept in contact throughout the past five years. There's been no need to call every week as he did when I was in Wyoming. But I keep him filled in on all that's been going on.

I've notified him that I'll be in Atlanta and will come by the church to see him and Carol. They're no longer in Douglasville but now minister in the counseling center in a large church in Sugar Hill.

Kirk has also been transferred there and is the senior pastor but he doesn't know I'm coming. Spending the night with Brenda I find my way to Buford. Many years ago I would travel through Buford going to Lake Lanier.

Buford was a spot in the road and that's why I'm so surprised this is where the Lord is sending me. Arriving, it's no spot in the road any more. It's a fast growing city so I'm not so leery about being sent here.

I find the church and Ben and Carol lavish hugs on me. I'm standing in the doorway of their office. Carol is sitting in her usual rocking chair. "You're different." I look at her, tired, but feeling a comfort at being back in Georgia. "I am different, Carol. The Lord has worked me over good!"

Waking early, the hotel has continental breakfast and I grab donuts and coffee to take with me as the Lord leads me through the streets of Buford. "*Turn left. Go straight, stop at that house.*"

I stop in front of a house with a for sale sign in the front yard. "Lord? Is this the house?" "*No. Write down the agent's name and number. Call him.*" Writing the agent's information down I return to the hotel to get some rest before starting the serious house hunting.

I call the agent. "I'm Sue Cass. I need to buy a house in the next four days. Are you willing to work with me?"

"Sure. How'd you get my name?"

"The Lord led me to you."

Here we go again. "The who?" The first house is a beautiful three bedroom, two bath. It's spotless and I really like it, until I go in the back yard. "No. I don't like that slope. Where's the next one?"

We've toured several houses and by the end of the day we're both tired. Randy is a Christian man and has accepted that I hear from the Lord. We are sitting in the parking lot of the Sugar Hill post office. "Randy, that's it. Do you have anymore?"

"That's all of them you picked. What's the Lord telling you?"

"Oh Lord. Now what do we do? Where's the house You want for me?" *"You've already seen it."*

Immediately I know which one. The first one with the sloping hill. Going back to his office we write up an offer. I have to leave tomorrow and we've been countering the offers back and forth.

The last offer was once again rejected. "Lord? What am I to do? They keep rejecting the offer." He tells me exactly what to put in the contract and they accept it. On the flight home, "Why did You let me run all over the place looking at all those houses when You knew that was the one?"

Not really expecting an answer, *"To let you have your own way."* "Okay, okay. Point taken." We can do things our way or His way. I've learned His way is best but on occasion I still try to assert my independence.

Eve has found an apartment she can afford. I've been helping her move in and have given her a few pieces of furniture that I was going to donate rather than take with me.

I stand amongst boxes I've managed to pack. "I guess I better call Michelle and see if she'll help me again." *"She won't be helping this time."* "WHAT? How am I going to do all this by myself?"

Sitting down on the couch I'm numb with the thought of trying to accomplish such a large task alone. "How am I going to do this? Lord, I can't drive the motor home and truck at the same time."

I don't want to hear His answer! *"You're going to sell the motor home. Call the movers you used to move you here. They'll take the car. You'll fly back."* I can't breathe. The last part of His instructions sound like they're coming from far off.

I am stunned beyond words. "Sell the Angel Buggy? I didn't hear that right. You didn't say that!" *"It needs repairs and gas prices are going to be very high. Sell it!"*

I burst out bawling. "I can't sell it! I won't sell it!"

Once again He's probably waiting for the explosion. "You've taken my husband! You've taken my home! You've taken my dogs! Now You want to take my freedom! What do You want from Me!?" "*Your life.*"

I swipe at the tears and I am still very angry. "I've given You my life! I've given up everything for You." "*Did you die for Me?*" Argument over. I can't express the devastation I feel at having to sell the Angel Buggy.

It represents freedom to me. When the pressure of life is too much I jump in it and go somewhere quiet. Somewhere I can relax in peace. No more Destin, Florida on the beach. No more Tybee Island bike riding and feeding the seagulls. No more, no more, no more.

This command, and it is a command, has knocked my knees out from under me. Advertising the Angel Buggy, removing everything from the closets, kitchen, bedroom is done in robot fashion.

It's tearing me apart. I can't imagine not being able to sit in an R.V. park listening to the birds and the slapping of a lake's waves or watching the tide come in as I bask in the sun on an ocean beach.

Anger begins taking form. "How dare He make me sell the Angel Buggy!" The anger turns to bitterness. I can't let go. As the Angel Buggy is driven out of my driveway by the new owner tears stream down my face.

Arriving in Buford before the movers arrive I'm staying in the hotel. Ben has loaned me his vehicle until mine arrives. Pulling into the parking lot of the church to visit with Ben and Carol, Kirk is walking toward the parking lot.

Recognizing me, he's quite surprised to see me. Walking over to the pick-up, leaning down to speak through the open window he says, "I didn't know you were back. Are you moving back?"

I didn't expect to see him right now. "Yes. The Lord's moving me back. I don't know what church I'll be in."

"Oooh. You aren't going to be at this one?"

"I don't know yet."

I'm leaving several things in boxes in the garage as I unpack. I'm not convinced this is the last move so I'm trying to make the next one easier. I pick up framed pictures that I'd normally hang on the wall and lay them back down. "*You can hang them. This is your last move.*" "Yea, right."

The hurt and anger of having to sell the motor home lingers and I'm not trusting like I did. Finally being convinced after several "this is your last move" statements the house is in order.

He's placed me in the large church with Kirk, Ben, and Carol. I've never been in a church with four to six thousand members and I'm having a very difficult time adjusting.

I feel swallowed up. Anonymous amongst so many people. Leaving the church in Redding has been very difficult. The services here are boring to me. Gradually I'm finding my "niche," as Kirk has called it, in the counseling center.

The Lord is leading me in a variety of different directions. The support group I started is over. "*No more support groups. I have other things I want you to do.*" I've started a new ministry. The Lord has told me to call it the Elah Ministry.

In Hebrew, Elah (Alah) means "Oak." Isaiah 61:3 is the scripture this ministry is based on. "... They will be called oaks of righteousness, ..." David kills the giant Goliath, in the Valley of Elah (see 1 Samuel 17) which is also significant.

The Elah ministry is a healing and deliverance ministry. Healing the wounds of the past. Delivering us from the "giants" in our lives. Spiritual "giants." Demonic "giants." Transforming us to be as strong as oaks. It's now grown and is a non-profit incorporated ministry.

Eve and I have kept in contact. She still wants to come to Georgia but can't. I've been calling her for the past week to no avail. I'm getting very concerned. Finally e-mailing Henry, "I've been calling and calling and she isn't answering. Is she alright?"

His reply almost knocks me off the chair. "Eve had a massive stroke. She's been on life support for nine days. They took her off yesterday. She's dead." Shock courses through me. I've only been home three months and she's gone?

Crying tears of loss the Lord opens my spiritual eyes and lets me see her one more time. Eve is dressed in a beautiful flowing gown. Her swollen body is now slender, healthy. No sign of illness.

She's looking up at Jesus with a glow illuminating her whole body as she and Jesus dance arm in arm to an upbeat song. She steps back as her arm reaches out with her hand in His and He twirls her under His arm.

Her beautiful gown floats around her silver clad feet and her smile, the love is like a soft glowing lantern in a dark room. The joy that is so evident fills my heart. "Good-bye my beautiful friend."

Speaking with a pastor I've been told is quite wise after a conference, I'm explaining what the Elah ministry is about. That part of its scope is ministering to those who have been sexually abused as children.

He finds it interesting but his comment leaves me speechless. Which is a very rare occurrence. In all his "wisdom," he states, "It's more traumatic for a girl to be raped in some alley than to be molested."

"What do you mean?"

He shifts from one foot to the other. "When a girl is raped it's a one time thing. Very traumatic. Molestation is all the time and they get used to it." My mouth opens. It closes. It opens again, no words will come.

I look like a fish when it's taken out of water. My mouth opens and closes as though gasping for air. Proverbs 10:14, "Wise men store up knowledge, but the mouth of a fool invites ruin."

The pastor smiles as I stare at him in disbelief. Turning he walks toward the other side of the room. Finally recovering my voice I want to scream, "Molestation IS rape! Every day and every night rape!"

People have no idea of the tremendous devastation, soul damage sexual abuse has on a child. Incest inflicts the worst kind of damage to the soul. Father figures are to emulate God.

How we see our biological father, father figure, is how we will see God. Loving? Trustworthy? Cruel? Controlling? Incest crushes the spirit of the child. For someone to trivialize this kind of devastation is an abomination! Especially coming from a clergy.

To tell a victim, "forgive and forget" is an insult and causes feelings of being raped again. "It happened a long time ago" trivializes the horror of the events. It behooves all of us to educate ourselves.

We cannot protect our children or help them through the devastation with a lack of understanding. Victims have great shame, great guilt. It takes tremendous courage to enter a pastor's office or a counselor's office seeking help.

34

These past years have been a tremendous growing period for me. The Lord has opened doors of new knowledge and teaching me about things I've had no idea existed. I never knew anything about generational sins for example.

Attending seminars, training sessions, conferences I've learned sins from our ancestors are passed down through the generations to us. How they can lead us into the same attitudes, behaviors, and sins they had. (See Exodus 20:5–6 and 34:7.)

For instance. If divorce is in our family line, it's more likely we will divorce. Abuse is definitely a generational sin. Be it child abuse, sexual and/or physical. Spousal abuse: "Daddy beat Mom so it's okay to slap my wife around." And the cycle continues.

We can pray renouncing, severing, and breaking these generational influences from our life. Breaking them from a thousand generations back to a thousand generations forward so they do not continue to affect our lives or the lives of our children.

My eyes have been opened to the forces of evil. So many know there's a devil but discount his power. Ephesians 6:12 tells us, "For our struggle is not against flesh and blood, but against the rulers, against the authorities, against the powers of his dark world and against the forces of evil in the heavenly realms."

We fight the battle by putting on the Full Armor of God. (See Ephesians 13–18.) Knowing God's Word, and acquainting ourselves with the truth about the demonic world.

The gifts of the Spirit (see 1 Corinthians 12), breaking un-Godly soul ties is another one.

Being taught about and now involved in prayer ministry. Prayer ministry is different from traditional therapy. Prayer ministry seeks God's wisdom and healing. Traditional therapy leans on our own wisdom.

These past five years have opened my spiritual eyes even more than before. Not only seeing angels but the demonic also. Seeing the demonic isn't pleasant. Whatever gift the Lord gives us is to be used for the benefit of others and His glory.

Taking me to hell was not to scare me. It was showing me the consequences of unbelief. The horror of being completely separated from the love of God. He doesn't send us to hell. That's a choice we make.

I didn't understand why He was showing me the church spinning on its axis and then disappearing into darkness until three years ago. He explained to me that when God is not the Master in a church it is going contrary to His will.

It follows man's wisdom, desires, and beliefs and enters darkness instead of His Light, falling from Grace. On the flip side of the coin, He allowed me to see my husband enter heaven.

That was/is encouragement for me too ". . . run with perseverance the race that is marked out for us . . . so that you will not grow weary and lose heart." (Hebrews 12:1–3) I can use that experience to encourage others.

Seeing my father being led to heaven by the angels testifies to the hope we all have in Christ. I prayed for my father to accept Christ as his Savior for many years. Don't stop praying for your loved ones. The visions, dreams, written messages continue.

Since I've been back in Georgia the Lord brought another woman to live with me and she stayed about a year when the Lord said it was time for her to leave the nest. Like the others the Lord has brought her enormous healing. She's teaching in a Christian school and continuing her college education.

We all can be His vessels. I am His vessel, He is the Healer. I take no credit for the healing of wounded hearts, for the miracles of putting another's life back together. He gives the opportunity and it's up to us to accept it or reject it.

The Lord has brought me a very long way from that woman that was angry, independent, and defiant. Most times I don't question but there are times He continues to test my faith.

Finally believing His promise that I don't have to move again, I've remodeled the kitchen and painted and decorated rooms. I've transformed the yard from barren to what many call my "Garden of Eden."

My home is finally exactly like I want it. I can rest and enjoy the blessings He's given me. When friends enter they feel the peace of God permeating every room. Several claim it as their "retreat." I'm comfortable, happy, and at ease with where I'm at.

Sitting out on the patio watching the chipmunk I've named Charlie, *"You're going to be moving."* I can't begin to express the shock I feel. "You promised! You said I never have to move again!"

He's explained His reason this time, circumstances have changed, but I totally reject it. All my mind is screaming is that He promised. I've told Him He's lied to me, knowing in my heart He can't lie.

I've told Him He's betrayed my trust and I can't believe Him anymore. In obedience I have packed. Being obedient doesn't help the sense of betrayal and hurt I feel. "All I ask for is a whirly. I just want a whirly. But if You see fit then I want . . ." I list everything I want in this next house.

When He said, "Follow Me" He didn't say "when you feel like it or if it pleases you." When He said, "Follow Me" doesn't mean we have to have all the answers to follow him. "Follow Me" doesn't mean we're going to understand His reasons or purposes.

For all this time I've not understood what the "five year odyssey" was about. What was I supposed to be learning? Why was I in all these different places? It has been a mystery that I couldn't solve.

Finally I've received some answers. The totality of the five years "on the road" was to teach me, "To trust Me, to wait on Me, and to obey Me." Those are lessons well learned and I adhere to them even now. I don't lean on my own understanding. I just do it and wait for Him to tell me why, if He chooses to.

I've been in nine different churches of various denominations over these past fifteen years. Why He led me to these churches I have not always understood. Some answers have come about that.

He told me recently that He's placed me in these churches for various reasons. He wanted my gifts to be exposed to others, to acquaint them with what they do not know. Another to minister to the hurting. Yet another to show me what a dead church is like.

Another denomination to increase my knowledge and grow me. To my joy He placed me in one where I could "spread my wings" in worship and feel free to express my love for Him without condemnation or judgment.

He let me see pastors that are worshipped instead of Christ and those who He did not call to pastor. Each and every church He has had a specific purpose for having me there.

He will have me in a class. "You aren't there for you, you're there for them." Once I asked, "When's it my turn,

Lord? When will others minister to me?" I suddenly find myself being ministered to. He always meets our needs.

Stretched out in the whirly in my new house, with everything I asked for, a thought suddenly drops into my mind out of nowhere. Eve was in a hospital dying. She was on a respirator. Not for just a day but for nine days.

The Lord knew I would be beside her bed. I would be there when they removed the life support. He had me move six months early to save me the anguish of sitting by her bed hearing the whoosh of the respirator, the beeps of the heart monitor.

The Lord knew the difficulty I would have in watching my friend die. The circumstances had changed. The revelation of "You're moving because the circumstances have changed" suddenly clicks.

Tears mix with the swirling water. Relief rushes through me like a tidal wave. "He didn't lie to me! He didn't betray me! He's looking after me." My tear-filled begging for forgiveness releases me of all the hurt and anger.

Testing my faith? You bet He does! I know the sudden remembrance of Eve dropping into my mind was not an accident. My hurt and anger was turning to bitterness against Him.

Satan, being the liar, deceiver, troublemaker if you will, moved in and was determined to destroy my faith and trust in Christ. He was hell bent on pulling me away from the only One I can truly trust.

The California house sold for a price that returned all the money I had lost on the other two houses plus a profit for me.

Michelle is still in Nebraska and it's up to the Lord if she helps me with any future moves.

Brenda married, has had a kidney transplant, and is living in Tennessee. She's still my "one woman groupie."

Ben and Carol continue to minister in the counseling center and Kirk has been transferred to another large church.

Mary is still in Wyoming and is now a beautiful ninety years young. We stay in contact often and I tell her each time we talk that I miss her and love her but I'm so grateful to be out of Wyoming.

This move has landed me in Cumming, Georgia. The Lord has placed me in a tiny old historic church. He's using me to assist the pastor and I've been told I will be in this house for a year and a half to two years. I've been told I have a new assignment—I don't know what it is. I don't ask. Psalm 22:5 says, "They cried to You and were saved; in You they trusted and were not disappointed."

I laid down my net and the journey continues.